Lois Keith is a writer and teacher and an active supporter of civil rights for disabled people. She is the editor of *Musn't Grumble: Writing by Disabled Women* (The Women's Press, 1994), winner of the MIND Book of the Year Award 1994 and the author of a teenage novel, *A Different Life* (The Women's Press, 1997), selected for Book Trust's 100 Best Books of 1998. Her book for children, *Think About People Who Use Wheelchairs* (Belitha Press 1998), was shortlisted for the Nasen Special Educational Award in 1999. She lives in London with her husband and their two teenage daughters.

Also by Lois Keith from The Women's Press:

Mustn't Grumble: Writing by Disabled Women (1994)
A Different Life (1997)

Lois Keith

Take Up Thy Bed and Walk

Death, Disability and Cure in Classic Fiction for Girls

First published by The Women's Press Ltd, 2001
A member of the Namara Group
34 Great Sutton Street, London EC1V OLQ
www.the-womens-press.com

British Library Cataloguing-in-Publication Data
A catalogue record for this book is available from the British Library.

ISBN 0 7043 4651 6

Typeset in Garamond 12pt/14pt by FiSH Books, London
Printed and bound in Great Britain by CPD (Wales) Ltd, Ebbw Vale

In loving memory of
Stephen Richard Keith 1947–1984
and
Ellie O'Sullivan 1947–1999

Acknowledgments

The title for this book was unwittingly given to me many years ago by my doctor Mr JIL Bayley, then director of the Spinal Injuries Unit at Stanmore. Recounting to him an unpleasant interview I had undertaken with a retired spinal injuries doctor (I was being assessed for compensation and he was examining me for the 'other side'), he remarked drily, 'Well, yes, he is a bit of a take-up-thy-bed-and-walk kind of man.'

Many thanks to Kathy Gale for her intial support for this book and to my editor Kirsty Dunseath for her intelligent and rigorous approach. Sue Gee, Jenny Morris, Mary Phillips and Ellie O'Sullivan read parts of this manuscript at various stages and offered a much needed combination of encouragement and sharp criticism. The staff at the Wellcome Institute medical library provided me with many valuable references which would otherwise have been difficult to find.

Thanks also to my friends for all kinds of support during the long process of bringing this book to completion. And most importantly, as ever, my thanks and love to Miriam, Rachel and Colin.

Books and Authors in Order of Publication

Contents

Introduction

Boys especially should not have childish tales with weak morality or washy piety, but should have heroism with nobleness before their eyes...Boys demand a pretty book with plenty of killing.

Charlotte Yonge, *What Books to Lend and What to Give*, 1887

My brother and I were children in the 1950s, teenagers in the 1960s. Like most children, our parents encouraged us to read what were generally considered to be 'good books', those written by well-established writers and published long before we were born. Our primary school didn't have novels you could borrow and there was no bus route to the local library, but we were bought books as presents and sometimes they were sent by my aunt in America – not hundreds of them, just enough to fill a bookshelf each.

I still own most of my childhood books and have inherited my brother's; cheap, cloth-covered hardbacks published by Dean and Sons Ltd or Thames Publishing Company and marketed as Regent Classics. The American books had better quality paper and plenty of illustrations which I adored. Few of the British ones had any pictures at all. If you were lucky, there would be one ludicrously anachronistic picture opposite the title page – my Regent Classics copy of *Jane Eyre* shows her in a long baby-blue dress with a blonde 1950s-style ponytail tied up in a pink bow, talking to Rochester, who looks like Cary Grant in a tuxedo. I thought it was great.

Apart from a shared collection of Enid Blytons, I don't remember reading my brother's books and I'm sure he didn't read mine. On his shelf were copies of *Robinson Crusoe* by Daniel Defoe, *Our Friend Jennings* by Anthony Buckridge, Jules Verne's *Around the World in Eighty Days*, *The Story of Davy Crockett* by Enid Lamonte, Mark Twain's *The Adventures of Tom Sawyer*, *The Man in the Iron Mask* by Alexander Dumas and Robert Louis Stevenson's *Treasure Island*. On my shelf there were much read and much loved copies of all of Louisa May Alcott's *Little Women* books and her lesser known novel *An Old Fashioned Girl*, Anna Sewell's *Black Beauty*, Susan Coolidge's *What Katy Did* and *What Katy Did Next*, *Jane Eyre* and *Wuthering Heights* by Charlotte and Emily Brontë, *Heidi* by Johanna Spyri, the sequel *Heidi Grows Up* written by her translator Charles Tritten, and a clutch of boarding school stories.

Books for boys and books for girls. While my brother had books of war, derring do, adventure and brave encounter, I had stories of family life, self-denial, love (without sex, of course), and personal stories of triumph over tragedy – the domestic dramas. In his stories, boys or young men went, often alone, to have adventures, wage wars or make fortunes. They were being taught how to be the arbiters of their own destiny. In my books, the girls either stayed at home or, if they were homeless, which was frequently the case, found a new one and almost always ended up as happy homemakers. There might not have been killings but there was certainly plenty of suffering and death in haunting, tear-stained scenes, most affectingly Beth March's in *Little Women* and Helen Temple's in *Jane Eyre*. The wars fought in my books were small, personal battles against character traits considered unsuitable for girls: hot tempers, ambition, too much cleverness or jealousy. Sometimes there were brave, dignified fights against injustice, like Jane Eyre's against her aunt and Mr Brocklehurst, or Katy Carr's calm handling of her distress when she was wrongfully accused of behaving provocatively towards the boys in the next-door school, and it was wonderful when my heroines won through, although there was often a heavy price to pay for their victory.

There was an advantage to only owning a few books because it meant that I really knew them well. By the time I left primary school, I had read and re-read these stories so many times that the lives of Jane Eyre, Helen Temple, Katy and Clover Carr, Heidi, Jo, Meg, Beth and Amy March were as familiar to me as those of the girls I walked to school with each day. Other children's classics I absorbed through television or film. I was so taken with Hayley Mills' cheesy but engaging Pollyanna that I saved up for a crystal mobile so that I could 'live all the time in a rainbow' and sent off to my aunt for the words of the American national anthem. I read Frances Hodgson Burnett's *A Secret Garden* but I'm not sure whether I've imagined seeing a BBC black and white television version too. The story had a lasting effect. Like most children, I was caught up in the romance and the mystery of the roses growing up behind that high-walled secret garden where only children could go.

What lived with me most in these books were quirky, odd details of personality, atmosphere and location; things which caught my imagination and stayed there. I remembered Heidi's meals of bread, melted cheese and fresh goat's milk which she drank out of bowls and her hayloft room with its round window looking out over the starry Alpine sky. Katy Carr's naughtiness at school, her climbing into next door's playground to retrieve her school hat and getting caught. Katy's cousin Helen with her calm saintliness, smooth shiny hair and beautiful presents. Jane Eyre in the red-room, her horrible bullying cousins, those terrible injustices at school meted out by cruel unthinking adults. Jo cutting off her hair and her disappointing failure to marry Laurie. Amy's brief passion for pickled limes; burning Jo's stories. Sweet Beth being given a piano with gold silk and candelabras, nearly dying but 'turning' and then finally leaving us all to cry for her. And Mary in the secret garden with just her friends, not a single adult knowing where she was.

As a child reader, I didn't see these books as old-fashioned or out of my time because I thought that books were always from a different place. It didn't occur to me that anyone might be writing about girls just like me, and my other reading (posh girls playing lacrosse at boarding school) confirmed this. It would have been impossible to imagine a book about a Jewish girl growing up in a London suburb, and I'm not sure I would have wanted to read one anyway. The books I loved were as different and distinct to me as each one was to its writer and I was only vaguely aware that there were any similarities between them. I think I understood that they were all about girls in families or searching for one and that a lot of these children seemed to be orphans, but I had no interest at all in comparing Heidi to Katy or Jo to Jane. I suppose if asked, I would have been able to say that all these girls were strong minded, battling with their own naughty and rebellious natures. I enjoyed this but since I was being brought up to be more of a Meg than a Jo, it was a secret relief to me when these lively rebellious girls grew up into sweet, submissive women. I certainly didn't notice that disability, illness (particularly paralysing illness) and cure are central to many of these stories, but this isn't surprising since most literary critics and commentators have similarly failed to notice it, or considered it, at best, worth only a passing remark.

I began to look at my books differently when I re-read them with my daughters. What made my reading different was not the passage of time, because my world as a child had been as different as my children's from the world of Katy, Mary and Pollyanna. They loved the stories as much as I did and for the same reasons but they brought a new knowledge to their reading. Since a road accident when they were very young, I have used a wheelchair and have legs which 'don't work'. None of us see me as a poor invalid who has to be taken care of, but we are also aware that no wheelchair smashed by a jealous goat-herd (*Heidi*), magic healing place (*The Secret Garden*), change of personality (*What Katy Did*), or miracle cure in a New York hospital (*Pollyanna*) is going to get me up and running about again.

At one point in my research for this book it felt like there was hardly a girls' novel since 1850 which didn't have a character who at some crucial stage defied their guardian and fell off a swing or out of a sled, became paralysed through tipping out of a carriage or was suffering from some nameless, crippling illness from which they could, indeed must, be cured. From the 1850s, up until very recently (and even now writers kill or cure their disabled characters with worrying ease), there were only two possible ways for writers to resolve the problem of their characters' inability to walk: cure or death.

In order for a cure to take place, for the story to end as the reader expected, the character almost always had to undergo some significant alteration – they had to become a different kind of person. Whether the paralysis was caused by injury, weakness, or a sickness of the soul, some personal, spiritual change was always central to the resolution of the story. Mostly it was the paralysed character themselves who had to correct some moral weakness but sometimes, as in *Pollyanna*, the function of the paralysis was to redeem another, flawed character and to bring unresolved elements in the plot to a neat close. Between 'once upon a time' and 'they lived happily ever after' this traveller, the crippled child,[1] was obliged to pass through what Northrop Frye calls 'various planes of existence'.

In these designs, nothing is merely accidental or coincidental. That is what design means; all inevitably falls into place, the right people meet, the necessary discoveries are made, the outcome ties up all the ends and our expectations of the significant pattern is fulfilled.[2]

There may be a 'descent into a night world' in the story but by the end there will always be 'a return to the idyllic world'. The wheelchair is literally or symbolically discarded, the character gets up and walks, and all is well in the world.

The ways in which the protagonists had to change in order to make the world idyllic again are as diverse as the stories themselves. They might, like Katy Carr, have to learn to be less boisterous and more womanly. They might, like Heidi's friend Clara, have to learn how to love themselves more and find a bit more zest for life. Or they might, like Colin Craven in *The Secret Garden*, have to learn to be less self-obsessed and more positive. One thing is for sure, for the story to reach its desired happy ending, each of these children has to learn some kind of lesson and

---

1. 'Cripple' is the word used by Victorian novelists to describe a number of physical and moral conditions, infirmity of body or soul, general bodily weakness, inability to walk and so on. Today it is a perjorative term and disabled people avoid it. In this book, I use it where the novelist themselves use it, and sometimes I use it ironically.
2. Northrop Frye, *The Secular Scripture – A Study of the Structure of Romance*, Harvard University Press, Cambridge, MA, 1976, p29.

we, the readers, need to understand the moral (and Christian) point of the lesson they have learned.

This cure is somehow so central to the outcome of the story, so expected, that I and generations of readers and countless commentators have failed to notice it or remember it as significant. But even as we failed to take account of it, we were storing up enough perceptions and ideas about disability to last a lifetime. We were learning that: (1) there is nothing good about being disabled; (2) disabled people have to learn the same qualities of submissive behaviour that women have always had to learn: patience, cheerfulness and making the best of things; (3) impairment can be a punishment for bad behaviour, for evil thoughts or for not being a good enough person; (4) although disabled people should be pitied rather than punished, they can never be accepted; and (5) the impairment is curable. If you want to enough, if you love yourself enough (but not more than you love others), if you believe in God enough, you will be cured.

Strong stuff then and strong stuff even now.

Unlike our ideas about women which have changed profoundly since these novels were written, society's ideas about disability and disabled people are not always so different to those held by the Victorians. Disability has always been a marginal issue to everyone except disabled people themselves and perhaps also to a certain range of professionals who make their living out of working with or being 'experts' in one area or another. There is still a tendency to see disability in medical terms – what is 'wrong' with someone – rather than in the social inequalities disabled people face. Whilst the different tasks, personal qualities and challenges writers ascribe to boys and girls in children's books is of enormous interest to both literary scholars and ordinary readers, interest in disability is marginal and 'specialist'. Perhaps this is why it has remained largely invisible.

Yet as the growing field of study in children's literature shows, the books that we read when we are young are in many ways the most important books we will ever read. In his essay 'The Lost Childhood', Graham Greene wrote that it is only in childhood that books have any deep influence on our lives. Many of the novels discussed here have stayed with me in the way that books I read as an adult rarely have, *Jane Eyre* and *Little Women* especially. I read them first when I was about eight or nine years old (*Jane Eyre* in a skilfully abridged Regent Classics edition) and re-read them continually until I reached my own adolescence. Adrienne Rich, talking about her own reading and re-reading of *Jane Eyre*, says, 'I have never lost the sense that it contains through and beyond the force of its creator's imagination, some nourishment I needed then and now.'[3] We take from books what we need and are able to understand at that time. Because I was a child when I first read *Jane Eyre*, the most powerful part of this book has never been her time at Thornfield and the love affair with Rochester, but Jane's own childhood: the terrifying scene in the red-room, the cruelty she had to endure at the hands of the relatives who should have loved her and cared for her in Gateshead, the injustices at Lowood School and her beautiful friendship with Helen Burns.

Like most women I know who read these books when young (some boys must have read them too but they have always been seen as 'girl's books'), my memory of these powerful and enduring stories is surprisingly selective. We wanted and needed strong, interesting girls and that's what

3. Adrienne Rich, 'The Temptations of a Motherless Woman, 1973', in *On Lies, Secrets and Silence: Selected Prose 1966–1978*, W.W. Norton and Company Inc., New York, 1980, p89.

we remember. What endured from my own many readings of *Little Women* was clever, unconventional Jo who sold her hair to help her family, was sometimes selfish and troubled but who was also enormously good fun. I remember my disappointment when Jo failed to marry Laurie and hitched herself instead to the much duller Herr Bhaer. It took a number of adult readings to realise that by the end of *Good Wives* (originally published as *Little Women Part 2*), Jo has married someone old enough to be her father and has literally taken up Beth's brooms and dustpans to become the 'heart of the house'. She doesn't exactly sing as she sweeps, but she does accept that sweeping is her job. She forgoes her dramatic lively stories and is only allowed by her parents to write if she limits herself to penning a family story, her own *Little Women*. I remember Katy Carr's wild antics over the school fence, not her marrying the boring but noble sea captain. I didn't read Ethel Turner's *Seven Little Australians* when I was young, but a friend told me that she did not remember Judy's death (the incredibly dramatic ending to this story), but only how naughty Judy was and all the mischief she got up to with her brothers and sisters. Similarly, I didn't consciously take from these stories any lessons about what kind of characters died in stories, how impossible it is to live as a disabled person and what they have to do in order to be cured.

Thinking and writing about books is essentially a matter of what questions you want to ask about them. The writer Michèle Roberts has talked about how, as a woman, she sees the world through 'gendered eyes'. I understand this to mean that she observes different things and asks different questions about the world from those which might be asked by a man. As a disabled women, I too look at the world differently and there are issues and ideas, apparently invisible to others, which are very real to me.

There are different things I observe when I read these books now and different questions I want to ask. I do not want to 're-write' these books or to indulge in what literary scholar Harold Bloom has disparagingly called the 'school of resentment'. I loved these books when I was young and mostly I love them still. I am not interested in asking why the writers didn't write a different kind of book, one in which the disabled character lived happily in their invalid status, but I am interested in being what Professor Jacqueline Rose has called 'a bit aggressive with a text'. I do want to ask questions about what readers have learned from these books and how these lessons might have affected our assumptions about disabled people. I want to look at the antecedents, and to understand the social framework which underpins the ideas in these stories. I want to know what the characters in these books have to do before they can be cured and assess the differences between those who are cured and those who die.

I am also curious about the fascination with spinal damage and spinal weakness. Until well into the middle of the twentieth century, people who broke their spines were not only paralysed for the rest of their lives but were very unlikely to live for more than a couple of years. Was the interest in walking and not walking in these novels merely symbolic, used as a device to bring the story to a happy conclusion? Were any of the medical conditions described in these books real to the Victorians? Mortality rates were high for children during this period and a scientific approach to medicine had not yet been established. There were no antibiotics and doctors frequently made things worse rather than better. A diagnosis of a condition like tuberculosis was received as a death sentence, cholera epidemics were widespread and an infection could kill a child in a matter of days. Children died in real life and they died in books. But the paralysed child whose legs do not move, who has to use a wheelchair and who becomes magically cured; where did this idea come from?

The novels I have chosen to write about are those which seem to have given a great deal of pleasure to their readers over the years. All the titles have been in continuous publication since they were first in print. In Great Britain they are all published in the Puffin Classics imprint of Penguin Books. You can find them in almost every bookshop which has a children's department and every library. New editions – illustrated, abridged, hardback, paperback – come out each year. I'm not sure what the modern young reader is making of them or even if they're reading them, but it is clear that they are still being bought. Perhaps it is the mums, aunties and grandmas who are buying them, remembering the pleasure of their own childhood reading and wanting like my own parents to instill 'the classics' in their offspring. All of these stories have been made into television series and/or films, sometimes several times over.

A surprising number of these titles have sequels and where I felt that they had something important to say, I have included them. Mostly I read the sequels when I was young, drawn on as writers and publishers hoped readers would be by the pleasure of the first. They were almost always disappointing. But sometimes, as with *Pollyanna Grows Up*, I was reading the sequel for the first time and was astonished by how central disability is to the story.

The first two books on this list were chosen because I cannot think of better examples of the power of novels to convince us that the good die young and that some creatures are just too saintly to stay on this earth. These are *Jane Eyre* by Charlotte Brontë (1847) and *Little Women* parts one and two – the latter more usually known as *Good*

Wives – by Louisa May Alcott (1868–69). *Jane Eyre* was not written for children and the author would probably have been surprised at the way her work has been marketed and sold since its publication, but for generations of girls, including my own, *Jane Eyre* was the most important book of our childhood. The next books, in order of publication, are *What Katy Did* by Susan Coolidge (1872), *Heidi* by Johanna Spyri (1880), *The Secret Garden* by Frances Hodgson Burnett (1911) and *Pollyanna* by Eleanor Porter (1913). All of these titles include at least one character who is not just ill or disabled in some general way but specifically is unable to walk and has to use a wheelchair. They are, for a time at least, portrayed as suffering and unhappy but by the end of the story they are up and running about. To this list I have added another family story which is now also published by Puffin Classics in Great Britain and has always been in print in Australia (and appeared on television, as a play and even a musical). This is *Seven Little Australians* by Ethel Turner (1894). This book's treatment of illness, accident, injury and death is so powerful and so unconventional that it seemed right to include it here. There are 66 years between the publication of the first and the most recent of these titles, 56 years between the birth of the youngest and the oldest of the writers. Not so long, perhaps. They seem to me to have much in common.

All of the books in this study have long been recognised as 'classics', a term we all accept but rarely question. John Rowe Townsend tells us that survival is a good test of a book and that 'the books that are likely to survive are those that have engaged the whole heart and skill of a writer or artist'.[3] Alice M. Jordan wrote in 1947

---

3. John Rowe Townsend, *Written for Children*, Penguin Books, London, 1974, pp11–12.

that it is the intensity of the imagination which is the important thing: 'Especially we feel, on opening the pages of a book that we are in a different world, and a world full of real beings about whom in one way or another we care.'[4] The titles which will be discussed in the following chapters are all the best known and best loved of their writer's achievements. Many of the authors were prolific in output: Johanna Spyri wrote over 50 books for adults and children, Louisa May Alcott published nearly 300 titles, Ethel Turner some 27 novels and Frances Hodgson Burnett had a total of 30 novels and countless short stories published as well as 14 plays performed, yet most people would be hard pressed to mention even one or two titles outside the books discussed here. Eleanor Porter is remembered only for *Pollyanna*, Susan Coolidge is only known for the Katy books and *Jane Eyre* is by far the most popular of Charlotte Brontë's four novels. Of all the books these writers produced, the titles discussed here are the ones which have in Townsend's words 'the vitality that will carry a book on through changing times and tasks'.

Of course there were other books written in this period which include a disabled character or one who is ill. Perhaps the most famous 'Victorian cripple' is Charles Dickens' 'good as gold' Tiny Tim (*A Christmas Carol*, 1843), who thinks that when people see him on Christmas Day it will be 'pleasant for them to remember who made lame beggars walk and blind men see'. Robert Louis Stevenson's *Treasure Island* (1883), with its one-legged Long John Silver and 'dreadful looking', 'deformed' Blind Pew, contains stereotypes of characters whose impairment signifies badness or evil, as does the

---

4. Alice M. Jordan, 'Children's Classics', in Virginia Haviland, ed., *Children's Literature – Views and Reviews*, The Bodley Head, London, 1973, p38.

'dreadful, dangerous' Captain Hook with his metal arm in J.M.Barrie's classic, *Peter Pan* (1904). I'm sure there are more. These are all characters to patronise and pity, or to fear and dread. They have much to offer in a study of disability in children's fiction but they are not included here. This is a book about novels which start at home and stay at home, where the disabled character is always a child, never a menacing adult, and where disability is primarily used as a metaphor for dependency and weakness, providing a time for reflection and learning. Whatever the trials, troubles and grief of the character – who is almost always a girl – things will be resolved, their reward is likely to be in their cure and all will end happily if not by hearth and home, then at least no further away than the garden.

Chapter 1
Punishment and Pity: Images and Representations of Disability, Illness and Cure

The evils that God inflicts are as real a part of his providence, as the blessings he bestows, as in the course of nature the darkness of night is by his order; as well as the light of the day: therefore they are always sent for some wise and holy design. Sometimes, they are sent only for trial, to exercise the faith, humility and patience. For the most part they are castigatory, to bring us a sight and sense of our state, to render sin more evident and odious to us.

from *How We May Bear Afflictions*, sermons collected by Samuel Annersley, London, 1676

In literature, as in life, people have found it hard to believe that there is anything good about being disabled. There have been some periods of time and some corners of the world where disabled people have been regarded as having a special gift, insight or purity of spirit, but far more prevalent has been the idea that there is something inherently 'bad' about a person who has an impaired body. People who were lame, deaf or blind, who could not walk, who had a curved spine or epileptic seizures were regarded as blemished and that blemish seen as a cause for exclusion and fear.

For as long as there has been recorded history, there have been three stock responses towards disabled people: they (or their ancestors) have been punished; they have been pitied; or through faith in God or self, they have been encouraged to 'overcome' what is usually seen as a burden of sorrow.

Punishment is inextricably linked to the idea of sin. Physical impairment, especially in a newborn baby, has been particularly open to interpretation as a sign of the wrath of the gods (or of God) or as a visitation of evil spirits. In its harshest form, punishment rests on the belief that disabled people have been bad in a past life, or in their present one, that their ancestors have committed sins, that they have shown disregard for the gods or have been touched by the devil.[1]

Throughout history there have been countless examples of the way society has rejected, punished and blamed disabled people, believing that their presence was, in itself, a sign of retribution. It was the ancient Greeks who inspired the myth of human perfectability and the idea that imperfection must be destroyed. In Greek mythology Hera, the goddess of hunting, gave birth to a son Hephaistus, who was so weak at birth that his disgusted mother dropped him from the height of Olympus to rid herself of the embarrassment that his painful appearance caused her. The Northern Salteaux Indians, believing the bodies of disabled people to be demon possessed, favoured torture and shot them with arrows, then burned the bodies.[2] The Jukan in Sudan believed impairment to be caused by the devil and left their disabled people to die.[3]

In Europe during the Middle Ages, many disabled

---

1. A friend of mine, Hindu by birth and paralysed in a car accident, was recently told by her mother-in-law that she must have broken someone's bones in the past, otherwise there could be no explanation of why her own bones had been broken so seriously. Those who followed the 1999 outcry at the comments of Glen Hoddle, then manager of England's football team (he claimed that families with a disabled member have to ask themselves what wrong has been done in the past) and those who know the Second Commandment of the Old Testament will be familiar with this argument.
2. K. Dovey and J. Graffam, *The Experience of Disability: Social Construction and Imposed Limitation*, Victoria College Press, Burwood, VIC, 1987.
3. L. Buscaglia, *The Disabled and Their Parents*, Thorofare, Charles B. Slack, New Jersey, 1975.

people were burned as witches. Superstition and witchcraft have always been used to exploit fear and thereby exert social control over things for which there are no rational or scientific explanations. The *Malleus Maleficarum* (*The Witches Hammer*), written in 1486, was a handbook on witch finding, and its influence lasted for the next 200 years, gaining support from the Vatican. The primary purpose of this text was the identification of witches and of those who had been affected by their spells. Physical impairment was the primary tool of identification. Witches could be recognised by physical features such as facial or bodily deformity, being lame or having marked skin.[4]

Ideas about witchcraft have had a profound effect on literature. The fairytales of northern Europe, with their physical depiction of witches (often in the guise of the wicked stepmother), continued the idea that a physical impairment was a sign of 'badness'. Illustrations in books designed for adults and children showed them as crook-backed, deformed and supported by crutches and sticks. Shakespeare's *Richard III*, the most famous literary 'hunchback', claimed that it was witchcraft that had distorted his frame: 'Edward's wife, that monstrous witch, consorted with that harlot-strumpet Shore, that by their witchcraft thus have marked me.'

Superstition frequently goes hand in hand with religion and although theologists will always argue against such a connection, it is often hard to make the distinction between the religious idea of the devil, leading humans astray, and the 'bad spirit' or 'evil eye' whose pleasure is to punish or deform. Jewish writer Isaac Bashevis Singer, a master of storytelling, often wrote about the superstitious, mythical ideas in the shtetls of eastern Europe and the damage that the dybbuks, golems and menacing spirits would willingly

---

4. Unpublished research by Anna Sullivan and Richard Rieser.

perform upon the innocent. In his story 'The Destruction of Kreshev', the voice of the devil speaks of the pleasure he has in making mischief:

> I am the Primeval Snake, the Evil One, Satan. The Cabala refers to me as Samael and the Jews sometimes call me merely 'that one'. It is well known that I love to arrange strange marriages, delighting in such mismatches as an old man with a young girl, an unattractive widow with a youth in his prime, a cripple with a great beauty, a cantor with a deaf woman, a mute with a braggard.[5]

But 'punishment' for being disabled is not something we can attribute solely to the long and distant past. In Nazi Germany in the 1930s and 40s, doctors developed 'euthanasia' programmes which gassed disabled people, especially disabled children, or gave them lethal injections. Until very recently in this country and right up until the present day in others, one way of punishing disabled people has been to lock them up in institutions, hidden away from society. In these institutions disabled children are deprived of family life, sociability, the chance of employment and many things others consider to be their right: a kind of life sentence for bodily impairment.

Compared to this, pity seems a fairly soft option. Whilst punishment suggests that disabled people or their ancestors are in some way to blame for their impairment, pity

---

5. Isaac Bashevis Singer, 'The Destruction of Kreshev' in Isaac Bashevis Singer, *The Collected Stories*, Farrar, Straus & Giroux, New York, 1982. My Polish grandmother used to wear a red ribbon on her underwear and made spitting noises if anyone paid a compliment to her family in order to ward off the 'evil eye'. When a neighbour praised my brother for his sweet nature on the same day he fell off the garden wall and had to have stitches, she was certain that this incautious flattery had made the evil eye jealous.

suggests that whatever the cause, they need the sympathy, care and charity of those more fortunate. In the Judeo-Christian tradition, which provided the moral framework for almost all the published literature of America and Europe in the nineteenth and early twentieth centuries, it is possible to hold the two approaches of punishment and pity side by side.

For example, the second commandment of the book of Exodus lays the foundation for regarding disabled people as the visible sign of punishment meted out for 'sins against God': 'For I thy God am a jealous God, visiting the iniquity of the fathers upon the children unto the third and the fourth generation of those who hate me.' However, the Old Testament also instructs its followers to take care of the sick and the needy. The book of Leviticus provides models both for the exclusion of disabled people from the religious and spiritual life of the community and for their inclusion as the recipients of kindness and 'care'. On the one hand, we are told that a man who is 'blind, lame, broken footed, crookbacked, a dwarf, or blemished' is not allowed to 'go into the vail, nor come nigh unto the altar' to receive the blessings or the 'Mitzvah' from the religious minister, and on the other there is the instruction that 'you shall not curse the deaf or put a stumbling block before the blind'. The idea that it is incumbent upon the community to remove 'stumbling blocks' became the model for charitable work within the Jewish community. But whilst a lot of good may be done in the name of charity, it also creates distance and inequality between the giver and the receiver; what disabled writer Nasa Begum has aptly called 'the burden of gratitude'.[6]

Whichever way one looks at the models of the past, it is

---

6. Nasa Begum, *The Burden of Gratitude*, University of Warwick, 1990.

clear that whether disabled people are to be blamed and punished or whether they are to be pitied, they are not to be accepted as full members of society. They are always somehow outside the boundaries of what is accepted as normal.

In literature, therefore, the portrayal of disabled people was likely to fall into a number of stereotypical roles. They would be terrifying and evil, like the devil himself, and our response would be to hate or fear them. Or they might be angelically pure invalids destined for an early death. Sometimes they might be ill but not dying and would need to embark on a difficult religious or psychological journey from which they would eventually be healed. We would pity these characters and either mourn their deaths or rejoice in their cure. Such portrayals taught readers not to fear or punish 'poor crippled children' but to be kind and caring, yet it was always clear that such children were not 'good creation'. God had his reasons for making children like this, reasons we could not always know, but it was understood that such children were somehow incomplete, not whole and not quite of this world.

The third response to disability 'overcoming' is also inextricably linked to a religious context, the moral teachings of the New Testament. Christianity is a religion which has always been exercised by the ideas of sin, punishment, forgiveness and healing, and the way in which these ideas have changed over the last 2000 years has closely affected the way we see and treat disabled people. It is also a flexible religion (a priest recently described it as a religion with 'woolly edges'), capable of changing along with the economic and social pressures of the day. But an idea which has shown an extraordinary capacity to endure is that of the representation of physical impairment as something which could be cured through *faith*.

The miracles of physical and psychic healing in Matthew,

Mark, Luke and John developed an idea which remains central to the way Western society continues to view the 'problem' of disabled people. In this paradigm, impairment is something to be healed or cured, not simply accepted as 'God's will', and the path towards this healing is absolute faith. The purpose of the miracles of the New Testament was to establish Jesus as the face of God on earth. In the healing miracles, the cripple walks again, the blind man learns to see, the woman who continually bleeds is healed, not, as one might think, because they have repented their sins, but because they have shown absolute and unquestioning faith in Christ as the authority of God. They possess these impairments in order for God's work to be revealed through them. When Jesus travelled through the towns and villages, visiting synagogues, preaching the good news of the kingdom and healing all kinds of diseases and sickness, he was demonstrating his divine power in the most obvious fashion:

> And getting into a boat, he crossed over and came to his own city and behold they brought to him a paralytic lying on his bed; and when Jesus saw their faith, he said to the paralytic, 'take heart your sins are forgiven'. And behold, some of the scribes said to themselves, "This man is blaspheming.' But Jesus knowing their thoughts said, 'Why do you think evil in your hearts? For which is easier to say, "Your sins are forgiven" or to say "rise and walk"? But that you may know that the Son of Man has authority on earth to forgive sins?' He then said to the paralytic, 'Rise, take up your bed and walk.' And he rose and went home. When the crowd saw it, they were afraid and they glorified God who had given such authority to men.[7]

---

7. New Testament, Matthew, 9: 1–8.

It is no coincidence that a large number of the New Testament miracle cures tell the story of the paralysed man walking again. 'Take up your bed and walk' has become a metaphor for the will to take responsibility for one's own recovery and life through faith – faith in oneself as well as in spiritual forces beyond the self.

There are enormous linguistic possibilities associated with walking or not walking. Words which relate to difficulties with walking and standing have taken on negative associations – bent, crooked, crippled, stooped, hunch-backed (a 'crook' is a criminal, a 'bent copper' is a corrupt police officer) – whereas those connected with walking are positive: straight, upright, firm, erect. In our common language, we have many expressions that equate walking with being strong and independent. We talk about 'standing on our own two feet', 'putting our best foot forward', 'keeping one step ahead,' 'walking tall' or 'taking it in our stride'. On a recent radio discussion on BBC Radio 4's *Today* programme, Professor Mansfield of Harvard University, who was expressing his concerns about the status of men in today's society, described masculinity as 'the ability to stand up – to step out'. When a character stops being able to walk, she or he symbolises our worst fears about dependency, expressed in Victorian fiction as having to 'lie on the sofa always, and be helpless and a cripple' (cousin Helen in *What Katy Did*).

Paralysis metaphorically denotes passivity, dependence, losing one's place in the world, being cut off and separate, no longer a complete human being. When we say that someone or something is paralysed, we mean that they are cut off from things, broken, silent, unable to do or to act. We describe someone without courage or strength of character as 'spineless', someone incapable of taking action as 'paralysed by fear'.

Paralysis and paralysing weaknesses which emanate from the central nervous system are capable of providing the greatest metaphorical possibilities for storytelling because there is something mysterious and hidden about the spinal cord. One minute a character may be upright, walking and 'whole', the next, the spine is broken and although not visibly scarred, the person is unable to move or to feel. Since the workings of the spinal column have always been so little understood, in literature at least, the cure can be made to appear dramatic and immediate. There are endless possibilities for happy endings, and clear moral points can be made if the reader believes that an unpleasant physical condition can be 'overcome', either by individual willpower or divine intervention. In stories where such a condition is portrayed as fated or irredeemable, the likely ending is death.

Louisa May Alcott's *Jack and Jill* (1880), Susan Coolidge's *What Katy Did* and Eleanor Porter's *Pollyanna* are all stories in which a girl at the crucial stage between girlhood and womanhood has an accident in which her spine is broken or damaged, becomes paralysed and later, sometimes several years later, is completely cured. *Heidi* and *The Secret Garden* also have as their centrepiece a miracle cure scene in which the wheelchair is discarded for ever and the character walks again, although in these stories the cause of the spinal weakness is not so clearly defined. Yet at the time when these stories were written, indeed right up to the present day, the spinal cord, which contains millions of nerve cells, has always been remarkably resistant to cure. In fact, until the middle of the twentieth century when antibiotics became readily available, people with spinal cord injuries did not usually live more than a year or two at the most.

*

Written records of spinal cord injury date back to the ancient Egyptians, who recognised that it caused paralysis of the arms and legs, bowel and bladder dysfunction and loss of erections. Although patients with signs of damage were recommended to apply meat and honey to the neck, the Edwin Smith Papyrus had no other conclusion but that spinal injury was 'not an ailment to be treated.' It was a view that was to prevail over the next 5000 years. The ancient Greeks were also fascinated yet mystified by spinal cord injury. Hippocrates (400 years BC) advocated a large intake of fluid and a special diet including four to nine pints of milk daily, with honey and mild white wine. He also developed methods to repair spinal deformities which were used by medieval and Renaissance physicians and continued to be used right up to the nineteenth century. His famous extension bench which employed stretching type traction to straighten the spine and treat fractured spinal columns was used by both Greek physician Galen (130–201 AD) and Oribasius (325–403 AD) who understood that injuries to the upper portion of the spinal column resulted in paralysis and loss of sensation which would lead to quick death.

Physicians through the ages have been intrigued by spinal cord injuries, though their treatments met with little or no success. In 1805, in the Battle of Trafalgar against the French–Spanish fleet, Lord Nelson was shot in the chest and the bullet entered his spine. He called for his surgeon to report that 'all power and feeling below my chest are gone'. The surgeon's mournful reply was, 'My Lord, unhappily for our country, nothing can be done for you.'

By the mid-1800s the use of ether and chloroform and the introduction of antisepsis techniques made surgery safer and more sterile, but as a treatment for spinal cord injuries, interventions remained controversial. In 1898, a rare example of a text on spinal cord injury was a German manual by Wagner and Stolper. There was no good news here either: 'In complete lesions it is the physician's forlorn task, even while knowing that the patient is approaching an early death, to keep him alive for weeks and months on end, only to see him wretchedly fade away, despite all skill and efforts.'[8] John Young, an eminent American SCI doctor, notes that right up until the Second World War, 'the view generally held was the sooner they died, the better for all.'[9]

Despite physicians' frustration with such injuries, there were very few developments in the treatment of people with spinal cord paralysis as the result of accident or concussion until well into the twentieth century and as a result, medical textbooks of the day devoted little space to this field. Standard texts often failed to mention it at all, or deemed it worthy of only a passing reference. A medical textbook by Dr Thomas Morgan Rotch, a professor of pediatrics at Harvard University – called *Pediatrics, The Hygienic and Medical Treatment of Children*, published in 1896 – has a lengthy section on paralysis in children which fails to mention spinal cord injury or trauma.

The most common paralysing illnesses of the day were chronic tubercular diseases of joints, particularly of the hip (known as 'hip-disease') or the spine (Pott's disease) and infantile spinal paralysis (poliomyelitis). These were un-romantic illnesses, resulting in lameness and deformity and with clear links to the conditions of poverty. In literature, such diseases were rarely mentioned unless, like Eleanor Porter in her portrayal of Jamie in *Pollyanna Grows Up* (1915), writers used disabling disease as a device

8. Wagner and Stolper, quoted in Sam Maddox, 'Spinal Cord Injury, A Primer', *Spinal Network*, PO Box 4162, Boulder, CO 80306, 1993, p23.
9. In adult literature, Somerset Maugham's play *The Saced Flame* (1929) and D.H. Lawrence's novel *Lady Chatterley's Lover* (1928), with their portrayal of paralysed, impotent males with beautiful, frustrated young wives, both upheld the view that people with spinal cord injury would be better off dead.

to present social issues to young readers and to make a point about the responsibility of wealthy Christian philanthropists towards the poor. A later British text, *Paralysis in Children*, also devotes only two lines to paraplegia. Under the section on the causes of spastic paralysis, paraplegia is described merely as 'affection to both lower limbs from a lesion in the spinal cord, or more rarely in the cortex, either of which may be due to trauma or inflammation.'[10] In the index, the one reference to 'spinal trauma' refers to defects caused by difficult births. There is no attempt to describe treatment, psychological effects or cure of spinal cord injury. It is very unlikely that children of this period did not have accidents which resulted in such injury and perhaps the lack of discussion in medical texts of the time was simply because there was no realistic treatment.

In fact, there was no talk of treatment and rehabilitation into a useful life until Ludwig Guttman, a refugee from Nazi Germany, founded the first Spinal Injuries Unit at Stoke Mandeville in the 1940s. The unit pioneered the synthesis of clinical procedures with social and professional rehabilitation, taking a 'whole person' approach. Guttman's objective was management of the condition rather than cure.[11]

As has been mentioned, up until the advent of the Second World War, when antibiotics were developed to treat previously lethal bladder and bowel infections, skin and lung infections (sulfonamides in America and penicillin in Britain), people with spinal cord injury rarely lived longer than a year or two. There was certainly no possibility for a 'cure' in someone with a complete spinal break. In a partial lesion to the spinal cord it has always been

10. R.G. Gordon and M. Forrester Brown, *Paralysis in Children*, Oxford Medical Publications, Oxford University Press, London, 1933, p6.
11. Sam Maddox, *Spinal Network*.

possible to survive beyond the first year or two and in these cases, there is also the possibility for recovery of movement and sensation below the point of the break. In an incomplete break, the pressure on the cord is not total and there is the possibility that sufficient nerve cells remain undamaged. Swelling or bruising to the spinal cord can reduce, and in such cases recovery can take place within the first four to eight weeks after the break. It is very unlikely, if not impossible, for this to happen beyond this time (and certainly not after five years as in *What Katy Did*) because after such a long period, a combination of factors – muscle atrophy and the growth of scar tissue which inhibits the re-growth of nerves, for example – make such recovery impossible.[12]

At the end of the twentieth century, for the first time in history, people with spinal cord injuries have the possibility of living full and active lives, but a severed spine means permanent paralysis and as yet there is no medical technique or surgery which has them miraculously walking again. Yet, as a literary device and as a metaphor for the power of self-will or faith to change the unacceptable, the idea of cure from paralysis still has resonance.

As we have seen, the real incurable and unromantic diseases of the time did not hold much appeal for the Victorian novelists. 'Spinal weakness', on the other hand, allowed great possibility for linking physical conditions with a troubled inner life. Paralysis was seen not just as physical limitations of the body, but as the removal of the 'vital energy' at the heart of a person. Causes and cures of disease were still largely unknown and, as Miriam Bailen points out in the introduction to her book, *The Sickroom in Victorian Fiction – The Art of Being Ill*:

---

12. Research from the International Spinal Research Trust, 8a Bramley Business Centre, Station Rd, Guildford, Surrey GU5 OA2, UK.

The transformation of suffering into balm is particularly striking at a time when medical science had little capacity to heal or even to alleviate the symptoms of a multitude of disorders to which people were then subject – when in many cases the treatment was far more dangerous than the cure.[13]

Linking otherwise inexplicable medical conditions to inner states of turmoil or distress was popular with the medical profession long before Freud and psychoanalytic thinking. Physical weakness was often linked to moral and spiritual infirmity, and emotion and temperament were used to explain both the causes and the symptoms of ill-defined conditions such as 'spinal weakness' ('*Neurasthenia Spinalis:* Functional Nervous Weakness of the Spinal Cord') and 'spinal irritation' ('*Rachialgia*').[14]

Equally Freud was not the first person to connect paralysis directly to sexuality, although earlier doctors were more likely to talk of it in terms of 'morals' and behaviour.[15] The illness is then, by implication, a punishment for frailty of character, and indeed, for seeking personal sexual pleasure. Richard Quain's standard text, *A Dictionary of Medicine* (first

---

13. Miriam Bailen, *The Sickroom in Victorian Fiction – The Art of Being Ill*, Cambridge University Press, Cambridge, 1994, p6.

14. The word 'nervous' itself has both scientific and emotional meanings. Used anatomically, 'the nervous system' describes the huge bundle of fibres which emanate from the brain and the spinal cord and control all bodily sensation and movement. 'Nervous' is also used to describe temperament and feeling. In its original use it meant muscular, vigorous and strong – positive, 'manly' terms – but subsqently came to mean the weaker, more 'feminine' characteristics of being timid, easily agitated, excitable and over-sensitive. A 'nervous disorder' or a 'nervous disease' can be real or imagined – it can be in the body or in the mind. This ambiguity was often used by the Victorian novelist in the development of female characters. 'Trauma' is also described in this way. A 'traumatic break', for example, can mean a broken bone or a broken heart.

15. Lord Byron's daughter Ada (1815–51), when in her mid-teens, that crucial age between girlhood and womanhood, suffered from what was assumed to be hysterical paralysis in her legs and was made to lie on a wooden bed. As soon as she recovered her powers of movement she fled the house, eloping with a tutor.

published in 1800), contains detailed descriptions of the causes and treatment of spinal problems. In his lengthy section on 'Spinal Cord, Special Diseases Of' he describes the causes of 'nervous weakness of the spinal cord' as representing:

> a condition of extreme nervous debility... not at all unlike some of those which may follow concussions of the spinal cord. Such symptoms are most likely to show themselves in those who are naturally of a neurotic temperament.[16]

This condition which, he argues, occurs most frequently in males is likely to be caused by 'sexual excesses (of a natural or unnatural order) either by extending in the form of habitual indulgence over a considerable period, or as more isolated but marked excesses'.[17]

Dr Quain also described 'spinal irritation', a more controversial condition of the day, as occurring 'chiefly in girls between the ages of fifteen and twenty-five'.[18] Although not mentioned in his writing, the ages of fifteen to twenty-five are, significantly, the time when girls and young women are developing into full sexual maturity and, as early marriage was the norm, were most likely to be sexually active. Many of the literary females in the novels of the nineteenth and early twentieth centuries who are paralysed or have difficulties walking at some point in the story fall into this age category.

---

16. Richard Quain, *A Dictionary of Medicine*, Longmans, Green and Co., London, 1800, p1498.
17. Ibid.
18. Margaret May in *The Daisy Chain* falls out of a carriage whilst driving. Katy Carr, Jill in Louisa May Alcott's *Jack and Jill*, Pollyanna and Judy in *Seven Little Australians* all have a blow to the spine after 'excessive movement', and Clara in *Heidi* and Colin in *The Secret Garden* seem to suffer from 'sensitive nerves to the spine'.

The causes Dr Quain gives for spinal weakness read like a list of all the things from which a refined Victorian girl was required to refrain: 'Excessive walking or driving; violent movements of the spine or a blow upon it; abuse of sexual intercourse; masturbation.'[19] As we shall see in Chapter 3, disability and illness were often used in the novels of the day to reinforce moral values and gender expectations.

The words used by Dr Quain to describe spinal irritation – 'a morbid excitability of the sensitive nerves of the spine' – suggest an emotional state as well as a physical one. In much the same way as novelists do, there is little attempt here to distinguish between states of mind and states of body. For example, in his description of injuries to the spinal cord, Quain does not make a distinction between cause and effect:

> Two distinct morbid states then follow a blow or some other traumatic agency on the spine. In the same way we find hysteria co-existing with spinal irritation. Indeed it is extremely rare to find that hysteria, beginning by any symptom will not soon be accompanied by some degree of spinal irritation; and on the other hand, in almost all cases of genuine spinal irritation more or less marked hysterical symptoms will appear, so that these two affections almost always are, at least partly, blended together.[20]

The suggested treatment for these conditions was remarkably optimistic. Dr Quain prescribed rest, 'especially in the direction of previous excesses', with lots of regular, sound sleep and plenty of fresh air – especially that of

19. Ibid.
20. Ibid., p1501

'elevated and bracing mountain situations'.[21] For the conditions which applied particularly to young women, a variety of medicines likely to make the condition worse rather than better – 'morphia' and 'strychnia' – were suggested, but most importantly, 'absolute rest' without movement for several weeks.[22]

Medical textbooks of the nineteenth century could be rather optimistic about cure but their recommendations often relied on the hope that the passage of time, preferably away from home, would bring about recovery. They tended not to ascribe it to self-will and energy in the way that novelists did. In novels, characters who had spinal weakness through one cause or another were likely to be cured by a combination of bed-rest and bracing fresh air as suggested by the doctors, but also through some kind of inner moral or spiritual change. In literature designed for children there was no question of any moral weakness being ascribed directly to sexual excesses, but there was often the clear message that weakness or failure of character was responsible for the calamity that had befallen them. It was essential for children, especially girls, to be morally pure and refined and to overcome excesses of energy or temptation. They had to learn not to put themselves first. On the other hand, too little energy and zest for life was also a problem for the Victorian girl entering womanhood, and re-directing energy away from selfish pursuits towards thinking about others was an important element in the process which would ultimately lead to cure.

With regard to sick or disabled children in stories, the clear message was that though such children should be pitied or cared for rather than neglected, punished or abandoned, in order for them to live into adulthood they

21. Ibid.
22. Ibid.

must be healed. In books, faith rather than scientific medical intervention was at the heart of this cure: faith in God as the ultimate source of power and goodness, but also faith in the self. These two apparently contradictory elements, the religious and the individualistic, run side by side in such stories since they were both important lessons that progressively minded writers of the time felt children needed to learn. Children needed to believe in God but their faith should not make them too passive. They also needed to believe that with sufficient energy and will they had the power to make their own lives better. In stories at least, it is the combination of these beliefs that results in healing.

Chapter 2

Too Good to Live: Deathbed Scenes in Charlotte Brontë's *Jane Eyre* and Louisa May Alcott's *Little Women*

I would gaze on Thee, on Thy patient face;
Make me like Thyself, patient, sweet at peace;
Make my days all love, and my nights all praise,
Till all days and nights and patient sufferings cease.

from, *A Sick Child's Meditation* by Christina Rossetti, 1885

The deaths of Helen Burns in *Jane Eyre* and of Beth in *Little Women* may occupy just a small space in the novels, but the parting scenes and the ultimate departure of Helen and Beth are crucial to the development of the story. Essentially different to the strong and life-loving central characters, these saintly girls, passive and resigned, serve to provide alternatives against which Jane Eyre and Jo March shape themselves. Removed from everyday concerns, reconciled to a short life within a safe, known world, they provide a clear contrast to the difficult journeys that their 'sisters' will have to make. Beth and Helen do not fight against the restrictions or unfairness of their enclosed worlds but submit humbly to their lot, believing that it is God's will to remove them from a difficult, bittersweet existence. To young readers they seem to be saintly girls, far better than any real children, possibly too good to live. We cry over their deaths but, like Jane and Jo, are able to move on in sadness because like the other characters in the story, we believe that they have gone to a better place.

The juxtaposition of the strong, difficult, potentially rebellious heroine alongside the sweet, passive and forgiving invalid was a common feature of nineteenth-century literature. In *Jane Eyre*, Jane has Helen to teach her that revenge and rage can be self-destructive, and in *Little Women* Jo has Beth to teach her patience and self-restraint. At the beginning of these stories, Jane and Jo are flawed, difficult, interesting characters. Both suffer from an excess of passion and strong feelings about the injustices of the world, and both have lessons to learn. Helen and Beth, apart from minor faults of untidy drawers or dreaminess, do not have to learn how to 'be' in the world; they are already well on their way to the next one. Neither Helen nor Beth engage with life; they are willing to submit to their removal from this earth with very little fuss. Death allows them to abdicate responsibility for having to make difficult choices, and they leave their stronger sister or friend free to continue on her own difficult voyage through life. Both of these stories use the metaphor of John Bunyan's *Pilgrim's Progress*: the idea of embarking upon a hazardous journey, where obstacles will be placed in your path and difficult decisions have to be made but where, in the end, you will return to your rightful place as a changed person, better, wiser and with more humility. By contrast, Helen and Beth's journeys are heavenward.

The deathbed scene in books intended for children started off as a way of teaching a moral lesson to those who needed to be saved from damnation and hellfire. They began as soon as books for children began, and continued to be popular whilst childhood deaths were still common. In the seventeenth century, the Puritans saw children as young souls to be saved and therefore a good deal of literature was aimed at the idea of rescuing them. One of their leading writers was James Janeway who, in 1671, published the snappily titled, *A Token for Children, Being an Exact Account of the Conversion, Holy and Exemplary Lives, and Joyful Deaths of Several Young Children*. Its preface asks the child reader, 'Whither do you think those children go when they die, that will not do what they are bid, but play the Truant and lie and speak naughty words and break the Sabbath? Whither do such children go, do you think? Why I will tell you; they which lie must to their Father the Devil into everlasting burning.'[1] In order to avoid this terrible fate and find a way to heaven, the book exhorts children to be dutiful to their parents, diligent at their book, learn their scriptures and their catechisms and live holy lives.

By the middle of the nineteenth century the deathbed scene was still a prominent feature in literature but had become softened and more sentimental. Readers were more likely to see good Christian children ascending into heaven in a gentle state of grace than falling into a pit full of fire and brimstone.

Charlotte Yonge's pivotal *The Daisy Chain* takes its title from the confident belief that loved ones will meet again in heaven. At the start of the story, the sisters Ethel and Margaret are in the unusual position in a Victorian novel of having both their parents alive. However, this is not to last. By page 25, there has been a terrible accident. The carriage has overturned, Mother has died, Father has broken his arm and Margaret is alive but paralysed. The doctor is called and looks anxiously at her. 'The want of power over the limbs is more than mere shock and debility... I cannot tell yet as to the spine.'

Margaret and Ethel are very different kinds of girls. Ethel is a model for many a later character in the domestic novel. Physically she is neither pretty nor angelic looking and has

---

1. James Janeway, *A Token for Children*, T. Norris & A. Bettesworth, London, 1709, Preface, point 3.

many similarities to Jane Eyre. She is a 'thin, lank, angular, sallow girl, just fifteen, trembling from head to toe with restrained eagerness as she tried to curb her tone into the requisite civility.' She is untidy (the state of her work-basket!) and hasty. After Margaret's accident, Ethel battles with her new domestic responsibilities, almost causing her little brother to be burned to death whilst paying too much attention to her 'books and Greek'. Meanwhile Margaret, who has been lying in bed for three months, struggles to accept her new condition. She is 'trying to prepare herself to submit thankfully whether she might be bidden to resign herself to helplessness or to let her mind open once more to visions of joyous usefulness'. Concerned with her slow recovery, her father calls in another doctor. In a scene which was to be almost duplicated in *What Katy Did* (published 16 years later), her father Mr May tells her that the doctor thinks she might get about again, though it may not be for a long time. The doctor says, 'he has known the use of the limbs return almost suddenly even after a year or two', and is able to give an account that convinces Mr May that his daughter Margaret will eventually be cured. She is now allowed to be lifted onto the sofa or carried downstairs. Whilst Ethel struggles against her nature which is to be 'wild and high flying', Margaret is for a while content with her lot. She understood that her period of disability and illness had taught her the lessons young women needed to learn and gains the invalid status of near saintliness. 'For herself Margaret was perfectly content and happy. She knew the temptations of her character had been to be ruler and manager of everything, and she saw that it had been well for her to be thus assigned the role of Mary instead of Martha.'

At the beginning of the story, Margaret was betrothed to Alan, who was away at sea, but she knew that the marriage would only be possible if she were to recover. However, the doctor's predictions have been over-optimistic and her health declines. It is now, of course, unthinkable that she might marry and when Alan dies on board his ship, she thinks: 'There had been so little promise of happiness from the first, that there was more peace in thinking of him as sinking into rest in Harry's arms than in returning to grieve over her decline.'

After seven years, she dies. When Ethel is summoned to Margaret's deathbed, she asks her father, 'Will there be no rally?' 'Probably not', he replies. 'The brain is generally reached at this stage...The thing was done seven years ago. There was a rally for a time when her spirit was strong; but suspense and sorrow accelerated what began from the injury to the spine.' Margaret's years of captivity have given her the status of the Angel in the House. Her selflessness has had an effect on everybody, and Charlotte Yonge sums up her life as only a Victorian novelist can:

> Over now! The twenty-five years of life, the seven years of captivity on her couch, the anxious headship of a motherless household, the hopeless betrothal, the long suspense, the efforts of resignation, the widowed affections, the slow decay, the tardy, painful death agony – all was over; nothing left save what they had rendered the undying spirit, the impress her example had left on those around her.

Margaret has gone to meet her Maker but she has died for a cause. And the cause was to teach the reader that it is one thing for a girl to think about being the kind of woman who can go boldly into the world, but it is a better thing to be the kind of woman who can suffer unselfishly, thinking only of the needs of others.

At the end of the book, Mr May is comforted by the

thought that his daughter has gone to be reunited with her mother: 'It seemed as if it were a home-like, comfortable thought to him, that her mother had one of her children with her. He called her the first link of his Daisy Chain drawn up out of sight.'

Sickness which led to death was presented in literature as largely clean and pure and the purpose of such illness was the calm, safe transition to a better place. Robert Louis Stevenson, a children's writer who had long periods of ill health as a child and whose own experience of sickness must have been far from gentle, nevertheless described invalidism as 'a gentle, merciful preparation for the long sleep as one by one our desires quietly leave us.'[2]

Most families in the nineteenth century would have had a child who did not survive into adulthood. Both Charlotte Brontë and Louisa May Alcott had experienced the death of at least one sister when they wrote their novels, and they drew heavily on their own experiences of suffering and death. In Charlotte's case two sisters died in childhood and her brother and other two sisters died as adults. Maria and Elizabeth Brontë died of neglected consumption a few months after their father sent for them to come home from The Clergy Daughters' School (on which Lowood is based), Maria in May 1825 and Elizabeth in June the same year. They were eleven and ten years old, and Charlotte was filled with rage and desolation. Lyndall Gordon describes Helen Burns as an 'exact model' of Maria Brontë who for Charlotte personified perfection. At the age of fifteen, Charlotte described Maria as 'a little mother among the rest, superhuman in

2. Robert Louis Stevenson, 'Ordered South 1881', in D.J. Enright, *Faber Book of Frets and Fevers*, Faber and Faber, London, 1989, p331.

goodness and cleverness'.[3] Charlotte was forced to watch Maria's repeated humiliation at the hands of a schoolmistress called Miss Andrews (the Miss Scatcherd of *Jane Eyre*). Although excelling at lessons and with a rare 'mind of grace', Maria was in constant trouble for untidiness, and her younger sisters Emily and Charlotte had to watch helpless when she was beaten with bunched twigs for having dirty nails, even though the frozen water made it impossible to wash. Charlotte shook with 'impotent anger' but Maria, like the fictional Helen, preached a creed of endurance. For her, the purpose of life was to look beyond life.

Louisa May Alcott's sister Elizabeth died in 1858 after a long and indefinite illness, ten years before *Little Women* was written, and another sister died in 1879. Louisa's remarks in her diary on the death of Lizzie indicate something of what she was trying to do in Beth's deathbed scene. In her search for a meaning to the horrible and painful death of her 23-year-old sister, who in life had always been so passive and undemanding, she wrote: 'So the first break comes, and I know what death means – a liberator for her, a teacher for us.'[4] The following year, alone in Boston hunting for employment, Louisa, lonely and depressed, saw the death of her sister as 'beautiful; so I cannot fear it, but find it friendly and wonderful'.[5]

The painful memories of these much-loved, gentle sisters, so different from both writers' own questioning and challenging natures, found their way into these novels. The extraordinarily mature words of the young Maria Brontë with her unquestioning faith in God could have been spoken at the deathbed of either Helen Burns or Beth

3. Lyndall Gordon, *Charlotte Brontë, A Passionate Life*, Vintage, London, 1995, p20.
4. Martha Saxton, *Louisa May Alcott, A Modern Biography*, The Noonday Press, Boston, 1995, p227.
5. Ibid.

March: 'God waits only the separation of spirit from flesh to crown us with a full reward. Why then should we ever sink overwhelmed with distress, when life is so soon over and death is so certain an entrance to happiness: to glory?'[6]

Helen Burns and Jane Eyre

Jane Eyre was not written specifically for girls, but for those who read it for the first time when they were young, it was perhaps the scenes of her girlhood which continued to inhabit the imagination. For such readers, the special force of this book was not her adult years at Thornfield or the time she spent with St John, Mary and Diana Rivers, but the first nine chapters of the book which cover the first ten years of Jane's life. For young readers, it can be argued, the central emotional experience of this book does not lie in Jane's relationship with Rochester but in her mostly unhappy and lonely childhood. Central to this are her early years with her cruel and unloving Aunt Reed and appalling cousins at Gateshead, particularly the scene in the Red Room where she is imprisoned as if she is a criminal and terrified by the sight of what she believes to be the ghost of her dead uncle. As a glimmer of hope in these dark times, the reader is offered the rare kindness shown by the apothecary and the servant Bessie. Jane's time at Lowood School, where she suffers terrible indignities and injustice but experiences being loved and valued for her own qualities for the first time, has extraordinary resonance.

However, as Adrienne Rich notes, it is not these childhood scenes but the Thornfield episode which is often recalled or referred to as if it *were* the novel *Jane Eyre*.[7] In

6. Lyndall Gordon, *Charlotte Brontë, A Passionate Life*, p16.
7. Adrienne Rich, 'The Temptations of a Motherless Woman, 1973', in *On Lies, Secrets and Silence: Selected Prose 1966–1978*, W.W. Norton and Company Inc, New York, 1980.

this truncated version the story begins where a young woman arrives as governess in a large country house, meets and falls in love with the master of the house, has her wedding day turned on its head by the discovery that the madwoman at the top of the house is in fact his wife, steals away, returns to find the house burned to the ground and the madwoman dead, and finally marries her lover now blinded and disabled by the fire.[8]

Jane Eyre, subtitled *An Autobiography*, is not an autobiographical novel in strict terms, but incorporates many elements of Charlotte Brontë's life. Charlotte was not an orphan like Jane and her home was with her father, brother and sisters. But The Clergy Daughter's School where she spent several years was much like the terrible Lowood. This school was designed for the daughters of poor clergymen who had to be prepared to earn their own living, mostly as governesses. The school was situated in an unhealthy and damp place and the children were fed a poor, sometimes inedible diet of stale bread and burnt porridge from a dirty kitchen. Stories such as those of the big girls forming a tight ring around the fire on their return from their walks so that the younger ones received no warmth are based exactly on the experiences of Charlotte and her sisters. The school's founder, William Carus Wilson, had much in common with the insufferable Mr Brocklehurst of *Jane Eyre*. Both believed that children, especially poor children, were essentially wicked and full of pride and both wrote Puritan tracts which encouraged children to believe that hell and damnation were just a moment away.

8. This is also the way the film industry deals with this story. In the most recent film of *Jane Eyre* the red-room scene, crucial in any understanding of Jane's struggle to break free of the injustices and restrictions of her own girlhood, is relegated to to the title sequence and entirely omitted from the main part of the film. Jane's girlhood takes up only ten minutes of a film which lasts an hour and three quarters, suggesting that its purpose is merely as introduction to the main story of thwarted love and ultimate reconciliation.

When Jane first meets Brocklehurst in Aunt Reed's parlour he seems to resemble a tall black pillar with a grim face at the top like a carved mask. This first meeting quickly establishes the difference between the received religious views and Jane's unique, independent spirit, even when she is intimidated and trembling with fear. When Brocklehurst asks her where the wicked go after death, she readily gives him the orthodox answer and tells him that they go to hell:

> 'And what is hell? Can you tell me that?'
> 'A pit full of fire.'
> 'And should you like to fall into that pit, and to be burning there for ever?'
> 'No, sir.'
> 'What must you do to avoid it?'

Jane knows that her answer will be considered 'objectionable' but when she replies 'I must keep in good health and not die', it is clear that she is refusing to play the adult's hypocritical game. She knows that Brocklehurst's response will be that she is a wicked girl who must pray to God to change her heart of stone into a heart of flesh, but she instinctively rejects the injustice of the adults who use God's name to justify their own cruelty. Her spirit will not allow her to accept a God who is so intolerant of questioning.

Both Aunt Reed and Mr Brocklehurst are in perfect agreement that Jane, who has no independent financial means, must be kept humble. 'Humility is a Christian grace, and one peculiarly appropriate to the pupils of Lowood . . . I have studied how best to mortify in them the worldly sentiment of pride', says Mr Brocklehurst. But Jane cannot easily be made humble. She has too much of the fighter in her, too much energy and spirit.

In the mid-nineteenth century, to describe a woman as having 'self-esteem' was an insult; it was synonymous with being selfish and wilful. But Jane's moral sense tells her that the sins she is accused of – self-interest, pride and deceit (and the accusation of falsehood is the most unfair of all) – are only sins if you are poor and dependent. Wealthy children like her cousins John, Georgiana and Eliza can be as proud and cruel and tell as many lies as they want. The spirit of religion is evoked not to comfort or shelter but to remind her that she is an orphan, without parents or friends; homeless even when she is living in the house of relatives.

As Mr Brocklehurst leaves, he presents Jane with a thin pamphlet entitled 'The Child's Guide'. He tells her to 'read it with prayer, especially the part containing "an account of the awfully sudden death of Martha G-, a naughty child addicted to falsehood and deceit."'

It is Jane's rebellious rage that enables her to survive this injustice. Her sense of fairness will not allow her to repent for sins she has not committed. However terrified she is, she knows that she must speak and before she leaves Gateshead she tells her aunt:

'I am not deceitful: if I were, I should say I loved *you*; but I declare I do not love you: I dislike you the worst of anybody in the world except John Reed: and this book about the Liar, you may give it to your girl Georgiana, for it is she who tells lies, and not I.'

When asked to justify her daring in speaking out like this, Jane replies passionately:

'How dare I? Because it is the *truth*. You think I have no feelings and can live without one bit of love or kindness; but I cannot live so: and you have no pity. I shall remember to my dying day how you thrust me back – roughly and violently thrust me back – into the red-room, and locked me up there, to my dying day, though I was in agony.'

Jane is exhausted by this but sees it as her first victory. Her action is an affirmation of the life force within her and her refusal to stay silent is a refusal to descend into a state of nothingness. Others believe that her passionate nature will mean that God will punish her. The servant Abbott comments: 'He might strike her dead in the midst of her tantrums, and then where will she go?' But Jane instinctively disbelieves this. To be silent would, to her, be the equivalent of death. As Adrienne Rich observes, 'It is at this moment that the germ of the person we are finally to know as Jane Eyre is born: a person determined to live, and to choose her life with dignity, integrity and pride.'[9]

Jane's sense of elation is short-lived. A Victorian child could not quarrel with adults without afterwards feeling remorse. Like aromatic wine, it seemed on swallowing to be warm and racy but its aftertaste was metallic and corroding and gave Jane the sensation of being poisoned. It was in this mood, but also with expectation and hope, that Jane began the next part of her journey and the second phase of her childhood at Lowood Institution.

From the beginning, the reader understands that Helen Burns is ill. Jane's first awareness of her is not a sighting, but the sound of a 'hollow cough'; unmistakable to the reader as a symptom of tuberculosis.

In mid-nineteenth century literature, tuberculosis was a straightforward and silent visitor which almost always

---

9. Adrienne Rich, 'The Temptations of a Motherless Woman, 1973', p93.

resulted in the death of its blameless victim. Helen's tuberculosis, the literary disease of the nineteenth century, is only referred to indirectly; we know only of the hollow cough, the pain in her chest of which she never complains, her pale face and thin cheeks. As Susan Sontag describes in *Illness as Metaphor*, consumption was often viewed as a lyrical, romantic taker of young lives, although in reality death from tuberculosis was ugly and painful. Helen embodies all the melancholy characteristics of the consumptive in literature: she is sensitive, powerless, a being apart. Like her name, she 'burns' with passion and suffering, but her passion is not for life. Nearly a hundred years later, Freud would describe Helen's state of mind as a death wish. In *Beyond the Pleasure Principle* he described the death wish as not unnatural but as a deeply pleasurable way to become nothing. But of course, Helen does not believe that she will descend into nothingness. Not quite life-loving enough to survive this world, she looks happily towards the next.

Jane's first view of this as yet unnamed girl is of her sitting on a bench, reading a book. Jane catches the title, *Rasselas*, and its strangeness interests her. She is used to reading only childish books, and this is serious and substantial. She is immediately attracted to the scholarly, self-reliant Helen who answers her questions politely but prefers to read alone.

Later that day, Jane witnesses the first of the many injustices meted out to Helen by the sadistic teacher Miss Scatcherd. When Helen is dismissed from class in disgrace and sent to stand in the middle of the large schoolroom, Jane expects her to show signs of great distress and shame, but to her surprise she neither weeps nor blushes. She seems to Jane to 'be thinking of something beyond her punishment – beyond her situation; of something not found before her.' The following day, Jane witnesses again

Miss Scatcherd's continual bullying of 'Burns'. Everything her friend does seems to irritate this teacher. Even when Helen gets all the answers right and Jane expects to hear praise, Miss Scatcherd cries out, 'You dirty, disagreeable girl! You have never cleaned your nails this morning!', and her passive and respectful response only causes further insults. 'Hardened girl!' exclaimed Miss Scatcherd; 'nothing can correct you of your slatternly habits: carry the rod away.'

Whereas Jane furiously searches for truth and fairness, Helen accepts the way others define her. Helen's response to Jane's cry that if she had been in her place, she would have snatched the rod from Miss Scatcherd's hand and broken it under her nose, is:

> 'Probably you would do nothing of the sort . . . It is far better to endure patiently a smart which nobody feels but yourself, than to commit a hasty action whose evil consequences will extend to all connected with you; and, besides, the Bible bids us return good for evil.'

When Jane questions her about her acceptance of Miss Scatcherd's cruelty, she replies that it is her own fault. Helen's form of Christianity is based on the idea of the sanctity of suffering and the total denial of the self. Jane cannot comprehend such passivity:

> 'When we are struck at without a reason, we should strike back again very hard: I am sure we should – so hard as to teach the person who struck us never to do it again.'

Three weeks after Jane's arrival at Lowood, Brocklehurst makes his first appearance. Denouncing Jane as an 'interloper and an alien', he places her on a stool so that they can see this 'liar' and instructs the girls not to speak to her for the remainder of the day. As Helen passes Jane, she lifts her eyes and an extraordinary sensation and light seem to pass from her into Jane, giving Jane the courage to master her rising hysteria and stay silent. 'It was as if a martyr, a hero had passed a slave or victim, and imparted strength in the transit.'

In a conversation which follows this incident, Jane tells Helen that she would rather die than live solitary and hated; to gain love from those she cared about, she would happily have a bone broken or a bull toss her. Helen's response is to try to calm Jane down:

> 'Hush, Jane! You think too much of the love of human beings; you are too impulsive, too vehement: the sovereign Hand that created your frame, and put life into it, has provided you with other resources than your feeble self, or than creatures feeble as you.'

Helen's role is to teach Jane restraint. Whilst Jane engages in a constant struggle with life, Helen finds it simpler to disengage herself from such concerns. She espouses a Christianity quite different to the hypocritical and harsh doctrine that Brocklehurst represents, and believes that life is too short to be spent in nursing animosity or in registering wrongs. When Jane recounts her ill-treatment by Aunt Reed and her cousins, Helen's advice is to try to forget the severity of her past treatment and to calm the passionate emotions which such injustices excite. Her spiritual beliefs allow her to rise above the brutalities of life. Her response to the cruelties of this world is to look towards the next: 'Revenge never worries my heart, degradation never too deeply disgusts me, injustice never crushes me too low; I live in calm, looking to the end.'

But Helen's life is not without its battles. Some months after Jane has joined Lowood, typhus begins to spread through the school, a result of its unhealthy location and the semi-starvation and neglected colds of the girls. Death becomes a frequent visitor and Jane, distracted by new interests, realises that she has not seen Helen for some weeks. Although she knows that Helen is suffering from consumption and not the typhus which is killing so many pupils, she does not understand the seriousness of this condition. One evening, seeing the doctor leave, she is struck by the knowledge that Helen is dying and that she must see her to give her 'one last kiss, exchange with her one last word'. Jane creeps into Miss Temple's room where Helen lies sleeping. She kisses her cold forehead and her cold, thin cheeks.

The following scene is moving in its simplicity. With the two nestling together in the cold bed, Helen has full confidence that she is about to enter a better world. She whispers calmly:

'I am very happy Jane and when you hear that I am dead, you must be sure and not grieve: there is nothing to grieve about. We must all die one day, and the illness removing me is not painful: it is gentle and gradual.'

Jane longs to understand and believe but her nature is not to accept the spiritual; she is too much in the real world. Earlier that day she has, for the first time, forced her mind to try to understand what she has been taught about heaven and hell, but when she tries to picture what this might be, she recoils in confusion. She can see only an 'unfathomed gulf' and her mind recoils from the thought of plunging into that chaos. For Jane, there is no simple or comforting vision of life after death and her mind can only comprehend 'the one point where it stood – the present; all the rest was formless cloud and vacant depth'. At Helen's bedside she is full of questions: 'Where are you going to Helen? Can you see? Do you know?' Helen is reassuringly certain of their joint future in heaven:

> 'I am sure there is a future state. I believe that God is good: I can resign my immortal part to Him without any misgiving. God is my father; God is my friend: I love him: I believe he loves me... You will come to the same region of happiness: be received by the same mighty Universal Parent, no doubt, dear Jane.'

Like this they fall asleep. Their last words are the simple words of friendship:

> 'Don't leave me Jane, I like to have you near me.'
> 'I'll stay with you, dear Helen: no-one shall take me away.'
> 'Are you warm, darling?'
> 'Yes.'
> 'Good-night, Jane.'
> 'Good-night, Helen.'

Helen's deathbed is symbolic of the loneliness of these two orphans: she dies, not in the bosom of her family, but with another child, the two of them wrapped around each other against the cold. What prevents this from being a typically mawkish and sentimental deathbed scene is not just its brevity but Jane's unconventional scepticism about the existence of God and heaven.[10] Jane cannot share Helen's view that by dying young she is 'escaping great suffering' or that death is 'so certain an entrance to

---

10. Susie Campbell, *Jane Eyre*, Penguin Critical Studies, Penguin Books, London, 1988, p23.

happiness – to glory'. Where Helen sees simple answers, Jane sees only questions and uncertainties. For both writer and reader there is a subtle casting off here; Helen's death marks the start of an independent self for Jane. Instead of turning heavenward, she embraces life, although she is by no means certain what kind of life this will be.

Helen Burns' role in the novel is often seen as teaching Jane to curb the negative side of her passion and to show her that it is possible to see injustice without the anger and despair she has known as a child; beating on the red-room door or raging against those who inevitably have control over her. She learns from Helen and her teacher, Miss Temple, that she cannot go out into the world with so much anger because socially she will have to occupy a lowly position and some humility is essential to her survival. She learns to distinguish between intense feelings which can lead to greater fulfilment and those which can only lead to self-destruction. But Helen's most important role is not just to 'counsel the indignant Jane in the virtues of patience and long-suffering', but to show her what she does *not* want to be.[11] Helen embraces death; Jane chooses life. Whilst Helen's only triumph over the daily tyranny and injustice of those around her is her own death, Jane wants to triumph by having the freedom and choice to regulate her own life. Helen's crucial role is to show Jane what she cannot choose to be, does not want to be, because her nature will not allow her to. As Lyndall Gordon writes of the relationship between Charlotte Brontë and her sister Maria, 'Maria was absolute for death, and as such, a formidable model against whom Charlotte was to choose her alternative.'[12] The same is true for Helen and Jane. In life Helen abdicates responsibility

---

11. Terry Eagleton, *Myths of Power: A Marxist Study of the Brontës*, Macmillan, London, 1988, p15.
12. Lyndall Gordan, *Charlotte Brontë, A Passionate Life*, p19.

for choices or decisions; her complete faith means that all is given over to God. Jane cannot help but think for herself. Her passionate desire for a more fulfilling life means that she has to look outwards to the world even though this involves taking great risks.

Jane Eyre, like most of the books which will be discussed here, is the story of a journey. Jane's progress, like that of Bunyan's hero, is full of pitfalls and difficult, painful choices, but she is clear about what she wants from life:

> Fears, of sensations and excitements, awaited those who had the courage to go forth into its expanse, to seek real knowledge of life amidst its perils.

'Reader, I married him' is Jane's famous announcement at the end of her story and it seems pertinent to comment here on the connection between Rochester's new status as a disabled person and their reinstated love. Jane, having fallen in love with her employer, flees Thornfield on the day of her marriage when she finds herself about to commit bigamy. A year later, having found safety but not happiness with the Rivers family, she hears Rochester's disembodied voice summoning her back. She returns to Thornfield to find it destroyed by fire. Enquiring of an old servant, Jane is informed that Rochester is alive, 'but many think he had better be dead', a common enough perception of the value of the life of a disabled person. He has been injured 'bravely' saving the life of the wife he once locked in the attic and pretended did not exist, and now has a full compliment of impairments: 'He is now helpless indeed – blind and a cripple.'

Brontë exploits the common idea in religion and literature that faith and love have the power to make cripples walk and blind men see, and Jane undertakes to 'rehumanise' the 'Bluebeard' of her past.[13] With the help of her arm he is able to walk again; with her unqualified love, he regains his sight and is able to look into the large, black eyes of his own son, a mirror image of his own.

Jo March and Beth March

Unlike *Jane Eyre*, *Little Women* was a book specifically written for girls. For years Louisa and her father Bronson Alcott had discussed the need for plain stories for boys and girls about childish victories over selfishness, and her publishers too wanted a 'girl's story', this being a newly discovered type of popular fiction. She agreed that 'simple, lively books were much needed for girls' and within a year she had produced perhaps the best-loved girls' book ever written. By the time *Little Women* came out in 1868, Louisa May Alcott had already published many stories and books, some in her own name and others, mostly racy melodramas and adventures, written under a variety of pseudonyms. *Little Women*, her first major book for children, outstripped all expectations and the character of Jo, the most unconventional and interesting of the four March girls, became the model for many literary heroines. As John Rowe Townsend points out, 'the very name of Jo still seems to bear her imprint.'[14]

Louisa May Alcott herself had four sisters, a loving and capable mother and a father who, despite his failings, she adored and respected.[15] The stories of the March girls in *Little Women* are clearly based on Louisa's own life. In her

13. John Sutherland, *Can Jane Eyre Ever Be Happy? More Puzzles in Classic Fiction,* The World's Classics, Oxford University Press, Oxford, 1997.
14. John Rowe Townsend, *Written for Children,* Penguin Books, London, 1974, p79.
15. Bronson Alcott, an idealist and transcentalist philosopher, kept his family in debt and poverty for most of his life.

journal she wrote: 'I plod away, though I don't enjoy this sort of thing. Never liked girls or knew many except my sisters; but our queer plays and experience may prove interesting, though I doubt it.'[16] Brigid Brophy describes Jo as 'one of the most blatantly autobiographical yet most fairly treated heroines in print.[17]

Louisa's own family life was, however, much more troubled than the fictitiously perfect March family. In one of the many studies of Alcott's life, Martha Saxton notes:

> Louisa adopted toward her parents a tone of sentimental pity that gave everything a heartbreak flavor, but that didn't necessarily correspond to reality. She chose to see them as baffled children buffeted mercilessly by arbitrary winds. This is the tone familiar to readers of *Little Women*, and it derives from Louisa's need to find a sentimental, loving vocabulary for articulating the family events. Rage, anger, and disappointment were not allowed.[18]

For all its affection and sentimentality, *Little Women* does not escape the didactic tone of earlier writings such as those of Charlotte Yonge and Maria Edgeworth. Every 'adventure' has its clear lesson, every sister (except Beth) an undesirable trait to overcome. Amy has to learn to be less selfish and vain, Meg needs to curb her desire for finery and learn that money cannot buy love, 'womanly skills' or true happiness, and Jo has to learn to dampen her wild, boyish energy and fiery temper and become what her father calls at

16. Quoted in Helen Jones, 'The Part Played by Boston Publishers of 1860–1900 in the Field of Children's Books', *Horn Blood Magazine*, June 1969, p331.
17. Brigid Brophy, 'A Masterpiece and Dreadful', in Virginia Haviland, *Children and Literature – Views and Reviews*, The Bodley Head, London, 1973, p69.
18. Martha Saxton, *Louisa May Alcott, A Modern Biography*, p196.

the end of the novel 'a strong, helpful tender-hearted woman'. The emotions the girls feel are strong but not passionate. The strongest are jealousy and anger but with effort they can be replaced by admiration and love. Self-denial is the order of the day, along with suffering and duty. Through these trials the four girls journey, often literally clutching their copies of John Bunyan's *Pilgrim's Progress*, hoping to reach Celestial City. As Reynolds and Humble point out: 'At one level each of Jo's sisters can be seen to represent one of the personality traits which needs to be overcome if the self is to learn to forget itself and become the intensely sympathetic, immensely charming and utterly unselfish, "Angel in the House".'[19]

Beth is set apart from the rest of her sisters by being entirely without ambition or self-interest. Like Helen Burns in *Jane Eyre*, Beth is presented to the reader as entirely blameless, a kind, saintly creature who never does anyone any harm. (Except the time she killed the poor canaries by forgetting to feed them, but her remorse was so great that we instantly forgave her.) Both struggle with ill health and have an unfailing belief that the next world will be a better place. Like Helen, illness visits Beth because she is not fully engaged with life. She too has an 'other-worldly' quality about her – a dreaminess which keeps her happily at home whilst others long to have adventures. Like Helen Burns, Beth is also part of the pilgrimage of another, stronger, life-loving character – in this case her unconventional, clever, difficult, older sister Jo.

The presentation of Beth's illness, like that of Helen Burns, plays on the stereotypical idea that what ill or disabled people need most is the pity and kindness of

---

19. Kimberley Reynolds and Nicola Humble, *Victorian Heroines: Representations of Femininity in Mid-Nineteenth Century Literature and Art*, Harvester Wheatsheaf, 1993, p154.

others. But in order to deserve this treatment, they must not burden those around them with strong emotions such as rage or disappointment. Their illness is sanitised and clean, their suffering spiritual rather than physical. Above all, they must be self-effacing, leaving plenty of space for the non-disabled character to develop and learn.

Beth's first line in *Little Women* establishes her unselfish (some might say self-righteous) personality. Whilst her sisters irritably complain about their poverty and lack of Christmas presents, Beth, sitting 'contentedly from her corner', reminds them 'we've got father and mother and each other'. This corner is significant. Beth remains in her corner both literally and metaphorically until her death three-quarters of the way through the second part of *Little Women*.[20] She is always sighing there so that only 'the hearthbrush and kettle holder can hear her', but such behaviour is always presented as unselfish and gentle rather than manipulative. When the others go off to have adventures, fall in love and get into scrapes they will always return to find Beth sitting in her corner ready to dispense love and sympathy. She is the peacemaker, particularly for troubled, clever Jo who wants more from life than an intelligent, robust, nineteenth-century female without independent means could possibly hope to get.

Beth's father calls her 'Little Tranquillity', and the name suits her 'for she seems to live in a happy world of her own, only venturing out to meet the few whom she trusted and loved.' She is thirteen years old, a crucial transitional time for girls in fiction, but Beth is not destined for womanhood. She is 'a child still', playing with her dolls, 'her little world peopled with imaginary friends'.

---

20. *Little Women* was first published in two parts: the first in 1869 and the second a year later. In England this second part is known as *Good Wives* but for the purposes of this chapter, I have referred to the books as *Little Women* parts one and two.

Jo and Beth are cast as opposites but there is a strong bond between them. 'To Jo alone did the shy child tell her thoughts; and over her big harum-scarum sister, Beth unconsciously exercised more influence than any one in the family.' Physically Jo (like many a heroine to follow) is the archetypal tomboy: tall, thin and coltish with a surplus of energy and zest for life. Her eyes are grey and sharp, by turns fierce, funny, or thoughtful. Beth is the very picture of passive femininity: rosy, with smooth hair and a shy manner, timid voice and peaceful expression. Jo, who always wants to be somewhere else, longs 'to do something splendid...something heroic or wonderful, that won't be forgotten after I'm dead', whereas Beth's most ambitious thought is 'to stay at home safe with father and mother, and help take care of the family'. In one of their many conversations where they play at being 'pilgrims', Beth declares her longing to enter the Celestial City of heaven where they will all go, by and by, if they are good enough. 'It seems so long to wait, so hard to do; I want to fly away at once, as those swallows fly, and go in at that splendid gate.'

Beth almost has her wish in the first volume of *Little Women*. Alcott takes Beth right to the point of death, but saves her at the last moment. The description of her near-death experience contains all the classic elements of such scenes: the family around the bedside, the midnight vigil, the promises to be better in the future, the doctor's presence, the sympathy of the natural elements – for example, a biting wind and falling snow – the fever that miraculously 'turns' in the early hours of the morning.

There are, of course, also some serious lessons to be learned from Beth's first battle with death, and Alcott does not leave the reader guessing what these might be. It happens when the 'Heart of the House', Marmee, has been called away to Washington to visit her husband, who is dangerously ill. Everything starts off well.

> For a week the amount of virtue in the old house would have supplied the neighbourhood. It was really amazing, for every one seemed in a heavenly frame of mind, and self-denial was all the fashion.

But after a week, Jo subsides on the sofa, reading and writing, Meg spends too much time in writing long letters or dreamily reading the dispatches from Washington, and Amy gets sick of the housework and goes back to her art. Only Beth continues with her duties. When she tries to persuade her sisters to come with her to visit the Hummels, a poor fatherless German family whom we met in the opening pages of the book, each sister has her own, selfish excuse. So Beth 'quietly put on her hood, filled her basket with odds and ends for the poor children, and went out into the chilly air, with a heavy head and a grieved look in her patient eyes.' She returns with the story of how the baby died in her lap before its mother returned home and with the first signs of scarlet fever. Jo is frightened and filled with remorse and in the absence of their mother, they send Amy to Aunt March's. Beth chooses Jo to stay and look after her and Jo devotes herself to her sister, day and night. Beth typically bears her illness with patience and without complaint, but soon the fever overtakes her and she cannot recognise the familiar faces around her. The 'shadow of death hovers over the once happy home'. Jo's lesson is to discover:

> the beauty and the sweetness of Beth's nature... and to acknowledge the worth of Beth's unselfish ambition, to live for others, and make home happy by the exercise

of all those simple virtues which all may possess and which all should love and value more than talent, wealth or beauty.

On the snowy first night of December when the year is symbolically 'getting ready for its death', the doctor tells Hannah the servant and Jo that it would be best to send for Mrs March. Jo is terrified when she learns how near to death Beth is. With tears streaming down her face she tells Laurie, 'she doesn't look like my Beth and there's no-one to help us bear it; mother and father both gone, and God seems so far away I can't find Him.' And later, 'Beth is my conscience, and I *can't* give her up. I can't! I can't!' He comforts her as best he can and they briefly debate God's motives for death. Laurie says hopefully that 'I don't think she will die; she's so good, and we all love her so much, I don't believe that God will take her away yet.' But Jo feels, 'The good and dear people always do die.' Both prove to be right, but Laurie is right first.

In an exhausting scene, guaranteed to wring every bit of emotion from the reader, both Meg and Jo promise to be better if only Beth lives. The doctor has been in to say that 'some change for better or worse would probably take place around midnight'. The snow falls, the bitter wind rages and all night the sisters sit by her bedside waiting for some change and for the arrival of their mother. The alert reader will recognise that in literature whenever a doctor warns that there will be some change around midnight for better or worse, the patient is likely to survive. Death in literature is rarely allocated a specific time; it either happens much more slowly, with the character drifting away as in Beth's actual death in the next volume, or much more suddenly, as in Judy's death in *Seven Little Australians* (see Chapter 6). The hour of midnight has a symbolic value in deathbed scenes. It

is the turning point between night and day and when the
clock strikes twelve in the March household, everything is 'as
still as death' and nothing but the wailing of the wind breaks
the deep hush. Beth's face is thin and wan and a 'pale shadow
seemed to fall upon the little bed'.

At past two in the morning, Jo, standing by the window,
turns to see Meg with her face hidden in the bed and assumes
that Beth has died. A great change seems to have taken place.
'The fever flush and the look of pain were gone, and the
beloved little face looked so pale and peaceful in its utter
repose, that Jo felt no desire to weep or to lament.' Jo kisses
the damp forehead of her favourite sister and says goodbye.
But sensible Hannah, startled out of her sleep, hurries to the
bedside, feels her hands, listens to her lips and exclaims in
servant's dialect much loved by writers of domestic dramas,
'The fever's turned; she's sleepin' nat'ral; her skin's damp and
she breathes easy. Praise be given! Oh, my goodness me!'

So Beth lives, for the time being at least. 'Never had the
sun risen so beautifully, and never had the world seemed
so lovely, as it did to the heavy eyes of Meg and Jo.' Then
mother comes home and everything is complete.

It is hard not to be moved to tears by Jo's response to
Beth's near death and the family's joy at her recovery, but
writer Brigid Brophy is having none of it. Infuriated by her
own tears after watching a weepy Hollywood film version of
Little Women, she wrote in an article called, 'A Masterpiece
and Dreadful':

> With Beth, I admit, Alcott went altogether too far.
> Beth's patience, humility and gentle sunniness are a
> quite monstrous imposition on the rest of the family –
> especially when you consider at what close, even
> cramped quarters they live (two bedrooms to four girls);
> no-one in the household could escape the blight of

feeling unworthy which was imposed by Beth...She brings Beth to the point of dying in *Little Women* then lets her recover; whereupon instead of washing her hands – as not ruthless enough to do it – of the whole situation, she whips the situation up again in *Good Wives* and this time does ('As Beth had hoped, "the tide went out easily"') kill her off.[21]

Christianity, as presented in children's literature in the mid- to late-nineteenth century, provided a comforting view of a sweet and beatific after-life. Characters like Beth were not wrested from life but drifted gently away. Death was a fairly clean and tidy business and this tradition, although largely gone from literature, lives on in Hollywood where in the romantic story the nastiest medical symptom any dying person is likely to have is a spot of blood, a croaking voice, a pale face or a fevered brow and where everyone who lives has some positive lesson to learn.

Beth's real death in the second volume does not involve another midnight vigil but is more of a slow, slipping away from life. From the beginning of this book, (*Good Wives*) the author makes it clear that Beth is unlikely to survive to the end:

Beth has grown slender, pale and more quiet than ever; the beautiful, kind eyes are larger, and in them lie an

---

21. Brigid Brophy, 'A Masterpiece and Dreadful', p69. Writer Elaine Showalter, speaking on the BBC Radio 4 arts programme *Front Row*, described her self-disgust at the way her emotions were manipulated in the 1999 film *Stepmum*, where the dying mother says her long goodbyes to each of her children, extracting a promise from them one by one. She didn't like the characters and felt the film was reactionary and sentimental, but it made her cry, it 'moved her' in some way she could not control. This is what Louisa May Alcott's deathbed scenes do to the reader, however often they read *Little Women*. At least Alcott's writing has the saving grace of being about girls for whom the reader genuinely cares. As Brophy says, 'We should recognise that though sentimentality mars art, craftsmanship in sentimentality is to be legitimately enjoyed', p70.

expression that saddens one although it is not sad itself. It is the shadow of pain which touches the young face with such pathetic patience, but Beth seldom complains and always speaks hopefully of "being better soon".

Meg is now married and is poor but happy and Jo, still battling with 'unacceptable' traits (bad temper and ambition in particular), is trying, as Louisa did herself, to find success as a writer. When she wins her first writing competition, she uses the money to send Marmee and Beth to the seaside for a month – this, along with the mountains, being the perfect literary place for cure and renewal. But Beth is not destined for cure and although Marmee returns feeling 'ten years younger', Beth is not 'quite so plump and rosy as could be desired'.

Jo's hopes for wider, more interesting horizons are dashed when Aunt March chooses more easygoing Amy to accompany her to Europe. She feels she is being punished for her strong-willed, direct nature. She tries to devote herself to literature and to Beth, but both girls are troubled and Jo confesses to her mother that she feels restless and anxious. She goes to Boston for the winter to work for a friend of the family and to develop her writing. She also meets the man who will become her husband, the middle-aged, philosophically minded German professor Herr Bhaer. Her rejection of Laurie, the handsome, fun-loving boy next door, remains a bitter disappointment to generations of her readers. Louisa May Alcott famously remarked in her journals, 'Girls write to ask who the little women marry, as if that was the only end and aim of a woman's life. I WON'T marry Jo to Laurie to please anyone.' But this remark turns out to be rather hypocritical, considering the lessons she had in mind for Jo following Beth's death.

When Jo returns from her time away from home, she

finds Beth much changed. Beth has never been fully part of this world but now her body reflects her more or less complete disengagement from life. Matter is being replaced by the spirit and the soul:

A heavy weight fell on Jo's heart as she saw her sister's face. It was no paler and but little thinner than in the autumn. Yet there was a strange, transparent look about it, as if the mortal was being slowly refined away and the immortal shining through the frail flesh with an indescribably pathetic beauty.

Beth is suffering from a nameless wasting disease, popular with sentimental Victorians and convenient for the novelist as the symptoms can be vague and relatively clean, unlike real illness.[22] Her dying lasts for many months, and in a style very different from the unsentimental, doubting lines in which Brontë describes Helen's death, Alcott writes:

Ah me! Such heavy days, such long, long nights, such aching hearts and imploring prayer, when those who loved her best were forced to see the thin hands stretched out to them beseechingly, to hear the bitter cry, Help me, help me! and to feel that there was no help.

---

22. It is interesting to compare this to the realistic set of symptoms of childhood illness described by Hippocrates a millennium or two earlier: 'In the different ages the following complaints occur: to little children and babies, apthae, vomiting, coughs, sleeplessness, terrors, inflammation of the navel, watery discharge from the ears. At the approach of dentition, irritation of the gums, fevers, convulsions, diarrhoea, especially when cutting the canine teeth, and in the case of very fat children and if the bowels are hard. Among those who are older occur affections of the tonsils, curvature at the vertebrae at the neck, asthma, stone, round worms, ascarides, warts, swelling by the ears, scrofula and tumours generally' (Hippocrates, *Aphorisms*, ?460–?377).

The reader almost drowns in the extended metaphor which sees the dying Beth as a traveller waiting to be taken across the river: 'Those about her felt that she was ready, saw that the first pilgrim called was likewise the fittest, and waited with her on shore, trying to see the Shining Ones coming to receive her when she crossed the river.' Finally, in the dark hour before dawn and 'with no farewell but one loving look, one little sigh', Beth's light goes out. Her peaceful death means that family and reader alike can 'thank God that Beth was well at last'.

Less sickly-sweet is the description in the following chapters of Jo's bitter despair at her sister's death. Jo is the only character in the book who is allowed any complex or subtle emotions and with Beth gone, she does not know what to do with herself. Nothing remains for her but 'loneliness and grief'. Amy is in Europe, Meg married and Jo does not know what 'useful, happy work to do' to take Beth's place. These are difficulties not easily solved and Jo (like Alcott herself) struggles with two opposing forces: the pressure on her to become the 'Little Woman' of the household, loved and remembered for her uncomplaining duty to others, and her desire for a more challenging, creative life which would necessarily involve separation from home and family.

But Alcott, unlike Brontë, does not allow Beth's death to be used as the start of a difficult journey, along which path Jo could become her real self. Such breaking free of family and home, she makes clear, could only lead to a loveless life. Shortly before her death, Beth foretold this as a route to unhappiness and she made Jo promise to take her place and be everything to Father and Mother: 'You'll be happier in doing that than writing splendid books or seeing all the world; for love is the only thing we carry with us when we go, and it makes the end so easy to carry.'

It is as if Alcott were denying the validity of her own life as a writer; as if the only real existence for a woman was love and domestic duty. Martha Saxton describes this as 'behaving spitefully towards her literary self and her readers'.[23] It is fascinating that most readers, even those who read the book many times over, remember Jo as our rebellious but loving heroine who forged a new way forward for herself. In fact Jo stays at home from this point, the only sister still remaining there, and modelling herself a little upon Beth, Jo learns to develop 'good womanly impulses':

> Brooms and dishcloths never could be as distasteful as they once had been, for Beth had presided over them both; and something of her housewifely spirit seemed to linger round the little mop, and the old brush that was never thrown away.

Alcott even has Jo humming Beth's songs as she cleans, brushes and sews. The 'splendid thing' she once wanted to do is now transformed into making her home as happy for her parents as they had for her and her sisters, even though nothing 'could be harder for a restless, ambitious girl than to give up her own hopes, plans and desires, and cheerfully live for others'. She doesn't quite turn Jo into saintly Beth, and Jo still finds it hard to carry out these duties entirely cheerfully, but the most difficult and therefore interesting sides of her nature – the hot temper, the vitality, the creativity, her indomitable self – are crushed by Beth's death, never to return.

Alcott, who would have preferred Jo to remain single, bowed to public pressure and married her to safe, older,

---

23. Martha Saxton, op. cit., p11.

unsexy Prof. Bhaer. They settled in Aunt March's old house and set up a school for boys. No wonder the sequels devoted to Jo (*Jo's Boys* and *Little Men*) are dull in comparison.

There is not a lot to be said about these last two sequels, which seem to have been written to please a voracious public rather than out of real commitment. The first of them, *Little Men*, contains a couple of disabled characters, but they are not central to the stories and pity is the sole emotion the reader is asked to feel about these two boys. The first, Billy Ward, 'a promising child changed to feeble idiot', is used to reflect the views of Louisa's father, Bronson Alcott, on education. Billy's father pressed him too hard and when he recovered from a fever, 'Billy's mind was like a slate over which a sponge has passed leaving it blank'. Jo tries to teach him simple things in order to 'give back intelligence enough to make the boy less a burden and an affliction', but presumably without success as he is never mentioned again. The second boy, Dick Brown, is cast in the 'Tiny Tim' mould of the cheerful cripple whose crooked body is tolerated because he bears it so cheerfully. Meg's little boy even asks him if 'crooked backs made people more cheerful'. His body would normally be considered abhorrent both to himself and others, but the Bhaers being of a philanthropic Christian frame of mind, 'soon led him to believe that people also loved his soul, and did not mind his body except to pity and help him bear it'. As with Jamie in *Pollyanna Grows Up* (discussed in Chapter 5) people try to ignore Dick Bown's impairment because his 'straight soul shone through it so beautifully'. Both boys die 'off-stage', and at the beginning of the next book, *Jo's Boys*, we are told that however kind these enlightened people were to them, their lives were scarcely worth living: 'Poor little Dick was dead, so was Billy; and no-one could mourn for them, since life would never be happy, afflicted as they were in mind and body.'

The deaths of Helen Burns and Beth March mark a particular point in literature about girls. As the century developed, writers were less likely to use the death of saintly, mild-tempered characters in order to give light and shade to the dilemmas of the strong heroine, and the 'burden' of illness and disability was more likely to be located in the protagonist. Death became rarer in domestic dramas and it was possible to have whole books in which nobody died. When they did, it was likely to be almost incidental, without any prolonged deathbed scene or sad mourning as in the case of Dick and Billy in the books mentioned above and Katy Carr's Aunt Izzie in *What Katy Did*.

The curing of the 'ill' fictional heroine had little to do with the progress of medical science or lower mortality rates for children and more to do with a more flexible, open-minded approach to children and the need for a happy, more child-centred ending to stories.

In the books which followed *Jane Eyre*, *Little Women* and *Good Wives* illness and accident were used to provide a space in which change could take place and through which the writer could explore a wide range of possibilities. These included: changing views about what could and should be expected of children, differing expectations for boys and girls, absolute faith in God to decide what is best for you, often set against the importance of the fictional child's own engagement with life and belief in self, and the rapid economic and social changes of the time.

Louisa May Alcott dealt with some of these elements in her story *Jack and Jill*, one of the many books for children which she wrote after the *Little Women* stories, but it does not bear comparison to her classic work. She called these later books her 'moral pap', and this is a fair description of her contribution to the paralysis/cure genre of children's fiction.

Jack and Jill was published in 1880, the same year as *Heidi* and eight years after Susan Coolidge's *What Katy Did*, to which it bears a striking resemblance. It is a long and rather pious tale of golden boy Jack, wild, dark, gypsyish Jill, and their many friends. At the beginning of the story, head-strong Jill persuades Jack to go sledging with her, even though he knows it is dangerous. When he refuses to go, Jill tells him, 'I won't be told I don't "dare" by any boy in the world. If you are afraid, I'll go alone.' Alas, down the hill come Jack and Jill, and Jill suffers serious injury. The details are suitably vague, but it is clear the problem is in her spine. She 'can't stir one bit', her 'backbone is cracked' and 'sprained', and they 'fear she might be a cripple for life'.

Her paralysis enables the transition from wild girlhood (she is about 14 or 15 at the time of the accident) to passive womanhood. She learns to be,

> so patient, other people were ashamed to complain of their small worries; so cheerful that her own great one grew lighter; so industrious that she made both money and friends by pretty things she worked and sold to her many visitors. And best of all, so wise and sweet that she seemed to get good out of everything.

When Jill learns obedience, she is given a back brace and allowed to sit up. Alcott overworks what Ellen Moers calls the distinctly female metaphor of the bird locked in the cage symbolising the longing for liberty.[24] This 'liberation' happens where it almost always happens in literature – in the open air. Jill is taken to the seaside and the first steps of 'a gentler Jill' are towards the shore. Ten

24. Ellen Moers, *Literary Women*, The Women's Press, London, 1976, p250.

years later she marries Jack and together 'they voyage down an ever widening river to the sea'.

It is not known if Alcott had some acquaintance with the earlier *What Katy Did*; if not, the parallels between the two stories are remarkable. Both deal with headstrong girls at a crucial age, both break their spines as a result of doing something they have been warned not to do, and both emerge from their long period in bed only when they have learned to be less selfish and more womanly. But it is *What Katy Did* which carries on the best tradition of the family story and it is this book which has survived.

Chapter 3

Learning to be Perfectly Good:
What Katy Did by Susan Coolidge

A little bird I am,
Shut from the fields of air,
And in my cage I sit and sing
To him who placed me there:
Well pleased a prisoner I be
Because my God it pleases thee.

From *Jack and Jill* by Louisa May Alcott

When *Little Women* was first published in 1868, Louisa
May Alcott was credited with writing the first classic
domestic drama for girls, but novels of family life were
being written at the same time in England, most notably
by Mrs Ewing, Mrs Molesworth and Charlotte Yonge.

Charlotte Yonge and her fellow writers wrote for the
middle-class girl at home, providing them with novels
which used the events of an ordinary home life to make
points about good and bad behaviour. It was felt that
stories offered to girls would be more likely to get the
message home if they dealt with a world that was
recognisably like that of their everyday lives, a world in
which their own emotional and moral problems were
reflected. Although the landscape of these books was
small and limited, the best of them have an enduring
popularity, proving that for a book to have the magic that
will sustain young readers, it does not have to be a story
of travel, danger and brave encounters in exotic locations
like *Robinson Crusoe* or *Huckleberry Finn*. Nor does it

have to have the magic and fantasy of books like that other mid-nineteenth century classic, *Alice in Wonderland*. Stories set in the much more familiar territory of home and family life, where the emphasis is not so much on overcoming wild territory and unknown enemies but on relationships, the psychological exploration of being a child in an adult world and learning how to grow up, also have the capacity to transcend the boundaries of time.[1]

The writers of these domestic dramas were beginning to reject the heavy-handed and crude didacticism of earlier evangelical books, where even the youngest child was expected to take moral responsibility for his or her own behaviour and where the punishments meted out were harsh, preferring instead something subtler which might be called the 'novel of character'. Nevertheless, faith, specifically Christian faith, was central to the novels of this period, and the belief that God is good and had the power to heal went mostly unchallenged. Sometimes at the most difficult moments of their lives, the troubled heroines would doubt their faith and fear that they had lost their way as Jane Eyre and Jo March do when faced with the death of a beloved friend or sister.[2] Like Heidi they might worry that they do not always say their prayers, or like Katy Carr and Judy Woolcot that they do not listen properly to Sunday School sermons like the 'good children in story books.' However, this doubt always serves the purpose of renewing and strengthening belief. In order to reach the end of their journey and to find a place in the world as happy and fulfilled young women, they must

---

1. Perry Nodelman, 'Utopia. Or, How to Grow Up Without Growing Up', in Sheila Egoff, ed., *Only Connect – Readings in Children's Literature*, third edition, Oxford University Press, 1996, p97.
2. *Jane Eyre* cannot, of course, be harnessed into the title 'domestic drama', but many of Jane's struggles as a young girl are replicated in the struggles of later heroines.

listen to the message God has sent them and must learn to be less questioning and more accepting.

To the modern reader, the religious and moral teaching of these writers might seem heavy handed, but this did not present a problem for Victorian writers, especially writers for children. As Joan Aiken says, 'In the nineteenth century, moral messages came naturally. Everyone wore them like bustles.'[3] For these writers, and most of those who wrote for the next six or seven decades, there were all sorts of problems and temptations which beset young people, but the way ahead was clearly lit by following the path of Christian teaching and listening to the adult, who was always ready to guide the child in prayer and atonement and to teach the difference between right and wrong.

Of course, in stories children often had to be imperfect, or at least misguided, in order to learn how to be good. There have been a number of studies on how girls in these enduring stories were given a time of freedom where they could be boisterous and lively but how, in the end, they always had to settle into their unselfish, comforting roles as wives and mothers.[4] Many of these fictional heroines were granted what Reynolds and Humble call a time of 'misrule and inversion' – a time when they were allowed to behave almost like boys, skating, playing out all day, climbing trees. This was especially true in books from

3. Joan Aiken, 'Purely for Love', in Virginia Haviland, ed., *Children and Literature – Views and Reviews*, The Bodley Head, London, 1973, p147.
4. In particular, Elaine Showalter, *A Literature of Their Own: British Women Novelists from Brontë to Lessing*, Virago, London, 1978; J. S. Bratton, *The Impact of Victorian Children's Fiction*, Croom Helm, London, 1981; Deborah Gorham, *The Victorian Girl and the Feminine Ideal*, Croom Helm, London, 1982; Kimberley Reynolds, *Girls Only? Gender and Popular Children's Fiction in Britain, 1880–1910*, Harvester and Wheatsheaf, London, 1990; Kimberley Reynolds and Nicola Humble, *Victorian Heroines: Representations of Femininity in Mid-Nineteenth Century Literature and Art*, Harvester and Wheatsheaf, London, 1993; Gillian Avery, *Behold the Child – American Children and Their Books 1621–1922*, The Bodley Head, London, 1994.

America, and Gillian Avery points out that English middle-class readers must have been fascinated by the sturdy, robust and confident children they found in these stories. Their English counterparts were still likely to have lives which were proscribed and limited and were unable to go anywhere without a chaperone. But even in American books, the rebellious girl could not grow up into a rebellious woman. Adulthood started early and by the age of 14 or 15, sometimes earlier, the energetic and lively girl would need to be tamed. Illness or accident were popular story devices in bringing about this change.

What Katy Did

Susan Coolidge was the pen name of Sarah Chauncy Woolsey. She was born in 1845 in Ohio and was only 27 years old when *What Katy Did* was first published in 1872. By coincidence she shared an editor with Louisa May Alcott, who had recently become very famous with the runaway literary success of *Little Women*, and it was suggested to her that she try her hand 'at the same kind of story'. It is often said that the first Katy book was inspired by *Little Women*, but it is in fact much closer to Charlotte Yonge's *The Daisy Chain* (Chapter 2), not just because of its description of a leisurely, sheltered childhood – which Gillian Avery suggests was rare in American children's books of the time – but also because of its themes of paralysis and redemption.[5]

In the known world of the domestic drama, energetic, creative, untidy Katy, the eldest child in a motherless family, is at the crucial stage of transition between girlhood and womanhood. Her 'accident' provides the turning point

---

5. Gillian Avery, *Behold the Child*, p168.

in the story. Through an enforced period of passivity, she leaves behind all ambition and the contradictions of her childhood. When she has learned to think less about herself and more about her responsibility to others, particularly her younger siblings, she replaces her mother to become the 'Heart of the House'. It is when she discovers a different, less selfish kind of strength that she finds the energy to walk again. The implication is that, with God's help, she has cured herself.

By the end of the first page of Coolidge's *What Katy Did*, the reader is already within the comfortable realm of the family story. We know that 12-year-old Katy Carr is the eldest of six children and lives with her brothers and sisters in a small American town called Burnett. Their house is large and square with roses and clematis growing round the door, a large garden to play in, a pasture running down to a brook and four cows. In the custom of such books, Katy's 'mamma' is already an angel in heaven, and her 'sad, sweet name' is spoken of on Sundays and prayer time. The children are looked after by that other classic literary figure, the spinster aunt – in this particular case, the slightly vinegary Aunt Izzie. She is not an unkind person but rather confused by the wild young things in her care. She would have preferred it if the children had been more like herself when she was a young girl: 'A gentle tidy little thing, who loved to sit as Curly Locks did, sewing long seams in the parlour, and to have her head patted by older people and be told that she was a good girl.' Unfortunately for her, Katy is the kind of girl who tears her clothes every day, hates sewing and doesn't care a button about being called good. With reference to storybook children from a more evangelical era, poor Aunt Izzie (we always think of her as 'poor Aunt Izzie') is constantly at a loss as to what to do with the six children in her care who are 'so little like the good boys and girls in Sunday school memoirs'.

Dr Carr, the children's father, is not much help in this matter. Firstly, like most fathers in Victorian novels, he is rarely around. He is, of course, a 'dear, kind, busy man', but he is away from home all day and sometimes all night too, taking care of sick people. Secondly, he seems to have decidedly modern ideas about child rearing. Aunt Izzie wants the children to be clean and tidy, quiet and still, and the only time she is really happy with her charges is in the half hour before breakfast when they are sitting in their little chairs, learning their Bible verses for the day. Dr Carr, however, has different views. He wishes the children to be 'hardy and bold, and encouraged climbing and rough plays in spite of the bumps and ragged clothes which resulted'. Of course, Dr Carr is not responsible for the washing and ironing of these clothes or else he might have been a bit more concerned about the 'sixty white pantalette legs hung out to dry every Monday morning'. However, we are soon aware that Dr Carr's desire for his children to be 'hardy and bold' is limited to but a brief period of childhood. By the time this book was written in the 1870s, there was a celebration of naughtiness in children's books, but it was mostly in books for boys. In books where the naughty child was a girl, her rebelliousness could be enjoyed but always with the knowledge that to enter womanhood, she would repent and learn quieter, more domestic ways.

At the beginning of the book, Katy, already knows the difference between being and doing, in essence the difference between masculine and feminine ways of seeing the world. 'Being' is how Cecy her friend and Clover her sister describe their ambitions. They want to be beautiful and good and have lovely things to wear – feminine things. Katy too wants to be good and have a lovely house but she also wants to *do*. Her ambitions are not only to be somebody but to do something 'grand':

> Perhaps it will be rowing out in boats, and saving people's lives, like that girl in the book. Or perhaps I shall go and nurse in the hospital, like Florence Nightingale. Or else I'll head a crusade and ride on a white horse, with armour and a helmet on my head and carry a sacred flag. Or if I don't do that I'll paint pictures, or sing, or scalp – sculp, – what is it? You know – make figures in marble. Anyhow, it shall be something.

But Katy, caught between these two irreconcilable desires, is almost always made uncomfortable by her own imaginative dreams of freedom and success. Not only do they get her into scrapes, but they also make her feel guilty. When she has had 'a bad mark or a scolding from Aunt Izzie', Katy consoles herself with the far more conventional, home-centred desire to be 'beautiful and beloved and as amiable as an angel'. The reader is made to share this ambivalence. We enjoy her ambitions, her rebelliousness against unreasonable Aunt Izzie and her lively naughtiness, but we already have the sense that whatever Katy achieves by the end of the book, it will not be something which separates her from her family nor will it go beyond what was possible for a middle-class Victorian female.

Indeed, from the very first page of the Puffin Classics edition we have already received the message that Katy's dreams of fame and conquering the world are bound to fail and that she will have to narrow her sights to a much smaller landscape. In these first two pages, written as if Susan Coolidge is speaking to her readers, we learn not only that the book is named after the repetitive 'Katy did, Katy didn't' sound of the North American grasshopper-like insect, but also are asked to believe that Katy in the novel is a 'real' girl Susan Coolidge once knew. This Katy 'planned to do a great many things and, in the end, did none of them, but something quite different – something she didn't like at all at first, but which, on the whole, was a great deal better.' What this wonderful 'better thing' is the reader can only guess, but the wording itself suggests some kind of suffering or relinquishing of self. The writer is, from the beginning, encouraging the reader into what Kimberley Reynolds describes as 'anticipating and desiring conformity for the heroine because it offers the only successful means of resolving crises and permitting a happy ending.'[6]

Katy's time of qualified wild exuberance lasts for half of the book. In the first seven chapters, her zest for life is enormous, her energy boundless and her childhood, along with that of her brothers and sisters, seems to be one of continual summer. Their garden is 'Paradise', a place of freedom and imagination, 'as wild and endless and full of adventure as any forest or fairyland.' As in *Little Women*, the games they play here are based on their reading of John Bunyan's *The Pilgrim's Progress*, with its Path of Peace and the Hill of Difficulty. This is the place where they can shout, run, jump and scramble at will and where they make up stories and imagine their future. Work, particularly work for Aunt Izzie, is something to be done as quickly as possible in order to get out and play. The garden has the same symbolic value as Frances Hodgson Burnett's *The Secret Garden*, or the Alpine pastures in *Heidi*. It is a place where children are beyond the ruling eye of adults. It is also

---

6. Kimberley Reynolds, *Girls Only?*, p129.

a place where delicious, table-manners-free meals can be eaten – picnics of buttered biscuits, thick meaty sandwiches, lemonade and wonderful toffee pies. Writers for children have for generations tempted their young readers with this idea of freedom and delicious things to eat, Enid Blyton and Roald Dahl famously carrying it on into the twentieth century.

Susan Coolidge writes with knowledgeable passion about the ambiguity of Katy's desire for danger on the one hand and her contrition on the other. At the start of one of several bad days when she has lost her algebra book, her slate and the string to her bonnet, she feels that Aunt Izzie has been unnecessarily horrid: 'They did run as fast as they could, but time ran faster. And before they were half way to school the town clock struck nine, and all the hope was over. This vexed Katy very much; for although often late, she was always eager to be early.'

Before the morning is over, Katy has misbehaved in class, but her 'conscience' makes her confess and she is punished in front of everyone. At recess she recklessly jumps over the school fence into the playground of the rival school next door in order to retrieve her hat, which has been blown away by the wind, and to great applause triumphantly returns to her own side. At lunchtime, in the absence of the teachers, she invents 'the Game of Rivers', a 'beautiful game' which creates such a noise and commotion, crashing and banging, that 'people stopped by and stared, children cried and an old lady asked why someone didn't run for the policeman'. By the time they are stopped by the head-mistress, chairs have been flung down, desks upset and ink is streaming on the floor, whilst the frantic rivers are still racing and screaming and Katy as Father Ocean is capering like a lunatic on the platform with her face as red as fire. Their behaviour is as far from 'ladylike' as it is possible to imagine. Katy confesses to Mrs Knight that it is she who has invented the game and Coolidge, reinforcing the moral point, reminds us that although Katy feels ashamed, 'there is a saving grace in truth which helps truthtellers through the worst of their troubles'. By the end of the day, her contrition is such that she is 'weeping like a waterspout, or like the ocean she pretended to be', and when papa in the evening recites the tale of 'For the want of a nail the shoe was lost...' the moral lesson is complete.

But before a week has passed, Katy is into another scrape, this time in a game of 'Kikeri', a cross between blind man's buff and tag which causes havoc and wreckage in the Carr household. Katy never means to do wrong and her contrition is again profound. When Aunt Izzie returns from a rare evening out, Katy confesses. Her 'crime' is not just that she has led the others into a scrape but that she has failed in her resolution to set an example to the younger ones. Her father reminds her 'more seriously than he has ever done before' that when her mother died, she had said that Katy must be 'a Mamma to the little ones when she grows up'. Hearing this, Katy, still only 12 years old, sobs 'as if her heart will break.'

Katy's transition from wild girl to replacing her 'angel Mamma', takes place through a dramatic incident, full of metaphorical possibilities. It happens on a particularly bad day for Katy. Their visitor, cousin Helen, permanently paralysed by a spinal break some years before, has left the previous night and Katy has gone to bed resolving to be a little more like her: 'I'll study, and keep my things in order, and be ever so kind to the little ones' even if it 'takes a thousand years'. But things go wrong right from the beginning. She goes to bed with plans to be an angel but wakes up the next morning 'as fractious as a bear'. She breaks her vase, the beautiful present from Helen, is made to tidy her drawers which are in a terrible state, shouts at her put-upon sister, Elsie, and gives her a nasty push, hurting her badly. Then, she defies Aunt Izzie's warning not to play on the new swing in the woodshed.

The swing needed a new staple to fasten it to the roof and Alexander the servant had been planning to do it that day, but irritable Aunt Izzie does not think it important to explain her commands to the children and Katy assumes that she just wants to spoil their fun. As she flies up in the air, Katy leaves the bad feelings behind and enters a kind of reverie: 'The place felt cool and dark, and the motion of the swing seemed to set the breeze blowing. I waved Katy's hair like a great fan, and made her dreamy and quiet. All sorts of dreamy ideas seemed to flit through her brain.' She flies higher and higher until through the small window of the cross-beam, she can see the pigeons pluming themselves on the eave of the barn and the white clouds blowing over the blue sky. Then suddenly, at the very highest point of the sweep, there is a terrible sharp cracking noise. The swing gives a violent twist, spins round and Katy is flung down. 'All grew dark and she knew no more.'

So a whole new episode begins: Katy's 'Dismal Days'. When she regains consciousness her head aches as if 'the hottest sort of a coal of fire was burning into the top of her head' and for weeks she is in a kind of fever of sharp, dreadful pain relieved only by sleep. After four weeks Dr Carr, no longer the absent father, gives her an explanation of surprising medical accuracy – surprising because in Victorian novels such medical conditions are usually left unclear and mysterious. He explains:

The spine is a bone. It is made up of a row of smaller bones – or knobs – and in the middle of it is a sort of rope of nerves called the spinal cord. Nerves you know, are the things we feel with. Well this spinal cord is rolled up for safe-keeping in a soft wrapping called membrane. When you fell out of the swing, you struck against one of these knobs, and bruised the membrane inside, and the nerve inflamed and gave you a fever in the back. Do you see?

By the time we get to the bruising which gave her a 'fever in the back', we are not so securely in the area of medical knowledge. But such vagueness has its literary place because it is important that both Katy and the reader believe in the possibility of some kind of magical resolution. When Katy asks how long she will have to remain in bed, her father answers, 'I can't tell exactly how long. The doctors think, as I do, that the injury to your spine is one which you will outgrow by and by, because you are so young and strong. But it may take a good while to do it.' He also tells her that the only cure for such a hurt is time and patience and in case Katy hasn't quite got the point yet, he reminds her that although going on the swing for a few minutes was just a little thing, it was also a 'little thing' to forget Aunt Izzie's order: 'Just for the want of the small horseshoe nail of Obedience, Katy'.

When Katy defies her aunt and falls off the swing, she is in a state of social 'wrongness'. She is a Victorian girl who is wild and unconventional. She cannot go forward into womanhood in this unrefined state and needs to be stopped in order to change. Kimberley Reynolds sees the function of the accident as a 'a period of dependency which acts as a preliminary to re-entering the world according to accepted social forms'.[7] The metaphor of paralysis will rein Katy in and for a long time she will be

7. Ibid., p130.

confined to one room in her home. After the accident, she will have to forgo not only ambition, but also her energy, her zest for life. She has, in Charlotte Yonge's words, to 'seek lowliness' and her own life must be laid aside. In her wilfulness, Katy made the wrong choices and now she must be deprived of freedom.

Such ideas, important in understanding the role of the Victorian girl, now seem confined to history. In modern fiction for girls, an independent, lively spirit is not something that has to be literally knocked out of girls in order for them to become women, but the source of the metaphor, the inability 'to do anything, or walk, or stand' as being a dreadful, pitiable state, a life of 'wasted years', still applies to how we collectively imagine the lives of disabled people.

Certainly Katy enters a long period of despair, with days full of dark misery and nights of long, hopeless fits of crying. Her 'once active limbs hung heavy and lifeless' and all she can think about is how wretched the rest of her life is going to be. For weeks on end Katy takes no interest in anything. She doesn't want to read or sew or to hear about the active life of her siblings. She is saved by cousin Helen, who the reader has first met several chapters earlier. Helen is one of the few characters in fiction who starts off disabled and remains so throughout the novel without being killed off or cured. Perhaps this is because Helen is already so near to heaven. Susan Coolidge is at pains to tell us that Helen is not a 'saintly invalid' because she 'didn't fold her hands and she didn't look patient', and in this sense she is different to those long-suffering, passive, invalid types who frequently inhabit the Victorian novel. But the reader does not entirely believe her. Helen is so perfect and so loving and understanding that the reader knows that she really is an angel.

The invalid was a popular feature of the nineteenth-century story. The bed-bound (and occasionally sofa-bound) invalid was the opposite of the wild girl who was always longing for freedom and independence. This saintly creature was always where she should be; in the home, providing comfort and solace to others. But she could never seek to fulfill her own dreams and ambitions. How could she? She was, to use the vocabulary still commonly used today, 'confined', indeed 'bound', to her sofa in the salon or her bed upstairs. From this position she could give guidance and advice to her confused and sometimes angry brothers, sisters and friends. She would remain virginally pure (the ultimate state of refinement) since in her condition it would be unfair and supremely selfish to expect anyone to marry her. As a middle-class girl, she was not expected to do any heavy lifting, cleaning or cooking, that's what the servants were for, so she could effectively manage the house from above, giving guidance to the staff, checking that the housekeeping books were in order, ordering the meals. She could be like a mother to her younger siblings.[8]

Helen fulfils many of these expectations but she is also, like Katy herself, the kind of character who inhabits the best of children's books; she brightens up the story and stays in your mind for years after you have read it. Helen is beautiful and perfect, gives wonderful presents, can read your worst thoughts and help you through them. When Katy, still in her wild, reckless state, rushes up the stairs with Helen's perfectly arranged supper tray, trips on her

---

8. Even in fiction, the invalid could only be tolerated if she were upper or middle class. For these women and girls, illness conferred refinement, delicate sensibility and even spiritual eminence. Less wealthy ill or disabled people would be locked away in institutions, far from view, or would die on the streets. There was no tolerance for the poor ill woman whose disability was likely to be caused by poverty itself.

untied bootlace and drops the lot to the resounding cries of Aunt Izzie's 'I told you so!', Helen pleads for her to have a second chance. And Katy, watching her eat this second supper, feels a 'warm loving feeling in her heart', for as Coolidge intuitively tells her readers, 'I think we are scarcely ever so grateful to people as when they help us to get back our self-esteem.' Here self-esteem is a good thing as it doesn't interfere with the needs of others. Like the best of the Victorian invalids, Helen is the truly wise maiden.

Unlike Katy, however, we know from the beginning that Helen will not recover from her spinal break. Despite being disabled, or maybe because of it, Helen is the realisation of the Victorian ideal state of refinement. Refinement, as Charlotte Yonge rather obliquely wrote, is 'the delicate aroma of Christianity'.[9] Helen is a devout believer in 'the one who is always with us', and her unquestioning faith becomes an essential part of her relationship with Katy. The refined female was required to show self-restraint, unselfishness, innocence and good taste (the last of these being essentially a matter of class and 'breeding'). The opposite of refinement or gentility included, as Charlotte Yonge says, 'rough, noisy and bouncing behaviour' and even worse, the qualities exhibited by Katy's brief friendship with the unsuitable Imogen: vulgar showiness and immodest behaviour towards men. Helen, despite her 'affliction', is always beautifully turned out, with smooth, glossy hair, pretty but modest clothing (she has learned to make even her nightgowns and wrappers as becoming as dresses by trimming them with lace and ruffles) and, however much in pain, she can always wear a 'sweet smile'. Refined females, rather ambiguously, were expected to be both modest and controlled, yet not too feeble or dependent on others. Helen, as a disabled person, fulfills the

---

9. Quoted in J.S. Bratton, *The Impact of Victorian Children's Fiction*, p180.

former by being in a permanent state of girlhood, yet although she is physically dependent on others, she avoids too much 'feebleness' by having a strong sense of who she is and by being aware of how much good she can do to others.

Helen is denied all prospects of a sexual life and deals with this with customary unselfishness. At the time of her accident she was engaged to a man called Alex and was very much in love. Her 'dreadful accident' meant that at first she was expected to die but then she grew slowly better and the doctors told her that she 'might live a good many years, but that she would have to lie on her sofa always, and be helpless and a cripple'. Alex offers to look after her, but she refuses and hopes instead that some day 'he would love somebody else well enough to marry her'. This, of course, he does and now he and his wife live next to Helen and are her 'dearest friends'. The reader then, as now, expects no different. However good and sweet Helen is and however much she is loved by those who know her, she will always be excluded from the main circle of family life. She must be 'taken care of' but she must not expect to be loved by a fit and handsome young man except in the most platonic way. How could this be otherwise? Even today people have problems with the idea of the sexuality of a 'crippled person'. Helen's job becomes one of caring for others and through loving God, she learns to know her place in the world.

When Helen visits Katy a few weeks after her fall she is shocked to find her in such a terrible state. Katy too is now in a state of exclusion. She has fallen, literally from her swing, symbolically from a state of grace. Her face is thin, her eyes red from weeping, her hair a 'frowsy bush' and her room a terrible mess. Katy cannot see how she is going to find the hope and patience her father has told her is essential to cope with the long illness ahead of her. Lying upstairs in a darkened room, she is not only physically and emotionally separated from her family, school and friends but also from the self she recognises. She has become estranged from her own body and has lost the sense of herself as the ambitious and lively girl who made plans for all 'the beautiful things she wanted to do when she was grown up'. She is also estranged from God, and without reconciliation to 'the Teacher who is always at hand' there could be no bright future. Helen's role in the story is to bring Katy back from estrangement to inclusion, and when she does it will be a completely new Katy who emerges.

In the pivotal bedside scene, Katy has entered a state of feebleness and dependency which is unacceptable. All her plans to 'study and help people and become famous' now seem like dreams. Most importantly, she can no longer keep the promise she made to her dying Mamma and take care of the younger children. She pleads with Helen to tell her what to do. Helen tells Katy that there is a special chance for her to learn to be 'wise and useful'. She now has the chance to go to 'God's school' where 'He teaches all kinds of beautiful things to people':

> 'It is called The School of Pain,' replied Cousin Helen, with her sweetest smile. 'And the place where the lessons are to be learned are to be learned in this room of yours. The rules of the school are pretty hard, but the good scholars, who keep them best, find out after a while how right and kind they are. And the lessons aren't easy either, but the more you study, the more interesting they become.'

The lessons she must learn are 'Patience', 'Cheerfulness', 'Making the Best of Things,' Hopefulness' and 'Neatness'. These are the lessons girls have been taught for generations and they are the lessons disabled people are still expected to follow lest they become a 'burden to others', 'bitter and twisted' or 'wallow in self pity'. They are lessons about learning not to put yourself first and being thankful for small mercies, but they also excuse society from any sense of responsibility for change, placing the onus back on the disabled person. 'God's school' is based on the Christian ideal that there are lessons to be learnt from suffering and that out of this torment, it is possible to become a better person.

In order to 'make the best of things', even when there doesn't seem to be anything to make the best of, Helen teaches Katy that everything has two handles, the smooth handle and the rough handle. If you take hold of the smooth handle everything comes up light and easily, but if you take hold of the rough handle, it hurts your hand and is hard to lift. This advice is given to help Katy to learn 'how people go' and how she should 'take hold of them', especially difficult Aunt Izzie and the children.

When it comes to explaining the importance of the lesson of 'neatness', Helen tells Katy a long story about herself and her own experience of sickness. In this story, Helen tells the disbelieving Katy how 'a girl she knew' had an accident which meant that 'all the rest of her life she had to lie on her back and suffer pain, and never walk any more, or do any of the things she enjoyed the most'. This girl did not understand how important it was for a sick person to be 'fresh and dainty as a rose'. Instead she kept her room in a dreadful state, full of dust and confusion, with the blinds shut. We understand that in this telling the erstwhile Helen, whilst literally keeping her room dark, was metaphorically shutting out the healing Light of God. When her father came to visit, he was distressed to find his daughter 'turning into a slattern' and instructed her to keep the room pleasant and clean, to get rid of all the unnecessary medicine bottles, to fill her room with light and flowers and to make herself look pretty, because 'a sick woman who isn't neat is a disagreeable object'.

Katy finds it hard to believe that beautiful Helen, with her smooth, glossy hair and her beautiful nightgowns and wrappers, can be talking about herself. Helen admits that it took her a long time to realise how selfishly she was behaving and to desire to do better. In a statement devoid of irony she tells Katy, 'After that when the pain came on, I used to lie and keep my forehead smooth with my fingers, and try not to let my face show what I was enduring. So by and by the wrinkles wore away and although I am a good deal older now, they have never come back.'

The lesson Katy is being taught is that for a 'sick person' to have any place in the world, they must strive to be better, more cheerful and more patient than anyone else, otherwise they will deserve to be alone and miserable. Susan Coolidge makes brief reference to the importance of Katy studying 'geography and sums' so that she will not fall too far back in her education, but her final, most important lesson is in how useful she can now be to the children and her father. When she was 'flying about' as she used to, she was of little use to them, but now she can be always on hand:

> You can make your room such a delightful place, that they will want to come to you! Don't you see, a sick person has one splendid chance – she is always on hand. Everybody who wants her knows just where to go. If people love her, she gets naturally to be the heart of the house.

As Gillian Avery has pointed out, the ideal girl of the Victorian novel was the one who waited on her father and brothers and by keeping them happy at home, prevented their feet from straying.[10] The female invalid, always at home, would be the perfect comforter, the one who was always there to listen. Helen's last word is to remind Katy that God is always there if ever the lessons seem too hard:

In this school to which you and I belong, there is one great comfort, and that is that the Teacher is always at hand. He never goes away. If things puzzle us, there He is, close by, ready to explain and make all easy.

That night, after Helen has left, God appears to Katy in a dream. She is trying to learn a lesson from a book whose pages will not open properly, written in a language Katy does not understand. Suddenly the forefinger of the Hand of God opens the page and points to line after line so that the meaning becomes plain. Katy no longer has to feel that she is alone.

Katy now remains tied to her bed, struggling to be good. To do all the things she wanted to do as a young girl, she needed the whole world, but to do all the things a woman is meant to do, she needs only the upstairs of her home. Katy's world has shrunk right down to a place where she is just heart and soul, where she has finally achieved lowliness. All that matters to her in her disabled state are her attachments to the other people in her life. (She is not actually an invalid at this point in the story; she can sit up, think straight and do things. All she cannot do is walk.) This is the defining state of womanhood: loving relationships with other people.

Carol Gilligan in her book *In A Different Voice*, points out that issues of dependency are experienced differently by women and men and that for females, their identity

10. Gillian Avery, *Behold the Child*, p171.

formation takes place in the context of ongoing relationships:

> For girls and women, issues of femininity and female development do not depend on the achievement of separation from the mother or on the progress of individuation. Since masculinity is defined through separation while femininity is defined through attachment, male gender identity is threatened by intimacy while female gender identity is threatened by separation.[11]

Katy's childhood dreams are about separation. Separation from her family, by going abroad; from conventional understanding of what women do by fighting battles and charging around on a white horse; and by developing potentially selfish individuality through creative skills like sculpting. Even in imagining herself as Florence Nightingale she is dreaming of going abroad, being answerable to no one but herself. These dreams are what Terry Eagleton describes as the character 'cutting herself off from the bonds of kinship'.[12] But her longing to be free is ultimately unacceptable. Her accident and subsequent paralysis are the devices through which she learns to forgo those dreams of separation and define herself through her attachments. It is only when she has accepted her essential presence in the family that she is allowed to walk again.

Interestingly, the dilemmas portrayed in stories such as this one were often the dilemmas of the writers' own lives. Some of the writers were young themselves; Susan Coolidge and Ethel Turner were both in their twenties when they wrote

---

11. Carol Gilligan, *In a Different Voice: Psychological Theory and Women's Development*, Harvard University Press, Cambridge, MA, 1982, pp7–8.
12. Terry Eagleton, *Myths of Power: A Marxist Study of the Brontës*, Macmillan, London, 1988, p26.

What Katy Did and *Seven Little Australians* and Charlotte Brontë was 31 when *Jane Eyre* was published. These struggles between ambition, independence, and the freedom to choose your own destiny on the one hand and fulfilling your God-given role as the moral and physical 'heart of the home', protected by a good and powerful man, on the other were a continuing theme in the American and English stories of the mid-nineteenth and twentieth centuries.

Since *What Katy Did* is essentially a novel about people rather than action, Susan Coolidge makes a lot of pleasurable, warm-hearted things happen throughout Katy's long period of capture upstairs, and her relationships with her brothers and sisters and the visitors to the house keep dullness and misery away from this section of the book. At Christmas, there are surprise presents for all the family, and on Valentine's Day Katy and her best friend Cecy arrange secret poems and little presents. The children remark that they never had such good times before Katy was ill and Katy hears this with mixed feelings: 'Her first long year of schooling had taught her self control and as a general thing her discomforts were borne patiently.'

About 18 months after the accident Katy's courage begins to flag, her spirits grow dull and she longs for 'something to happen'. What happens is that poor Aunt Izzie dies, off-stage, without any kind of deathbed scene:

> Katy's Aunt Izzie may be the first of an illustrious line of people who died quietly in the night... Mentally, as far as the book is concerned, the death is in a bracket, because its purpose is to show Katy rising to the challenge of doing the housekeeping efficiently, despite her disability.[13]

---

13. Juliet Dusinberre, *Alice to the Lighthouse: Children's Books and Radical Experiments in Art*, Macmillan, London, 1987, p134.

Actually, Katy is doing the housekeeping not despite her disability but because of it. If she were not an 'invalid' she would still be a girl, at school all day, running with her friends and allowed at least another year or two of freedom and girlhood. As it is, after a brief period of regret when the children all wish that they had appreciated Aunt Izzie more when she was alive, Katy begins to manage the house-keeping from her room upstairs even though she is only 13 years old (14 in 2 weeks' time). It is her invalid status which allows her to throw off any vestiges of childhood and mature into a refined and reformed young woman.

Katy remains upstairs for four years altogether, significantly between the ages of 12 and 16. She is paralysed as a girl and cured as a young woman. After six months, her father buys her a kind of moveable chair-bed where she can be pushed to the window so that she can watch the seasons change, but unaccountably, since she seems well in every way but her ability to walk and is efficiently running the whole household, she remains more or less flat on her back for another three and a half years. When she is finally given a wheelchair (an expensive item but, one assumes, well within Dr Carr's budget), she is delighted with the limited freedom this brings, although it is clear that she still has much to learn. When she calls her sisters by ringing her bell, we are told:

> Katy came to meet them as they entered. Not on her feet; that, alas! was still only a far off possibility; but in a chair with large wheels, with which she was rolling across the room. This chair was a great comfort to her. Sitting in it she could get to her cupboard and bureau drawers, and help herself to what she wanted without troubling anybody.

When cousin Helen visits she is able to be helped to

move all over the house but Katy, otherwise fit and well, must remain not only upstairs but confined to one room in the house until she is thoroughly transformed. She does not even explore the upstairs of the house in her wheelchair, but remains in her own room until the last chapter of the book, when she is able to walk again. During this time, she learns how to care for others. 'Considerate' is the word Coolidge uses repeatedly to describe this new Katy. At the end of this section, we are reminded of how thoroughly 'good' Katy has become, and by implication, how different from her old self. Her sister Clover remarks wistfully, 'Sometimes I think I shall be really sorry if she ever gets well. She's such a dear old darling to us all, sitting there in her chair, that it wouldn't seem so nice to have her anywhere else.'

Katy's 'cure' comes on fairly gradually and there is no single dramatic miracle scene. Just as her transformation from wild girl to tame woman has been slow and steady, so is her transformation from paralysis to walking. The energy to walk again comes only when her own life has been 'laid aside' and she has replaced self-love with love for others. The first sign of Katy's recovery is when she rings her bell and Clover and Elsie rush to her room and are amazed to find her standing. Despite the fact that from the very first, the reader has been led to expect that in time Katy will walk again, her recovery is presented as an act of will rather than a medical development. Katy is given responsibility for her own recovery as if her disease was caused by a state of mind, rather than a physical fall. Like Sleeping Beauty, who finds redemption in the kiss of a handsome prince, Katy 'wakes up' from her own dark dismal days: 'It seemed as if her will had been asleep and now that it had waked up, the limbs recognised its orders and obeyed them.'

After two or three weeks she can walk all over the upstairs and takes great pleasure in her exploration. The 'celebration' day for her to come downstairs for the first time since her accident is appropriately September the eighth, her Mamma's birthday. Katy chooses this day herself. She has the dress of a woman, not a girl, a mature 'soft, dove-coloured cashmere, trimmed with ribbons of the same shade', and it is clear that her role is now that of 'little mother' to the household: 'Katy was evidently the centre and the sun. They all revolved around her and trusted her for everything.'

The nearest thing to the 'miracle cure' moment is when Katy, coming downstairs for the first time, sees Helen on the sofa waiting for her. Amazed, she lets go of her father's arm and runs towards her. Helen is described as perhaps the happiest of the party. Her final words to Katy sum up the central purpose of the book. Describing to Katy her pleasure in the changes she sees, she says,

> I want to tell you how pleased I am to see how bravely you have worked your way up. I can perceive it in everything – in Papa, in the children, in yourself. You have won the place, which you recollect I once told you an invalid should try to gain, of being to everybody 'The Heart of the House.'

The implication is that Katy has redeemed herself through these changes. She has 'made the best of things', and her hopes for the future now lie not in the wide world but in her own home.

This view of women now seems outdated in Western society, but it sits more comfortably with ideas about disability which are much slower to change. Katy learned the lesson that disabled people are supposed to learn. She smiled through her tears, learned patience, was grateful for the care she was given and did not discomfort others by bad temper or aggression. But unlike Helen, who as a permanent invalid was destined to a life of solitary virginity, Katy was encouraged not to give up hope for a cure. Helen's life was worthy but hardly the stuff of a happy ending. Katy must be cured not just so that she can leave her one room upstairs but, more importantly, so that she can become a real woman: a wife and mother. Love and romance come for Katy in the form of a handsome sea captain and is only two sequels away.

Susan Coolidge's sequels, *What Katy Did at School* (1873) and *What Katy Did Next* (presumably inspired by the extraordinary success of *What Katy Did*) are an attempt to give Katy back her lost girlhood and then take her down the traditional path of love and marriage whilst on a tour of Europe. Although she has some brave battles with injustice while away at her boarding school, it is a sadly chastened and serious Katy we meet in these books, and Coolidge's attempts to give Katy back her girlhood do not ring true.

Chapter 4

The Miracle Cures: Clara in *Heidi* by Johanna Spyri and Colin in *The Secret Garden* by Frances Hodgson Burnett

Let us only place the rising generation, from its cradle up, under the mighty influences of divine nature, so that her intuitive language may penetrate to our children's souls and awaken an echo in them, and mankind will soon be better able to solve the riddles which contain the key of life.

From *Child and Child Nature*, Baroness Marenholtz Buelow, 1879.

Heidi and *The Secret Garden* are books that celebrate life, the freedom of the spirit and the restorative powers of the open air. In both stories, children learn to thrive in the natural world and the fear of death is renounced. Faith and healing are central to these stories; a straightforward faith in God, combined in *The Secret Garden* with a less conventional faith in nature and 'Magic'. Closely linked to these ideas is an exploration of punishment for past sins, repentance and the renewal of belief.

Heidi, written by Swiss author Johanna Spyri in 1880, and *The Secret Garden*, written by American-British writer Frances Hodgson Burnett in 1911, come from different countries and different times but they have many elements in common. Written within the European, Protestant tradition, they share ideas about the importance of giving children independence and the freedom to play, and have something to say about old-fashioned attitudes towards children which required them to be kept inside and quiet.

Also central to these books, but largely overlooked, is the theme of the tragedy of a child who cannot walk but who is miraculously cured by faith. In both stories healing occurs place in a nearly enchanted place where these children have experienced their first taste of freedom. In *Heidi* it happens in the high pastures of the Swiss Alps and in *The Secret Garden* in the enclosed, private garden the children have made their own.

Clara in *Heidi* and Colin in *The Secret Garden* both learn to walk again when they have learned to have faith. But faith in God on its own is not enough to fulfil the writer's purpose, which is to show that children should not be passive receivers of life but must believe in their own power to change things for the better. When Clara learns to walk again, we are asked to believe that this is the result of two apparently contra-dictory factors: that God has judged the time to be right for the healing to take place and that Clara, deciding that she no longer wants to be dependent on others, has found the energy to take matters into her own hands. In the words of Heidi's grandfather she has 'made the effort and won the day'.

The Secret Garden, published 31 years after *Heidi*, also deals centrally with faith and healing but in this book 'faith' is more complicated than a simple belief in the all-seeing, all-knowing power of God. In *The Secret Garden*, the psychological dimension is more important than the religious one. Trust and belief in God are largely replaced with confidence in the self. Colin cannot walk because he is literally paralysed by fear and believes that he is being punished in some way. When he learns to take control of his own life and learns how to love himself then he too can miraculously walk again.

For child readers this provides the standard, expected happy ending. For critics and commentators, the issue of walking/not walking in these novels is most often understood as merely a symbolic representation of the psychological or spiritual healing of unhappy children – children who are orphaned, unloved and with too many adult-imposed restrictions on their lives. In such a reading, illness and the eventual cure of the disabled child are not recognised as significant issues in themselves but as the metaphorical equivalent of sadness, powerlessness and dependency. Such a reading of *Heidi* gives Clara to us as a motherless girl, loved by her Grandmamma and her father but locked in the dark, unnatural world of the town. She lives in the city of Frankfurt, surrounded by bricks and mortar in a place where one can hardly see the sky. Her illness makes her passive and excludes her from the possibility of rebellion and misrule, and in this sense she is more like Beth March and Helen Burns than Katy and Pollyanna. But Johanna Spyri's motive is healing and redemption, so Clara must be made whole.

Clara accepts the idea of an all-seeing, all-knowing God although she does not understand why He has chosen to afflict her in this way. When she makes the journey to Heidi's home high up in the Alps and is surrounded by the beauty of Creation, she is able to feel God's purpose and finds the will to walk. Her walking, along with the symbolic destruction of the wheelchair by the jealous goat-herd, means that when Clara stands on her own two feet she is for the first time truly herself. Her healing plays a part in restoring religious faith to the previously errant grandfather. It teaches the reader to understand that God always knows what is best even though we may not understand His reasons, and it gives Heidi the role frequently allocated to the orphaned, previously homeless heroine – the power to bring light where hitherto there has been darkness.

A similar reading of *The Secret Garden* would include an understanding of Colin's first steps and the regaining of his physical strength as a throwing off of his earlier negative and destructive self-image. The literal key to the garden found by Mary at the beginning of the book becomes the symbolic key which unlocks Colin's belief in himself. In bringing the dead, dark garden to life, the children discover their own Arcadia and in watching the plants grow, they too grow and blossom into happy, healthy, plump children full of life and energy. Colin's walking is a result of faith in himself and faith in others.

A modern reading of *The Secret Garden* also includes a psycho-sexual interpretation, as shown by the reviews of Agnieszka Holland's 1993 film version of the book. The clearing of the garden and the growth of the flowers from bud to full bloom is thus symbolic of the ten-year-old children's developing sexuality. Colin's walking and his relationship with Mary is seen, not just as a co-operative friendship between two lonely children but also as a sign of their sexual development. As Colin learns to walk he becomes physically and mentally stronger and can leave behind the dependence of childhood. The final image of him running forward to meet his estranged father shows him upright and, more than just a boy, ready to enter adulthood.

Of course in life, both these writers would have known real, disabled children quite unable to throw away their wheelchairs (if they were rich enough to have one) and be cured by faith. Frances Hodgson Burnett had extensive dealings with 'crippled' children and adults. Her first husband was frequently described as 'lame' and her cousin's son, Willie Daniels, was disabled by an incurable hip disease. (In her divorce proceedings her husband was described as 'less than ordinary stature and a cripple', whilst she was 'of pleasing appearance and much personal magnetism'.) She worked closely with a charity called Invalid Children's Aid and in an article published by *Scribner's Magazine* wrote of the prevalence of spinal and hip diseases among the poor children of London; of sick children lying on dirty boards under rough sacking and of crippled children, fed on dry bread, unable to play, unable to move and with nothing to do.[1] In her later books there are a large number of crippled children, and she seems to have had a particular fascination for 'hunchbacks'.

Less is known about the life of Johanna Spyri, but paralysing illnesses were common in this period and it is unlikely that she did not know some disabled children who were not able to be cured either by medical knowledge or by religious belief.

Fiction for children that relies upon the miraculously walking child for its happy ending transmits a number of messages beyond the obvious one of fulfilling the reader's expectations. Perhaps the most important of these is that children who cannot walk are to be pitied and cared for but they can never be *accepted*. In order for them to live into adulthood, they must be cured. An ending where the non-walking protagonist is reconciled to her or his impairment and loved and accepted by all around is not seen as a possibility and writers, readers and film-makers still find it difficult to comprehend a story which ends without the lame person walking and a symbolic discarding of the wheelchair. 'Overcoming' stories, whether from fiction or life, have the important role of lessening the fear that disability holds for people. They assure the world that normal is right, to be desired and aspired to.[2]

---

1. Anne Thwaite, *Waiting for the Party: The Life of Frances Hodgson Burnett*, Virago, London, 1974, p137.
2. Jenny Morris, *Pride Against Prejudice: Transforming Attitudes to Disability*, The Women's Press, London, 1991, p101.

As discussed in Chapter 1, another message from these stories is that faith, whether in God, nature or self, has the ability to produce cure. The healing miracles of the New Testament were based on an absolute and unquestioning faith and this formed a social and moral code in Protestant countries which continued throughout the nineteenth and well into the twentieth centuries. But there was always another dimension to 'faith'; what might now be called 'mind over matter' or the 'power of positive thinking'. This belief in human ability to change events by the force of our will can be traced as far back as Virgil and the *Aeneid* (30–19 B.C.): 'mens agit molem' – mind moves matter. In the eighteenth century it was the subject of an entire system of philosophy when Bishop George Berkely wrote that nothing in the world exists unless it is perceived in the human mind. Even in the most all-inclusive forms of Christian teaching and in all but the most authoritarian of Victorian moral tales, children needed to be taught that they had some power to change the circumstances of their lives.

The relationship between the power of God to decide what is best and the power of the child to change the circumstances of her or his own life by positive thinking or self-will formed two halves of the developing and changing ideas about childhood in the period in which these books were written. Absolute faith in God, and in Christ as the face of God on earth, was an essential part of the teaching of Christian children, but they also needed some measure of self-reliance in order to cope with the increasing demands made upon them. The developing, post-Calvinist view of the child as an organic whole who needed to be loved, nurtured and developed into an independent being, capable of making her or his own decisions, required a child who was fully engaged with life. The passive, unquestioning, invalid child would either remain an invalid or, like Helen Burns and Beth

March, would die. Both these options were unacceptable endings for the central character of a story. If their faith was energetic enough, they could be cured.

Heidi

Little is known about *Heidi*'s author Johanna Spyri. She was born in 1827 in the hamlet of Hirzl near Zurich and was sent to the village school, which she hated. The foreword to the sequel *Heidi Grows Up*, produced by her translator, Charles Tritten, and published by Collins in 1958, suggests that perhaps Spyri's teacher mistook her shyness for inattentiveness and humiliated her before her class for being dull, but whatever the reason, some of her ideas about how children suffer and fail to learn when they are locked up in schools or in the hands of foolish tutors inform the story of *Heidi*.

As a child, Spyri spent time in the high village of Maienfeld, where she played in the upland pastures and lunched at the herdsman's hut, and these happy memories find their place in Heidi's high playground above the fictional village of Dorfli. Spyri didn't begin to write until she was in her forties, apparently in order to help the refugees from the Franco-Prussian War who were flooding into Switzerland. Like most of the writers discussed in this book, her literary output was enormous – she wrote more than 50 books for adults and children, but it is only for Heidi that she is remembered today.

Heidi was first published under the strikingly long title of *Lehr und Wanderjahre: eine Geschichte fuer kinde und auch fuer solche welche die Kinde lieb haben*. It came out in England in 1884 and was an immediate success. Anne Thwaite, in her biography of Frances Hodgson Burnett, notes that in the year that it was published *Heidi* (together with *Treasure*

Island), was listed as the bestselling novel of the year.[3] There were no specialist lists for children at this time so it is safe to assume that like *The Secret Garden*, *Heidi* was first read and enjoyed by both adults and children. *Heidi* has remained an international bestseller. There are currently many editions: abbreviated, illustrated, paperback and large glossy hardbacks. *Heidi* has been televised, serialised and filmed (video copies of the 1937 version starring Shirley Temple are now a collectors' item). Switzerland Tourism organise trips to 'Heidi Village' where you can visit 'The Original Heidi's House', and tourists and fans are tempted by the possibility of taking photos 'with Heidi sitting at her table' or lying on the bed 'where Heidi slept'.

Heidi holds its own because its central character is good-natured and kind and the story is never dull. But perhaps the most important reason it has endured is its extraordinary evocation of place. Elizabeth Enright writes in her 1950s article 'At 75, Heidi Still Skips Along':

> And over and above the action of the characters tower those other mighty characters, the mountains, with their fiery snowfields and high pastures all jeweled with rock roses and gentians. For a child who has never seen it, a new land is created: high, airy, exciting. His inward ear can hear the world of air and brooks; his imagination's eye can scan the deeps or see the eagle in the air.[4]

On Heidi's first day in the mountains with her grandfather, everything delights her: the clean spare hut

---

3. Anne Thwaite, *Waiting for the Party*, p95. The British Library catalogue lists almost 50 English-language editions of *Heidi*.
4. Elizabeth Enright, 'At 75, Heidi Still Skips Along', in Virginia Haviland, ed., *Children and Literature – Views and Reviews*, The Bodley Head, London, 1973, p79.

with a place for everything, her cosy bed in the hayloft where she can lie looking out of a round window and see right down the valley, the shrill whistle which means that grandfather's two goats are home and best of all the delicious meal of golden toasted cheese, bread and fresh milk drunk from a round bowl. As Elizabeth Enright comments, many a child has developed a taste for bread and cheese after reading this book! The next morning Heidi roams the mountain with Peter and the goats and is amazed at the colours and the beauty. That night when she sees her first sunset, she thinks that the rocks are on fire and is amazed at the beautiful, crimson snow. She feels a complete sense of happiness in her new home.

Like the goats and the birds, the flowers and the insects, Johanna Spyri's child is a part of nature. Heidi gambols around like a little strong, brown goat, she eats good, simple food and grows and blossoms like the flowers. The Puritan idea of the child as a soul to be saved or damned was losing its power by this time and thinkers like Jean Jacques Rousseau (1712–1778), had begun to develop ideas about the naturalness and simplicity of children. Children were unspoiled until adults made them so and in order to grow into the ideal adult, they needed a childhood in which they could develop a body which was strong and active and a mind unclouded with prejudice.

It was Rousseau's follower Friedrich Froebel (1782–1852), a student of the Swiss educational reformer, Johann Heinrich Pestalozzi (1746–1827), who developed the idea of the child as an organism like any other natural species. Childhood was a process, and the organic child needed to grow and develop naturally through action and play. Froebel first proposed the idea of schools for very young children, places which would nurture and develop the young. He called them 'Kindergartens', literally children's gardens, also known as nurseries. His disciple, Baroness Marenholtz Bulow, urged that every child should be given a garden of his or her own:

> To be a child who has never called a piece of ground his own, has never tilled it with the sweat of its brow, has never expended its fostering love on plants and animals, there will always be a gap in the development of the soul, and it will be difficult for that child to attain the capacity for human nurture in a comprehensive sense.[5]

This became a central idea in both *Heidi* and Frances Hodgson Burnett's *A Secret Garden*.

Juliet Dusinberre argues that the insistence of Froebel's followers on the need for more understanding of the child's nature generated a new insight into the relation between mind and body in the healthy child:

> Johanna Spyri's emphasis in *Heidi* on the health-giving properties of the mountain air and fresh milk for the invalid goes hand in hand with the belief that Clara began to walk because when she fed the goats she experienced the pleasures of independence, of caring for something else rather than always being cared for.[6]

The assumption here is, of course, that there can only be an independent mind where there is a healthy body.

Like many other books of this period, and this includes *The Secret Garden*, *Heidi* starts with a journey. Orphaned Heidi is being taken up the mountain by her cousin Dete to live with her grandfather, who is nicknamed 'Alm Uncle'. On the way, Heidi sheds her clothes one by one,

5. Baroness Marenholtz Buelow, *Child and Child Nature*, translated by Alice M. Christie, W. Swann Sonnenschein, London, 1879, p32.
6. Juliet Dusinberre, *Alice to the Lighthouse: Children's Books and Radical Experiments in Art*, Macmillan, London, 1978, p18.

shedding the old life where she was neither wanted or loved. Heidi is a homeless child in search of a home. Unusually for such books she is still a little child, only five years old, but her intelligence and spirit make her seem older. On the first day, her grandfather realises that she has taken exact note of where everything goes so that she will remember and be able to help. With her 'loving little heart' she will eventually bring comfort and cheer wherever she goes, even to Peter the goat-herd's blind grandmother, who has not known any joy for a long time.[7]

Heidi's grandfather does not at first sight seem the ideal surrogate parent, living alone at the top of a mountain, isolated and bad tempered. He has not led a good life and for this he has been exiled. In his youth he played the grand gentleman and went around the country drinking and mixing with bad company. He drank and gambled away the whole of his property, reducing his brother to beggary. His parents died of sorrow, one shortly after the other. His young wife died soon after their marriage and although his son Tobias grew up to be a steady young man and married, he died when a beam fell on him as he worked. When his wife Adelaide saw 'the poor disfigured body', she fell into a fever from which she never recovered. Their orphaned daughter Heidi was looked after by an aunt and her older cousin, Dete.

In Old Testament style, the general opinion is that these disasters were the punishment he deserved for the godless

---

7. *Heidi* is the only novel discussed in this book which English-speaking readers know through translation. For this chapter I have used the edition I read as a child (Regent Classics, Thames Publishing Co., J.M. Dent and Sons). The Puffin edition, translated in 1956, seems linguistically more feeble, less true to the sometimes stern mid-nineteenth century Protestant outlook. Clara's grand but benevolent 'Grandmamma' becomes the housewifely 'Mrs Sessemann', Heidi's grandfather, known everywhere as 'the Alm Uncle' becomes 'Uncle Alp.' Clara is no longer 'crippled', the word used by all Victorian novelists to describe the state of not being able to walk, but 'an invalid'. Clara's 'miraculous walking' is dissipated into the mild 'something attempted, something won' rather than grandfather's strong affirmation of self-will: 'You have made the effort and won the day.'

life he led. A minister exhorted him to repentance 'but the old man grew only more wrathful and obdurate and would not speak to a soul'. He went up the Alm and lived the life of a near hermit.

The belief in punishment for past sins was an important part of the unforgiving and Calvinistic approach to Protestantism. The villagers of Dorfli seem to have taken on a literal interpretation of the second commandment in the book of Exodus – 'For I thy God am a jealous God, visiting the iniquities of the fathers upon the children unto the third and fourth generation.' The 'Alm Uncle' seems to accept the view that his sins have caused the death of those he (presumably) loved and has turned his back on religion. Heidi's gentler, more forgiving New Testament Christianity, taught to her by Clara's grandmother during her stay in Frankfurt, sets an example which eventually reconciles grandfather to God and man.

From the beginning grandfather is 'not himself' in his behaviour towards Heidi, but is always kind and gentle towards her. She, in turn, begins to grow 'so strong and healthy that nothing ever ailed her'. She spends every day with Peter on the mountains tending the goats and does not go to school as her grandfather is frightened that she may have inherited her mother's nervous disposition. Despite his attitude to the rest of the world, he under-stands what Heidi needs to be happy. He takes care that she does not get cold in the winter or go hungry. He worries whether she will be scared by the howling winds around the hut and when he looks at her in her hayloft, 'her cheeks rosy with sleep, her head peacefully resting on her little round arm, and with a happy expression on her baby face as if dreaming of something pleasant', he cannot help but love her and want to protect her.

Into this paradise, nasty cousin Dete returns and virtually kidnaps Heidi. She is now eight years old and Dete has found a position for her in Frankfurt which will impress her own wealthy employers. The position is as companion to sickly Clara, who is first described to us in these conventional terms:

> An only daughter, young and an invalid, who was always obliged to go about in a wheeled chair, and was therefore very much alone and had no-one to share her lessons so the little girl felt dull.

Grandfather is furious at this proposal and, shouting at Dete to be gone, he storms out of the hut. Heidi is tricked into believing that she will be allowed to return to the Alm as soon as she wants and is whisked away from her beloved mountain.

Clara, whom she meets the next day, is the typical storybook invalid, lying on her couch all day, occasionally wheeled from room to room. She has a thin, pale face and soft blue eyes and is both patient and passive. Although Clara is a kind and generous girl, some years older than Heidi, she is rather dull and it is only her sickness which makes her interesting. She is too sensible and ordinary to be a fully fledged romantic invalid like cousin Helen in *What Katy Did*. Clara, too, is motherless and her father Herr Sessemann, like other fictional fathers, is a good, kind man but often away on business. Unlike the poor crippled children described in Frances Hodgson Burnett's articles who were hidden away in bare institutions or lived in dirt and near starvation, Clara is the kind of wealthy invalid who was tolerated and protected, even loved. She is, like other fictitious invalids, confined within her house, her 'weakness' making it impossible for her to be independent or venture out. She has a 'long illness' which requires her to have extensive periods of rest, and her doctor has very little hope of her final recovery. Again, the vagueness of the unspecified illness allows the possibility that it is 'in the mind' and can therefore be reversed.

Although Clara tries to be a good friend to Heidi, her stay in Frankfurt is a period of great unhappiness for her. Like all the really good children's writers of this time, Spyri has a deep, instinctive understanding of what makes children unhappy or scared and how they react when they have no one who listens to them. Fraulein Rottenmeier, the acerbic housekeeper, is the foolish and small-minded villain of the piece. She has old-fashioned ideas about children, believing that they should be quiet, grateful and still. Punctuality and neatness are what is important. Emotions, if children must have them, are best kept hidden and tears must be swallowed. Heidi, unusually in literature of the period, is not a middle-class child and does not understand the ways of the town or the hierarchy of servants and masters within the grand house. Without meaning to, she creates chaos. She wanders out of the house and gets lost, misses meals, doesn't understand the rules. When an organ boy she has met brings a bundle of kittens to the house, Fraulein Rottenmeier calls her an utter barbarian and threatens to lock her in the cellar with the rats and black beetles.

With painful accuracy, Johanna Spyri describes what happens to a homesick, desperately unhappy child who learns to lock all her feelings inside her so that no one perceives her sorrow. She now becomes the metaphorical bird locked in the cage. When she tries to catch a glimpse of the sky she can see nothing but walls, windows and stony streets. Heidi longs for her grandfather and the beautiful mountains, but as the seasons pass and it becomes spring once more, she realises that she has been lied to and cannot choose to go home. People are kind to her and she does not wish to seem ungrateful to Clara (who despite her kind, patient, invalid status seems quite unable to perceive Heidi's troubles) or to the good Frau Sessemann, Clara's 'Grandmamma'. Her secret feelings stay locked inside her, but when 'the weight of trouble on her little heart grew heavier and heavier, she could no longer eat her food and every day she grew a little paler'.

One of the purposes of this long, unhappy time is to develop Heidi's (and, by implication, the reader's) faith in God. She has not been brought up with any religion and has never been taught how to pray. Grandmamma Sessemann, on her visit to Frankfurt, gives Heidi beautiful picture books and through these Bible stories, she learns how to read and speak to God:

Dear child, let me tell you what to do: you know that when we are in great trouble, and cannot speak about it to anybody, we must turn to God and pray to Him to help, for He can deliver us from every care that oppresses us. You understand that, do you not?

When Heidi tells her that she is not used to praying, Grandmamma explains that this is the reason she is so unhappy. If she prays to God and tells him her troubles, 'He can help us and give us everything that will make us happy again.'

So, Heidi enthusiastically prays to be allowed to go home to her grandfather, but when she finds that her prayers are not answered, her eyes begin to look sad again and she stops telling God her troubles. Now Heidi is introduced to the moral and religious idea of 'God's plan'. Grandmamma explains that God will give Heidi her wishes but only when He judges the time to be right. He cannot give her everything she wants right now because she may later come to realise that it was not the best time for her to have it:

He thought it was better for you not to have at once what you wanted, He said to Himself: Yes, Heidi shall have what she asks for, but not until the right time comes, so that she may be quite happy.

Despite all this teaching, it is psychological rather than religious reasons which eventually bring Heidi home. She begins to sleepwalk, terrifying the whole household who believe that the unlocked front door each morning means that there must be a ghost. One night Herr Sessemann and his friend the doctor stay up to find out and are astonished to see the tiny white figure of Heidi in the open doorway, trembling from head to foot. The doctor sees how ill she has become. Like her mother before her, she has 'over excited nerves' which pills and powders will not cure. When he asks her the questions that should have been asked long ago, she tells the doctor how Fraulein Rottenmeier forbade her to cry and how all her feelings have been kept inside her, so that she has felt as if a great stone is weighing on her heart. Dramatically, the doctor announces to Herr Sessemann that unless she is sent back to the mountain air immediately, she may not go back at all.

So begins the second half of the book, of which the most significant element is healing. Heidi is healed the moment she is back in the mountains; the grandfather is healed by repentance of past transgression and makes his peace with God and man; the doctor is healed of a broken heart at the death of his beloved daughter and, most important of all, Clara is healed and learns to walk again. Heidi's 'loving heart', the landscape of natural beauty and the realisation of 'God's Plan' are the significant elements in this restoration.

Clara's visit takes longer than planned – she has had a 'bad attack, although she bore it so patiently' , but eventually she is brought up the mountain in a sedan chair. She arrives in May, the time of growth and rebirth.[8] The last snows have disappeared and the colours of the flowers are starting to show. Like cousin Helen in *What Katy Did*, Clara brings with her the thoughtful gifts of the wealthy invalid – everyone from Peter's grandmother to Heidi herself is presented with expensive, loving presents.

The reader has received several hints concerning the forthcoming healing. Clara's letter announcing her arrival tells Heidi of the doctor's words, 'no-one can help getting well up there', and when Heidi visits Peter's grandmother to give her this news, she is asked to read aloud a little hymn:

All things will work for good
To those who trust in Me;
I come with healing on my wings,
To save and set thee free.

To Heidi, healing means 'that which cures everything and makes everything well', and grandmother confirms that 'everything will come to pass according to God's good purpose'.

From the minute of her arrival, Clara is entranced by all the beauty around her. Almost her first words are 'if only I

8. Both Clara and cousin Helen in *What Katy Did* travel in search of a cure. Both go to take waters, Clara at the town of Ragatz, which is still open.

could walk about with you . . . if I could but go and look at the fir trees and at everything'. She longs to join Heidi on the higher slopes where she could see for herself the flowers and the smells Heidi describes: the red centaury, the bluebell flowers, and the bright yellow rock roses. Her 'cure' happens when she has been in the mountains for three weeks. Grandmamma has left and Clara is being nursed by the Alm Uncle who is surprisingly good at it, having nursed his own captain who had been 'crippled' fighting in Sicily. He takes care of all Clara's needs with gentle care, although of course, since this is a nineteenth-century novel, we are not told any details of what this personal care might be. Although described as a child or a 'little daughter', she is actually about 14 years old, the crucial transitional age between being a girl and being a woman. But in her invalid state she is forever the child and it is appropriate to think of the grandfather attending her 'as if his chief calling had been to look upon sick children'. She will not be on the path to young womanhood until she is made whole by walking.

Clara's health begins to improve almost from her first breath of mountain air. At her first lunch in the mountains she takes a second helping of golden toasted cheese and many references are made after this to her increased appetite. At the end of her first day, Clara lies with Heidi on the soft bed in the hayloft and exclaims in delight, 'Heidi, it's just as if we were in a high carriage and were going to drive straight into heaven.' This encourages Heidi to deliver a little religious homily in which she tries to explain that seemingly insoluble problem of why people need to pray if God has the future already planned. She tells Clara, 'We must never forget to pray, and to ask God to remember us when He is arranging things so that we too may feel safe and have no anxiety about what is going to happen.'

The 'high life-giving mountain air' gives Clara new energy and she wants to stay for ever in this 'great stillness' and beauty. She is almost at the end of her visit before grandfather names the possibility of her walking: 'Won't the little daughter try if she can stand for a minute or two?' Clara attempts to please him, but without success, and she has to content herself with listening to Heidi's descriptions of the flowers she cannot see for herself and the wonderful light from the evening sun. When Heidi begs her grandfather to push Clara's wheelchair up the mountain so that they can be with the goats, again he coaxes her with the reply that he will: 'But if I do, the little daughter must do something to please me: she must try her best again this evening to stand on her feet.'

Somehow, everyone has failed to notice the growing jealousy of Peter the goat-herd. Until Clara's arrival, Peter, who is poor, not very bright and often abused by the adults around him, has enjoyed having Heidi as his special friend. He bitterly resents Clara and cannot bear the thought that for the first time that summer (we seem to have gone from early spring to full summer in three weeks) Heidi will not be exploring the mountain but sticking by Clara's side all day long and ignoring him. Ironically, since all through the book the weak and passive Clara has been presented as someone to be pitied, Clara's wheelchair is to Peter both a symbol of her wealth and superiority and an indispensable part of her ability to stay on the mountain. When he sees it standing ready outside the hut, waiting for Clara to be lifted into it, he regards it as a powerful enemy and thinks that with it gone, Clara will have to go back home: 'There stood the chair on its high wheels; Peter seemed to see something proud and disdainful about it, and he glared at it as at an enemy that had done him harm and was likely to do him more still today.' In a furious temper, he hurls the wheelchair down the mountain and hiding behind a bush, he watches it racing faster and faster down the hill until it smashes into a hundred pieces. He is sure that 'Heidi's friend would be obliged to go away, for she would have no means of going about'. Heidi will be free to come out with him again and everything will be all right. But as Johanna Spyri cannot help but remind the reader, 'Peter did not consider, or did not know, that when we do a wrong thing trouble is sure to follow.' As a moral lesson, Peter's plan is foiled in all respects. He suffers several days of panicky fear and is eventually found out, and Clara is not sent home and is carried onto the high slopes by grandfather, where she will have the best day of her life.

The mountain pastures where the girls are taken becomes their garden of Paradise; nature is at its most perfect. The snowfield sparkles as if set with thousands of gold and silver stars, the sky is dark blue, the mountains lift their lofty heads and the great bird is poised aloft. They are at the top of the world, almost in heaven. As in the parallel scene in *The Secret Garden*, there are no authoritative adults around to limit them in their desires. What time or place could be more perfect for a miracle? Clara, sitting alone for a few moments feeding one of grandfather's little goats, feels something akin to a religious vision. The vision is for her own future as an independent young woman:

She suddenly felt a great desire to be her own mistress and to be able to help others, instead of herself always being dependent as she was now. Many thoughts unknown to her before, came crowding into her mind and a longing to go on living in the sunshine, and to be doing something that would bring happiness to another, as now she was helping to make the goat happy.

Whilst Clara is thinking about the kind of woman she hopes to become, Heidi is planning ways to help Clara see the flowers beyond her reach. In vain, she tries to help Clara onto her feet, but Heidi is too small and Peter too stiff to support her weight. Then, with Heidi's encouragement, Clara finds that with determination to go beyond her pain, she is able to do it alone. Suddenly and miraculously, she finds that she can 'take up her bed and walk':

> And Clara went on putting one foot out in front of another until all at once she called out, 'I can do it, Heidi,! Look! Look! I can make proper steps.'

Heidi can think of no greater joy than for Clara to walk about and not have to be pushed around in a chair. Clara agrees, 'for she could think of no greater pleasure in the world than to be strong and able to go around like other people, and no longer have to lie from day to day in her invalid chair'.

Although there are a few further references to not tiring herself and leaning on grandfather's arm for support, it is clear that we are to understand those first few steps not as the beginning of a long journey towards health and recovery, but as a sudden and miraculous healing. Sitting at the top of the mountain only moments later, Heidi 'suddenly remembers that Clara was cured; that was the crowning delight of all that made life so delightful in the midst of all this surrounding beauty'.

When grandfather goes to fetch the children from the mountain and hears from Heidi what happened that morning, his first words to Clara are, 'So we've made the effort, have we, and won the day!' His first response is that Clara has walked because she found the energy and will to do so. But to this idea is added another more weighty one:

that her healing is a 'blessing bestowed by God'. Later that night, in the second of her homilies to Clara, Heidi explains that God has now shown why he did not answer Heidi's prayers to take her away from Frankfurt. If she had left when she wanted to, Clara would never have come to Switzerland and if this had been the case, she would never have got well. Heidi explains that He 'always intends something better for us than we know or wish for', and that people must always continue to pray just to show that we 'have faith in God to make everything alright in the end'.

The absolute power of God to decide what is best and the power of the individual to change the circumstances of her or his own life by acts of self-will or the 'power of positive thinking' are two quite separate views of life, but they highlight the delicate balance between dependence and independence for the Victorian girl as she approached womanhood. On the one hand the invalid (in-valid, not worthy, not real) could provide a role model for the Victorian ideal of the woman as self-sacrificing, passive and dependent on others, and this could be symbolically represented through the character confined to bed, or in a 'wheeled chair', unable to walk and accepting the will of God. On the other hand, this was an inadequate representation of the Victorian ideal for womanhood which also required her to be domestically active, vibrant, not only in charge of the hearth and home and acting as moral guide for her husband and children, but also going outwards to engage in good works for those less fortunate, someone like that most perfect of perfect mothers, Marmee in *Little Women*.

The 'poor little, white, sickly, Clara' of the earlier chapters in *Heidi* would not be able to grow into an adult upon whom there would be many demands and responsibilities. Like Marmee or Clara's own indomitable grandmother Frau

Sessemann, the middle-class woman of the day needed tremendous resources, skills and energy to run their domestic empires. They had to supervise the servants, run the house, make endless decisions about domestic matters, be financial managers, supervise the religious guidance of their own children, obey their husbands and use their powers to minister good and transform the lives of others. Since the Victorian woman needed to be both a passive believer in the divine right of God (and men) and a person who did not always accept fate but could make things happen by her own acts of will, it was possible, indeed desirable to hold two apparently contradictory beliefs at the same time.

Clara, like Katy Carr before her, walks when God has judged the time to be right for her to stand on her own two feet and she has 'made the effort and won the day'. When Clara walks again she metaphorically steps into her dead mother's shoes. Tears spring into Herr Sessemann's eyes when, seeing his 'new' daughter for the first time, he finds in her the image of his departed wife: 'Just so had Clara's mother looked, the fair-haired girl with the delicate pink-and-white complexion.' Like 15-year-old Katy Carr who comes downstairs on her dead mother's birthday in order to take up her rightful place, 14-year-old Clara is now well on the way to leaving behind the dependence of childhood and becoming the 'Heart of the House' in Frankfurt.

Heidi is an important book which has had a powerful effect on generations of readers. Its ending is entirely happy and positive. Clara's pleasure at her new-found independence, the joy of her grandmother, father and the doctor when they visit her and unexpectedly discover her complete cure, the Alm Uncle's religious transformation, Clara and Heidi's lasting friendship and over and above the continuing beauty and magic of the place all add to its enchantment.

On readers who themselves cannot walk, its effect is curious. One story which I think is quite common, particularly for those disabled children who spent large portions of their childhood separated from the rest of the world in 'special' schools, was told to me by a woman who, like Clara, used a wheelchair as a child. *Heidi* was a favourite book, she loved the story and the strong sense of place and believed that like Clara, she would walk before she reached adulthood. Since neither literature nor life had given her images of the independently minded non-walking adult, she too waited and longed for God's divine blessing to be visited upon her. As an adult she is no longer waiting and has instead become an active campaigner in civil rights for disabled people. A dream story came from a different disabled child, also a fan of *Heidi* and also a wheelchair user, who was taken on holiday to Switzerland when she was nine. Having looked forward to visiting the mountains, once there she began to have a series of panicky nightmares in which her legs developed a life of their own and would run away from her with her body still attached. Usually she woke in terror with the image of her legs running off down the mountain. Sometimes in the dream she could exert feelings of control and self-preservation by imagining that she chopped off her legs and let them run away by themselves, leaving behind her body, the 'real' part of herself.

When Peter dramatically hurls Clara's wheelchair down the mountain in a fury, he unwittingly becomes the instigator of her cure. Along with him, we watch the wheelchair turning and spinning, rolling over and over to its complete destruction. The wheelchair is the cage, not the liberator. Sitting alone in the wide open space of the mountains, free from the shackles of her wheelchair, Clara is not panicked by the thought of what will happen to her if nobody comes to fetch her, but for the first time contemplates the possibility that she can change her own life. The wheelchair, not the nameless illness, is the symbol of her dependency and once it is gone, she is able to set herself 'free'.

The Secret Garden

Frances Hodgson Burnett had written 30 novels, 14 plays and countless short stories by the time *The Secret Garden* was published in 1911. Surprisingly, it met with a mixed reception on publication and when Burnett died in 1924, it was not even mentioned in her obituary in *The Times*. Yet today it is the most enduring and popular of her titles, reproduced on television and in film many times over and published in hundreds of different editions. For many people, *The Secret Garden* is *the* favourite book of their childhood.

Although the novel is set at a time when Christianity was central to the lives of most people and most stories, religion is remarkably absent from this book, or at least conventional religion. In contrast to *Heidi*, God is not mentioned at all, although Burnett frequently summons something she calls 'Magic'. Mary and Colin never go to Sunday school, no one lectures them about how Jesus can see and understand their every thought and there is not even a hint of the vicar or a reverend. There are lots of ideas about what makes children happy and, even more important for the time, what makes them good, but the morality is surprisingly secular. The central philosophy of this book is 'New Thought' rather than Christianity. This was a belief, similar to but not the same as Christian Science, that the mental and physical problems of life should be met, regulated and controlled by the suggestion of 'right thoughts'. Burnett believed passionately that with energy and determination, bad and negative thoughts could be replaced with good, positive ones. The movement Burnett ascribed to also believed that there were forces inside and outside the human body which could be harnessed to cure mental and physical illness – an idea not a million miles away from the ever popular 'mind over matter'.

In *The Secret Garden* both Mary and Colin need a system of belief which makes them feel that they can have power over their own lives because they do not receive any worthwhile moral or spiritual guidance from the adults around them. Both are orphaned and although Colin has a father, he has been absent for most of his life. Colin's beautiful, laughing mother died when he was born and his grief-stricken father, described as a 'hunchback', has placed his baby son in the care of the servants, unable to take care of him or even look at him. The servants who look after him are too scared of this difficult child to offer any guidance or love and he has learned that hysterics and tantrums are the only way to get attention.

The orphan convention was so widely used in Victorian fiction that, as Reynolds and Humble remark, 'we could be forgiven for assuming that orphanhood was the typical condition for children of that period'.[9] With the exception of Jo March, all the characters discussed in this book are motherless and even when the father is alive, he is usually distant and distracted. There was an unfailing attraction in the motherless orphan battling against society, having to make their own way in an uncaring world, fighting their own battles. The struggle was, of course, different for boys than for girls. The fictional orphaned boy set off on his adventurous journey without any sense of callousness or irresponsibility to a family left at home. He proved himself by his self-reliance and his success in conquering the

---

9. Kimberley Reynolds and Nicola Humble, *Victorian Heroines: Representations of Femininity in Mid-Nineteenth Century Literature and Art*, Harvester Wheatsheaf, London, 1993, p24.

world. Of course Colin is not a 'typical' orphan boy in that he is highly feminised at the start of the book. Yet even he, once cured, will go off to see the world. Success for the orphan girl, on the other hand, lay in an ending where a new family had been created, preferably one where a few long-lost blood relatives could be discovered. The orphan brought light where hitherto there had been darkness. Jane does this at Thornfield, Pollyanna converts her sourpuss aunt in a small American town, Heidi works miracles in the Alps, and Mary, of course, transforms Misslethwaite Hall, bringing Colin's father back into the family fold.

Like Colin, Mary is a neglected, unloved child. She has been brought up in India with a beautiful mother, who clearly did not like her own, plain child, and an absent, ill father. The only adults in her life are a series of Ayas whom she treats, as she has seen adults do, with imperialist contempt. Colin and Mary have to learn for themselves how to be good and how to be well. Their secret garden is the vehicle for this change because it is in this space that they gain freedom from the stifling world of adults – servants and housekeepers mostly – whose idea of child-rearing is already old-fashioned.

The Secret Garden is a book about healing and cure. It is, as Juliet Dusinberre argues, a book in which the lugubrious Victorian death story has been turned into a child's celebration of living.[10] Mary and Colin have both been 'sickly' from childhood. Colin has been an 'invalid' all his life, and Mary arrives at her new home unattractive and yellow as a result of being jaundiced and neglected. They are thin, pale and weak in the manner of literary invalids of the previous century but they are certainly not saintly or

10. Juliet Dusinberre, *Alice to the Lighthouse*, p131.

cheerful. Burnett's portrayal of unhappy, unattractive children who have been denied love by their parents, and who have in their turn become difficult and hard to love, seems very enlightened in its understanding of why neglected children behave badly.

The story opens in an unusually dramatic way. Nine-year-old Mary is in India at the centre of a cholera epidemic. She hears her beautiful mother's voice and catches a glimpse of her lovely clothes. She hears the servants scream and cry but nobody talks to her or explains anything. The next day there is panic everywhere and during the confusion, Mary hides herself away. She has been forgotten by everyone: 'Nobody thought of her, nobody wanted her, and strange things happened of which she knew nothing.' Some time later when the soldiers come to lock up the house, they are amazed to find this child all alone. They had heard rumours that the beautiful Mrs Lennox had a child, but no one had ever seen her. This background is designed to help the reader to understand Mary and feel some sympathy for this difficult girl.

The real beginning is in the orphaned Mary's journey to find a home. Her travels are unusually long and lonely. She has to make her way from India by boat, train and carriage until she arrives in the huge, lonely Misslethwaite Hall in Yorkshire. Mary has become the ward of Mr Craven, an uncle she has never heard of and never seen.

Mary makes an unlikely heroine. She is not a bright-eyed, cheerful orphan like Heidi or Pollyanna, nor is she the energetic, untidy lively heroine in the style of Jo or Katy. She is an 'ugly cross little thing', stiff, plain and silent. The opening paragraph of the book describes her as:

The most disagreeable-looking child ever seen...she had a thin little face and a thin little body, thin light hair and a sour expression. Her hair was yellow and her face was yellow because she had been born in India and has always been ill in one way or another.

Her nearest literary equivalent is Jane Eyre, whom Charlotte Brontë describes on the first page of her book as lacking in that 'attractive and sprightly manner' which children, especially girls, were required to possess. Jane Eyre was not 'light, frank and natural' with adults, and neither is Mary. They have much the same reasons for this difficult, edgy approach to people: they have been ignored and have learnt how to be solitary rather than sociable. Both have a sense of not belonging anywhere, of living in other people's houses with no one who really cares for them.

Misslethwaite Manor, a huge, dark house on the edge of the moors with many shut doors and secrets, seems at first sight to be an unlikely place for Mary's psychological and physical healing. Significantly, she arrives at the end of winter when everything is still bare and bleak and nothing is growing. Most of the hundred rooms are locked up and the housekeeper, Mrs Metlock makes it clear that Mary is to keep to her own rooms. Mrs Metlock is not exactly unkind, but does not understand children and has no time for them; she wants neither to see Mary nor to hear her. In the common pattern of children's stories of the time, Mary's first real friends are the ordinary, lowly servants: Martha, the young servant girl who attends to Mary, her brother Dickon, a boy who can literally speak to the animals, and the irascible old gardener Ben. These are plain Yorkshire people who speak dialect, don't know and don't care about fancy manners and underneath their bluff exterior have hearts of gold. Martha Sowerby, with her 11 brothers and sisters and wonderful, 'healthy minded' mother (the idealised Susan Sowerby), has no patience for

Mary's cross and selfish ways. She will not be spoken to in the way Mary is used to speaking to the servants in India and is amazed at Mary's dependence on others to perform tasks as simple as getting herself dressed.[11]

It is Martha who first introduces Mary to the idea of the secret garden. She does it to relieve Mary's loneliness and to help improve her appetite and strength by playing out of doors. She is a firm believer that running around in the fresh air is just what Mary needs, but the Yorkshire weather is dull and cold, so she entices Mary with the story of the garden which has been locked up for ten years: 'Mr Craven had it shut when his wife died so sudden. He won't let no one go inside. It was her garden. He locked th'door an' dug a hole and buried th' key.'

Mary's healing starts when she begins to think of people and things beyond herself. Like Clara, she is cured by a combination of fresh air, wholesome food and a desire to be independent and make decisions for herself, and as in *Heidi* it is the natural world which restores her health. The unpromising Yorkshire landscape is an important part of this. The wintry moor at the beginning of the story acknowledges a debt to the moors of the Brontës. The wind 'wuthers' around the house and when Mary first meets it on her journey towards Misslethwaite Manor, (much as Jane Eyre travels towards Thornfield), the moor seems 'like a wide expanse of black ocean'. But it is the moor that restores her to health and happiness. As spring approaches, the purple heather and the golden gorse blossom and begin to grow, just like the alpine flowers bloomed for Heidi and Clara. The moor stirs Mary's blood, awakens her appetite and 'blows the cobwebs out of her brain'. It is nature – the

---

11. There are a number of appalling comments about the 'natives' in this book. Burnett subscribed to the contemporary position that the population of India was a quite different species to that of Yorkshire.

'cool fresh air of the English moor' rather than the 'hot and languid' air of India – which brings Mary to life and stirs her imagination. Everything works to help her: her friendship with the friendly robin, her strange, edgy relationship with the old gardener Ben Weatherstaff, who makes no secret of the fact that when he first meets Mary he thinks he has never seen 'an uglier sour-faced young 'un', and her relationship with Dickon – the boy of nature with whom she can share her secret.

But it is the locked garden itself which is the 'key' to Mary's transformation from plain, lonely child to cheerful, round-faced one. Like a fairy godmother, it is the robin who first shows Mary the key to the garden. Symbolically, Mary has woken to a beautiful blue sky and realises that springtime is coming. She puts the key into her pocket and holds it like a talisman. The next day, skipping around the garden with her new skipping rope, 'Magic' is evoked. The wind blows away the ivy and under it, Mary sees the lock of the door and in a moment, she finds herself in 'the sweetest, most mysterious looking place anyone could imagine'.

The appeal of this garden to generations of readers is that it is entirely a child's world where children can have their own secrets and where they can make things happen for themselves. This is particularly important for children (then and now, although for a very different set of reasons) who have no freedom from the adults around them, who are kept shut inside and who are chaperoned everywhere. When Mary first finds the secret garden, what she likes most of all is the feeling that 'when its beautiful old walls shut her in, no one knew where she was. It seemed almost like being shut out of the world in some fairy tale place.'

The garden is also the place where lonely, isolated Mary, 'an odd, determined little person', can do two more things which help her to heal: she can make things grow and, perhaps more importantly, she can share this secret with the first friend of her childhood. Firstly alone, she instinctively clears a space around the little green shoots appearing through the brown earth, because it feels like they have no room to breathe, and later, with Dickon, she learns that if you know how to look, you will find that things which seem dead are really alive and growing. It is through making the garden come alive that Mary comes alive herself.

Physically Mary changes from a thin, sallow, lank-haired child to a round-faced, rosy-cheeked, smiling girl. The links between a healthy body and a healthy mind are clear. Like Colin later in the book, Mary finds psychological health and simultaneously regains physical strength. Emotionally she has been unable to show any love and affection because she has never known any herself, but as soon as she is able to look beyond herself and make good relationships with others, she becomes physically stronger. The 'key' to Mary's psychological health lies in her growing self-love and her love of others. In the way that only an unloved, lonely and insecure child needs to do, she asks Dickon, 'Does tha' like me?' When he replies without hesitation, 'Eh! I likes thee wonderful', she is well on the way to being healed.

At this point in the story, about halfway through the book, Burnett seems to lose interest in her heroine and gives her attention to an equally unlikely hero, Colin Craven.

When Mary first meets Colin, he is literally in a 'night world' from which he must be released. Like Jane Eyre at Thornfield, Mary hears cries along the dark, empty corridors of Misslethwaite Manor. The servants look terrified when she asks who is crying and tell her it is just the sound of the 'wuthering wind' but Mary, curious and lonely, does not believe them. Late one night she hears this plaintive crying again and goes to investigate. What she finds is the sad spectacle of a boy locked in against life. Colin has all the physical characteristics of a fictional Victorian invalid. He is romantic looking with a pale ivory face and sharp delicate features, huge grey eyes rimmed with thick black lashes and long, dark, curly hair. But he is neither saintly nor patient enough to fill this role – he is a thoroughly 'bad' invalid who rules over everyone around him like a young rajah. In 1833, Charles Lamb wrote that to be sick is to enjoy monarchical prerogatives: 'If there be regal solitude, it is in the sick bed. How the patient lords it there; what caprices he acts without control.'[12] Colin, at the beginning of the book, is as authoritarian and controlling as any monarch, but there is no pleasure for him in his isolated kingdom.

From the beginning, the reader understands that Colin's paralysis is psychosomatic and 'hysterical', brought on by emotional neglect and fear rather than illness. There has been no fall or accident, no typhoid fever or tuberculosis, and there is not even a vague diagnosis of a 'weakening disease' as in *Little Women* or *Heidi*. Colin cannot walk because he believes he cannot walk. He believes that he is going to die young because he has overheard the servants talking about him. He knows that his father has never been able to look at him, that his 'beautiful, laughing mother' died shortly after his birth, and that everyone believed that if he grew up, he would be a 'deformed and crippled creature'.

It is not clear whether Frances Hodgson Burnett knew the work of Freud, but it was very likely that she was aware of his ideas. In the first decade of the twentieth century, his

---

12. Charles Lamb, 'The Convalescent', 1833, in *The Faber Book of Fevers and Frets*, Faber and Faber, London, 1989, p341.

work was widely received and much talked about, particularly in New York, where Burnett spent much of her adult life. Freud's *Studies in Hysteria*, written with Joseph Breuer, was published in 1895, sixteen years before *The Secret Garden*. This book was the first to show that hysteria was psychological rather than physical. The body could be seen as a container of psychological distress, and illness was not necessarily material in origin. Freud's work proposed that since negative, unconscious memories cannot be expressed normally, their emotional effect is dammed up and must be expressed elsewhere in the body. Burnett also looked for explanations of behaviour and illness within the personal, psychological history of the individual. For Freud, the soul was mental rather than spiritual, and although Burnett had some faith in forces outside the self, she too regarded the centre of a person and the responsibility for healing as within the human mind rather than in religion.

Whether or not Burnett was directly influenced by Freud's writings, she was certainly taken up with what she called 'the new wave swelling upon the century's shore': ideas about how the power of the mind could influence the body and the heart. Colin's hysteria is not strictly Freudian, although it does have a psychological dimension unusual in children's books of the time. He is not really 'paralysed'; his memories of bad things are not repressed, neither do they seem sexual in origin. But he does have traumatic memories which are pathogenic. He knows that his father hates him and associates the birth of his sickly, weak son with the death of his strong, happy wife. One of the first things Colin tells Mary is, 'My mother died when I was born and it makes him wretched to look at me. He thinks I don't know but I've heard people talking. He almost hates me.' Colin's disease is an expression of his inner self – or more accurately, of the inner self of his depressed father. Archibald Craven is described as a 'hunchback' who from the very first was 'set wrong'. He knew a brief moment of joy but when his wife died, all his rage and self-hatred reasserted itself and was turned on his baby son, who he predicted would be 'deformed and disfigured' like himself.

Burnett seemed to have a particular interest in the 'hunchback' which she saw as an ugly, physical deformity which corrupted the body and the spirit but which, miraculously, could be 'overcome' with splendid and uplifting thoughts. In her children's book *The Lost Prince*, a naturally noble upright boy Marco Loristan, unaware that he is the uncrowned prince of a Baltic state, makes his way through Europe disguised as a poor urchin, secretly carrying the message that war-torn Samavia will be free after hundreds of years of captivity.[13] He makes this long journey in the company of a character known as 'The Rat'. At the beginning of the book, The Rat is 'a hunchback' and despite a good brain, he seems scarcely human. He spends all day in a kind of cavern and pushes himself along the ground like a rodent:

> He was a strange creature with a big forehead and deep eyes which were curiously sharp. But this was not all. He was a hunchback. His legs seemed small and crooked. He sat with them crossed before him on a rough wooden platform set on low wheels, on which he evidently pushed himself about.

---

13. Samavia is based on Serbia. Burnett had met a displaced member of the Serbian royal family, and this story is clearly based on the centuries-old struggles in that region. Writing about it as the war in Kosovo pulls another Baltic state apart, it is disturbing to read this intensely patriotic story of the battle over the rights to a country, against what is portrayed as an ancient and 'uncivilised' enemy.

The Rat (he never loses this name) hero worships the princely Marco Loristan and his father and as he develops a purpose in life – he vows to serve them until death – he is spiritually and physically uplifted until the point where without any medical treatment or even a better diet, he can not only walk on crutches but is capable of crossing uneven landscapes and climbing mountains to deliver crucial messages. Like Jamie in Eleanor Porter's *Pollyanna Grows Up*, he never quite loses his self-hatred for being 'a cripple' but somehow his 'hunchback' completely disappears and, through the power of his own will and patriotic zeal, he can make himself an upright hero who can 'stand face to face' with Marco and 'poise very erect'.

Another children's story by Burnett, *The Little Hunchback Zia*, published in 1916, is more obviously based on Christianity and uses the story of the birth of Jesus and the later healing miracles to make the point that physical deformity can be overcome by faith. In this story Zia is a poor beggar boy, 'a little deformed creature' with the 'blight of Jehovah's wrath upon him'. The witch-like creature in whose house he lives has told him that he must not look her in the face. She declares that evil spirits look out from his shining eyes and that he is possessed of devils. But an unearthly beauty shines out from these eyes which might 'behold the Messiah'. As if this and his 'accursed hunchback' are not enough to bear, poor Zia breaks out in spots and cracked skin and is declared a leper. A complete outcast, he travels to Bethlehem where he meets the Virgin Mary. He follows her radiant light and the next morning, in the stable, touches the hand of the baby Jesus and is made whole: 'He moved, he rose, he stood upright – the hunchback Zia who had never stood up before! His body was straight; his limbs were strong. He looked upon both his hands, and there was no blemish or spot to be seen!'

With his straight body and strong limbs, he now becomes luminary and 'the shepherds come and make obeisance to him as a king's son'.

'Hunchbacked' is a description of a physical condition such as scoliosis or curvature of the spine which can cause the curving or bending of the shoulders, back or ribcage – in dictionary terms 'having a protruberant or crooked back'. This can develop in childhood or adolescence, as is said to have happened to Archibald Craven in *The Secret Garden*, and causes a permanent change to the structure of the body. It is therefore only in literature that this condition can be completely altered by faith, exercise or willpower.

The *Shorter Oxford English Dictionary* gives the earliest use of the term 'hump-backed' as 1681, although it was pre-dated by 'crump-backed' and possibly 'hulch-backed'. Since the dictionary definition of 'hump' is 'a fit of ill humour', and is further described as 'normal in a camel, a deformity in man', its use was never value free.

The term 'hunch backed' is attributed to Shakespeare in 1712; Henry VIII's jester, William Somner, was a hunchback and so was Richard III, perhaps the most dramatic representation of the completely evil character who is misshapen and monstrous in both body and soul. In *Henry VI*, Part 3, Richard presents himself as an outcast who rejects pity, love and fear. At the end of the play, he says 'I am myself alone.' Sometimes his 'cruel body' is ascribed to his difficult birth and at others to bewitchment and sorcery by his sister-in-law Elizabeth. This, he believes, has made it impossible for him to 'make my heaven in a lady's lap' or to be a 'man who is beloved'. In the famous 'Now is the winter of our discontent' speech, he informs the audience that since his physical body means that he cannot be a lover, he is determined to be a villain, one who can 'murder while he smiles'.

The most famous literary hunchback is, of course, Victor Hugo's Quasimodo (1831). Unlike Richard III he is victim rather than villain. However, he too is believed to be touched by the devil, and the mob's response to him is a mixture of superstition and fear. He is 'deformed and grotesque', an 'unholy monster', and young women are required to light a candle in church if he accidentally crosses their path. Quasimodo – the name means 'half-formed' – is the bell-ringer in Notre Dame Cathedral in fifteenth-century Paris. In French, the book is titled *Notre Dame de Paris*, without the use of the word 'hunchback', and the title we use today seems to have its source in the film industry rather than the novel. Quasimodo does not appear until the fourth chapter and the story is of hypocrisy and super-stition in medieval Europe. In England it has largely endured because of the 1939 film starring Charles Laughton, who plays Quasimodo as a tragic but hideously ugly victim, humiliated by the mob who are both terrified and fascinated by him. The 1996 Disney cartoon film (seven feature films have been made of this story) brought him to the public's attention again, and in this sentimentalised version he is less frightening but still a pathetic outcast. When the evil Frollo first looks at him as a baby, he proclaims that he is a 'monster'. In all versions, Quasimodo loves the beautiful Esmeralda but as in the many variations of the traditional fairytale, where the ugly beast loves the beautiful princess, the most he can hope for is her pity. In the final scene of the 1939 film, Charles Laughton's heartbroken, lonely Quasimodo clings to the wall of the bell tower, wishing that like the grotesque gargoyles around him, his heart were made of stone.

It is hardly surprising that when Mary first hears the description of her uncle, she is filled with fear:

He lives in a great, big, desolate old house in the country, and no one goes near him. He's so cross he won't let them, and they wouldn't come if he would let them. He's a hunchback and he's horrid.

Her only experience of 'hunchbacks' so far is in the French fairy story *Riquet a la Houppe*, about a 'poor hunchback and a beautiful princess'. When she hears that her uncle wants to see her a few weeks after her arrival at Misslethwaite, she turns pale with fear. But he turns out not to be a Bluebeard after all. He does not even have a 'hunchback', only 'high, rather crooked shoulders' and is not even ugly at all, only sad looking and distracted. His 'problem', as the reader learns later, is more a matter of depression and moral cowardice than physical impairment. When he learns to face life again, symbolically and literally he will stand 'upright'.

Colin's problem is also not a 'hunched back', although his fear of it is real enough. All through the early part of his story, he taunts himself and all those around him that when he feels the lump begin to grow, he knows that he will die. All his energy is negative and self-destructive, and his 'cure' will rely on developing a capacity for self-love. Colin's view of himself is reinforced by those who whisper around his bed that he would be better off dead.

Into this world comes Mary. She is unconvinced by Colin's illness and sees only that he is sick because he wants to be sick and thus, logically, he can make himself better again. All his life, Colin has been the victim of out-dated, inappropriate medicine. The family doctor and a relation, Mr Craven (who will inherit the property if Colin dies), keeps him lying down, sometimes entrapped in a big, useless back brace – a medical practice dating back hundreds of years.[14] He lives in

---

14. Richard Quain, *A Dictionary of Medicine*, Longmans, Green and Co., London, 1800, p1505.

a huge, dark, airless room, surrounded by people who are
ignorant and tired of him. He is scared of everything that
might heal him – exercise, fresh air, other people – and has
never known the company of children.

Mary is the first person to confront him with his fears and
she does it with the rage of an equally unloved child. She tells
him that he is too nasty and horrible to be about to die. She
refuses to show any sympathy and makes him sit up in order
to look at his spine. For the first time in his life she proves to
him that 'there's not a lump as big as a pin – except backbone
lumps, and you can only feel them because you're thin.' No
one has thought to tell him this before.

From this point, Colin and Mary join Dickon in their
ecstatic celebration of living and healing. Colin moves from
the closed, dark claustrophobic atmosphere of the house
into the idyllic, bright world of the garden and for the first
time feels that he could 'live to grow up'. Dickon is the
symbol of everything which is simple and alive. Contrasting
him to Colin, Mary says, 'He's always talking about live
things. He never talks about dead things or things that are
ill. He's always looking up in the sky to see birds flying – or
looking down in the earth to see something growing.' The
garden becomes the children's private world. Colin gives
instructions that he is to be carried downstairs and placed in
his wheelchair but in order to preserve the secret, no one is
allowed to follow him. In the style of Johanna Spyri there
are rapturous and detailed descriptions of spring turning
into summer – the buds unfurling into the wonderful
colour of English rather than Alpine flowers; iris, white
lilies, campanula, delphiniums, poppies and most
spectacularly of all, cascades of roses that, like the children,
'come alive, day by day, hour by hour'. It is in this garden,
the 'wild garden of the English romantic imagination,'[15] that
the children are most themselves.

But unlike *Heidi*, this awesome power of nature is not described as the work of God but as 'Magic'. 'Magic' is everything which is good. The children believe it is what makes the flowers grow and, even more importantly, what is helping to turn Colin into an entirely different kind of boy. 'Magic' is invoked by thinking good, brave thoughts rather than negative, frightened ones. The children's faith is not in 'God's plan' but in the power of the self to evoke 'good thoughts' and thereby make good things happen. As Burnett explains in an unusually didactic passage which seems to include both Freud and Mary Baker Eddy, the founder of Christian Science:

> One of the new things people began to find out in the last century was that thoughts – just mere thoughts – are as powerful as electric batteries – as good for one as sunlight is, or as bad for one as poison. To let a sad thought or a bad one get into your mind is as dangerous as letting scarlet fever into your body.

In a kind of New Age mantra, the children summon the force of 'Magic' by sitting in a circle and chanting an ode to Nature. Its aim is to get Colin up and walking:

> The sun is shining. That is Magic. The flowers are growing – the roots are stirring. That is the Magic. Being alive is the Magic. The Magic is in me…

And so on. This 'prayer' to nature is not very far removed from the Christian interpretation of 'cure' as part of God's plan. Perhaps the balance of the forces is slightly different, but Colin's miracle healing, like Clara's, is still the result of

15. Angela Carter, 'Walter de la Mare: Memoirs of a Midget', 1982, in *Expletives Deleted*, Chatto and Windus, London, 1992, p59.

the combination of the power of a force outside oneself, the force which manifests itself in the 'beauty of nature' and the power of the forces inside – self-will and determination.

Colin getting on his feet for the first time, however, actually has very little to do with the spiritual forces or the 'Magic' of good thoughts and much more to do with (masculine) hurt pride. All his life, his sense of self, his 'ego' has been battered by the view of himself as a 'poor, bent, crippled boy'. Whispered around the house are descriptions of him as 'a humped backed boy with helpless limbs', and, assuming that the two go hand in hand, that he is also 'not right in the head'. On the rare occasions that he was taken out of the house, for example a trip to the seaside, he hated the staring pity of strangers.

In a set piece, similar to Clara's walking scene, but with more energy and decisiveness, Colin's 'miracle cure' happens on his first day in the garden. Instead of the benevolent old Alm Uncle, we have the crusty old gardener Ben Weatherstaff, who looks over the wall of the secret garden from his ladder and is furious to find children playing there. When he sees Colin in his 'wheeled chair with luxurious cushions and robes' sitting up like a young rajah, he cries, 'Lord knows how tha' come here. But tha'rt th' poor cripple.' When Colin hotly replies that he is not a cripple, Ben, remembering things he has heard, asks, 'hasn't tha' got a crooked back? Hasn't tha' got crooked legs?' Furious at this, Colin pulls back his covers and – with Mary whispering under her breath, 'He can do it! He can do it!' over and over again – Colin stands, for the first time in his life:

There was a brief, fierce scramble, the rugs were tossed on the ground, Dickon held Colin's arm, the thin legs were out, the thin feet were on the grass. Colin was standing upright – upright – as straight as an arrow and looking strangely tall – his head thrown back and his strange eyes flashing lightning.

For the first time also, he commands people to look at him and Dickon is the first to agree that 'he's as straight as any lad in Yorkshire!' Within minutes he walks to the tree and with the imperious anger of someone who knows he is speaking to his social inferior, he commands Ben to look at him and Ben, with a 'queer rush of tears' and much dobbing of hat, thoroughly agrees that he is 'not a hunchback or a half-wit'.

This walking because of hurt pride is the first 'step' in Colin's important journey towards a state of 'upright' masculinity. When he is ill and frightened, he is not like a boy from a 'boy's book'. His illness feminises him and makes him petulant and subject to passionate but useless outbursts. He is the victim of his emotions, entirely dependent on others and frightened of everything, even the fresh air. Until Freud's work was published in 1895, it was believed that only women could suffer from hysterical symptoms such as paralysis; the word itself comes from the Greek word for 'uterus'. Throughout the period of Colin's illness his appearance is feminine and romantic but from the moment he stands up, he begins to become the 'real boy' his father never thought he could be.

When the children affirm that Colin is standing 'upright', not 'crooked' and without a 'bent bone in him', and deny that he has ever been 'a cripple' or a 'hunchback', even though all the world saw him as 'a poor half-witted lad without a straight bone in him', they are not simply describing his physical condition; the language of 'straight' and 'bent' has clear moral implications. 'Straight' and 'upright' mean honest, honorable, frank and trustworthy. To describe someone, particularly a man, as completely 'straight' in the context of character is always positive – it means that you know where you are with him and that he is unlikely to let you down. When Dickon, the most dependable, honest boy in all of Yorkshire, declares that 'Colin is as straight as I am', he is not just referring to the shape of his backbone.[16]

From this point on, Colin affirms his place as a real boy in the wild and mysterious walled garden. Everything is now designed to help him become straighter and stronger so that he can surprise everyone and meet his father as a man. Fresh air is a vital part of this process and Burnett was as fervent about the healing powers of nature as was Johanna Spyri. Following the Rousseau-Froebel movement, she too believed that children needed freedom to play and some land of their own in order to grow strong and independent.[17] Like many writers of the period, Burnett was also enthusiastic about food. As Colin gets stronger, his appetite grows and the children, under the supervision of the wonderful Mrs Sowerby, eat as much 'healthy' food as they can: bread, fresh milk, eggs, jam, hot potatoes, butter and currant buns are described in loving detail.

Colin wills himself to become well again, to triumph over death, but he needs something more manly than just tending the flowers, and Dickon organises lessons from a local champion wrestler Bob Hawarth (a very Brontë name). He practises 'muscle exercises' every day to strengthen his arms, legs and every muscle in his body. Nothing seems

---

16. 'Bent' is also a pejorative term for a homosexual and whilst 'straight' is often used ironically by gay people in this context, meaning heterosexual and 'normal', the word 'bent' is never used by them, since there is no context where it can be positive.

17. For at least a century there had been the belief in the healing powers of the fresh air, particularly in the escape from cities where the air was heavily polluted. Open Air Schools for delicate children existed in England well into the middle of the twentieth century and were places where children were required to eat, learn and sleep out of doors all through the year and were only taken indoors in the coldest part of the winter.

impossible for him now. He imagines all sorts of possibilities
and adventures for himself: 'Athlete, Lecturer, Scientific
Discoverer' – all manly, ambitious, non-domestic pursuits
which will take him outwards into the world. Mary is half-
forgotten – no one asks how she feels about the
reconciliation between the boy and his father and we do not
know what lies in store for her. We can only hope it isn't
responsibility for the running of Misslethwaite Manor.

The story ends with the happy reconciliation of Colin
and his father. All the time he has been imagining himself
well, the thought that has stimulated him more than any
other was 'what his father would look like when he saw
that he had a son who was as straight and strong as other
father's sons'. All Colin's self-hatred had been focused on
himself as a 'weak backed boy whose father was afraid to
look at him'. Burnett is clear that there can be no self-
respect and, even more important, no love where there is
an imperfect body, not even from a parent.

Archibald Craven is summoned back to Misslethwaite
by the force of the 'Magic'. For years since the death of his
young wife, he has been wandering alone in Europe, unable
to settle or to think 'good thoughts'. But one day in the
beautiful Austrian Tyrol (very much like Heidi-land) he
begins to feel that he is 'alive'. Although he does not know
it, it is the same day that Colin has gone into the secret
garden and called out 'I am going to live for ever and ever
and ever!' From this point Mr Craven begins to change, and
in a dream he hears the voice of his dead wife calling him to
the garden. He rushes back to find Colin, upright and
strong, the embodiment of young manhood: 'He was a tall
boy and a handsome one. He was glowing with life and his
running had sent splendid colour leaping into his face.'

The previously gloomy, depressed man listens as his son
tells his story and makes his assertion, common to the

ending of all such stories – 'I am never going to get into the chair again. I shall walk back with you.' Craven becomes the loving father, full of approval for his now fit and whole young son.

Although Burnett clearly wanted an ending which would take Colin on the road to manhood, there is a strange twist at the end of the story – a sense of Colin becoming, or at least replacing, his mother. This is a fairly common ending in domestic dramas, particularly in stories where the leading character has been miraculously cured of malady or paralysis, but rarely does it happen to a boy. All through the story there have been numerous references to the physical similarity between Colin and his mother. When Mrs Sowerby first sees Colin she cries, 'tha-'rt so like thy mother, tha' made my heart jump'. His 'grey eyes rimmed with black lashes' had also been the main reason Mr Craven was unable to look his son in the face, since his wife's laughing eyes were too great a contrast to his son's sad ones. Archibald Craven returns home because he has heard the voice of his dead wife, and when he reaches the garden, it is as if she falls headlong into his arms. It is Colin's eyes which make him 'gasp for breath'. But this is a temporary illusion, because what he sees is 'a tall boy and a handsome one . . .'

Perhaps in this story of the celebration of life, Frances Hodgson Burnett was trying to reconcile herself to the idea that the spirit of the dead live on in this world and can continue to do good. Her own beloved son Lionel died when he was 16, and it was important to her to feel that Lionel, like the beautiful, laughing Mrs Craven, was still able to look over her shoulder and help her. The secret gardent she created is possessed by the spirit of the dead and the magic of the living.

Chapter 5
A Study of Disability, Class and Gender: *Pollyanna* and *Pollyanna Grows Up* by Eleanor Porter

Disability Syn. Unfitness, incapacity, inability, weakness, decrepitude, incompetence, impotence, infirmity, feebleness, defect, disqualification, inadequacy, uselessness. Ant. Fitness, capacity, qualification, suitableness, ability, power, efficacy, energy, capability, potentiality, mightiness, strength, effectiveness, adaptability.

A Dictionary of Synonyms and Antonyms by Joseph Devlin, 1987

Eleanor Hodgman Porter had an overnight success with *Pollyanna*, which was first published in 1913. It sold over a million copies within the first year and its sequel, *Pollyanna Grows Up*, was published two years later. Margery Fisher, writing in 1975, describes Pollyanna as 'Possibly the most exasperating heroine in fiction. Fair, freckled, trusting and indomitably optimistic, she seems the epitome of everything that is priggish and sentimental in the fiction of fifty years ago.'[1] A quarter of a century later, Pollyanna's power to irritate the reader remains intact, yet as Fisher continues, it is impossible to dislike this relentlessly 'glad' girl whose game reflects the courage of a truly unhappy child.

Like many girls of my generation, my first encounter with

---

1. Margery Fisher, *Who's Who in Children's Books: A Treasury of the Familiar Characters of Childhood*, Wiedenfeld and Nicholson, London, 1975 p287.

Pollyanna was with the actress Hayley Mills in the excruciatingly sentimental film version of 1961. I am ashamed to say that I liked it a lot. There was something very appealing about a little girl more or less the same age as I was then, who had the power to change people and circumstances with the force of her personality. She was a sort of messenger, spreading love and warmth where there had only been misery and darkness. She reconciled differences, cheered people up, turned houses into homes, rekindled romances, made sceptical vicars rejoice in the Lord and found a place of safety for unwanted young boys, puppies and kittens.

Like Enid Blyton's novels, *Pollyanna* is a difficult book to read once you are past ten years old. Her boundless cheerfulness, her pursuit of invalids to cure and her endless need to find things to be glad about have a grating quality, like a nail being rubbed the wrong way on a blackboard. But nevertheless the story has qualities which engage. For the child reader, or at least the child reader of the early twentieth century, the repetition may have been part of the attraction of the book. Every time Pollyanna meets a stranger she tells them the story of the 'Glad Game'. When her father was still alive, she hoped to receive a doll in the 'charity barrel' where she usually received all her second-hand clothes. But instead of the doll she longed for, there was only a pair of crutches. Like all children in this situation, she finds it hard to be cheerful until her father encourages her to find a reason to be glad even in her disappointment. Following the Christian principle that there's always someone worse off than you, she realises that one 'should just be glad because you don't – need – 'em!'. In each telling, and there are many in both *Pollyanna* and its sequel, we relearn the point that even though she was disappointed in the way any child would be, she could still be glad that she had no need for the crutches and could run around and play. When early on in the first story she meets the lifelong invalid Mrs Snow, she declares that she's 'glad she's got legs to hurry with', and when Mr Pendleton breaks his leg, she tells him that, unlike Mrs Snow, broken legs mend so he can be glad of that.

The whole idea of walking or not-walking seemed to hold a particular fascination for Eleanor Porter. It is a central theme in *Pollyanna* and becomes almost an obsession in *Pollyanna Grows Up*. In the first book it is handled conventionally and in the second with a surprising degree of social awareness and realism. Crutches run through both stories like a leitmotiv, symbolising dependency and weakness, together with the impossibility of 'gladness' or hope.

Although Eleanor Porter is not considered one of the heavyweights of children's writers of the first decades of the twentieth century, *Pollyanna* is still published and presumably read, still referred to as a 'classic' and still praised. Peter Hunt argues that although the writing is rather mechanical, 'the skill of the author is undeniable; there is a satisfying of evil by good on virtually every page'.[2] Even for those who don't know the book, Pollyanna lives on as a word in the English language: a synonym for an almost relentless cheerfulness. When Ruth Picardie, a funny and talented 33-year-old writer and mother of young twins, was finally confronted with the fact that her cancer had spread to her lungs and her liver, she described her state of mind as 'Pollyanna commits suicide'.[3]

---

2. Peter Hunt, *An Introduction to Children's Literature*, Oxford University Press, Oxford, 1994, p24.
3. Ruth Picardie, *Before I Say Goodbye*, Penguin Books, London, 1998, p39.

Pollyanna

Pollyanna was first published in 1913, 40 years after Susan Coolidge's *What Katy Did* and 33 years after *Heidi*, but apart from the fact that Pollyanna's accident happens because she is run over by one of those 'new fangled motor cars', rather than falling off a swing, this book seems to be cast in an older mould.[4] Pollyanna, like Katy, Jo, and Judy in *Seven Little Australians*, is full of energy and curiosity about people, but unlike them she is not a young heroine full of rebellious thoughts, struggling with a difficult and wilful nature. She is an almost desperately cheerful child, anxious to please and still crying into her lonely pillow at night. At the point where we meet her for the first time, she has had a difficult life and her ability to be cheerful in adversity has obviously stood her in good stead. Pollyanna's 'mamma' is an 'an angel in heaven', joined long ago by her two other daughters Polly and Anna, who died as babies. (Pollyanna is an amalgamation of the names of her two older sisters.) Her sweet papa, a poor but good clergyman, has only recently gone to join them, leaving Pollyanna at the mercy of the relentlessly do-gooding charitable workers, the 'Ladies' Aiders'. Pollyanna has for much of her young life been a sufferer of what politically active disabled people now call 'the burden of gratitude', but her own faith in God and in human nature is unquestioning. Her God is not the fearful, judgemental spirit of earlier evangelical novels, nor the God who decides who is worthy of a charity handout and who is not, but a God who seems cheerful, loving and kind – like Pollyanna herself.

The reader first meets Pollyanna when she is 'coming home'. Like *Rebecca of Sunnybrook Farm, Anne of Green*

---

4. Gillian Avery, *Behold the Child – American Children and Their Books 1621–1922*, The Bodley Head, London, 1994, p181.

Gables, even *Heidi* and *The Secret Garden*, the story of *Pollyanna* starts with a female orphan without a home, looking for protection and love. In the American version of this story, they are all bright, lively, independent-minded girls whose role is to bring happiness where hitherto there is only gloom.[5] They are displaced children travelling by train and horse-drawn buggy to stay with a spiky, irritable and above all unmarried female aunt who is to be their protector. In Pollyanna's case, her protector is Aunt Polly. Miss Polly Harrington lives in Beldingsville, a small American town in Vermont much like the fictional Burnett in *What Katy Did*. The Harrington family have prided themselves on their wealth and good breeding for years, and Aunt Polly has reluctantly agreed to look after her dead sister Anna's child (one might speculate why Porter only managed to think up two first names for five female characters) out of a highly developed sense of Christian duty rather than love. Love has not been part of Polly Harrington's life since she sent her fiancé packing after an argument many years before. The identification of this lover is one of the long, drawn-out 'mysteries' of the novel and its discovery and resolution will rest largely on Pollyanna's 'terrible accident'.

Like many other characters in children's novels of the time, Pollyanna has a much better sense of what children need to be happy than do the adults around her. Adults in these stories often seem unaware that fresh air and freedom to play is important to the health and happiness of children. Aunt Polly, more old-fashioned and narrow minded than the author or her protagonist, wanted each day to be 'profitable', that is, organised like a timetable with all the activities carried on indoors and informed by what she

---

5. Ibid., p197.

believed was good for Pollyanna rather than what was fun. This schedule included: reading aloud to Aunt Polly at nine o'clock every morning, sewing, cooking and music lessons. When Pollyanna hears this she is dismayed: 'Oh, but Aunt Polly, Aunt Polly, you haven't left me any time at all just to – to live.' Her idea of living is to do the things a child wants to do: playing outdoors, sleeping under the stars, reading to herself, talking to the people she meets in the street and the garden and discovering the world about her. Aunt Polly's stifling 'sense of duty' does not include giving Pollyanna a real place of her own within the house, nor the freedom to play outside, and as in *The Secret Garden*, Pollyanna's only real allies in her need to have a proper childhood are people without 'refinement or good breeding': the servant Nancy and the gardener Old Tom.

In the end Pollyanna does gets her time just to live (between two and six o'clock each afternoon), not because of any change of heart, but because her Aunt Polly finds her irrepressibly cheerful and literal-minded niece too exhausting to deal with for more than an hour at a time. Pollyanna needs the freedom to roam not just because it gives her the space to be happy, but because her function in the story is to transform the lives of others. Until the point of her accident three-quarters of the way through the book, the novel is a series of encounters with strangers: the sick, poor, lonely or misguided, who all discover how to play the 'Glad Game'. The stories of these encounters run through the novel, overlapping each other until everyone is a little more reconciled to their place in life and everyone has become a devoted member of the unofficial Pollyanna fan club.

The first of these encounters is with the fretful Mrs Snow, a bed-ridden invalid who is always moaning and never grateful for the charitable gifts she receives from the 'good women' of the town. Porter does not feel the need to cure Mrs Snow (like Peter's grandmother in *Heidi*, Mrs Snow is 'old' and therefore the best of her life is past), but she will be transformed through love. On her second visit, Pollyanna encourages her to be glad with the unselfish thought that other folks weren't like her – all sick in bed. Mrs Snow, not surprisingly, is unimpressed by this approach to her invalid status but little by little Pollyanna wears her down by bringing her three choices of charity dinners so that she cannot say she hasn't been brought the very one she wanted, doing her hair, setting up prisms in her room so that she could feel that she was 'living in a rainbow' and just by being Pollyanna. By the end of the book, as her daughter Milly tells Aunt Polly when she visits the house following Pollyanna's accident, Mrs Snow is much happier, taking care of how she looks, knitting things for fairs and hospitals and keeping her room bright and cheerful. In *Pollyanna Grows Up*, we find that she is no longer stuck in bed all day, but getting around her house in a wheelchair – a rare example of the wheelchair as an object of mobility rather than restriction.

Two of the most important people whose lives are to be 'gladdened' by the unstoppable Pollyanna are Mr John Pendleton, an extremely wealthy but reclusive Beldingsville citizen, and Jimmy Bean, an orphan in need of a home. Mr Pendleton is an unfriendly stranger whom Pollyanna passes on the street nearly every day. One day she discovers him in the woods near his house. He has fallen and broken his leg and she is the brave little heroine who enters his scary, lonely house and rings for help. During his convalescence she visits him and learns that he is miserable because he is lonely – his adult life has been scarred by unrequited love for her own mother who many years before rejected him for the poor but perfect Reverend Whittier. He confides that for years he has been a cross, crabbed, unloveable, unloved old man who needs 'a woman's hand and heart or a child's presence' in order to turn his house into a home. Sweet, enthusiastic Pollyanna is the child whose presence he wants, and sensing that Polly Harrington doesn't really love her, he offers to adopt her.

Alongside this relationship runs the story of the robust and engaging Jimmy Bean. Jimmy, whom Pollyanna discovers on one of her solitary wanders around Beldingsville, is much the same age as her, ten going on eleven, but unlike Pollyanna, Jimmy has no relatives and since the death of his father a year before, he has lived in the Orphan's Home. He knows that no one cares about him and has run away from the orphanage in the hope of finding a 'home with a mother in it, instead of a Matron'. Pollyanna, certain that everyone will be as glad to find Jimmy a home as she would be herself, takes him first to Aunt Polly, who prides herself on her own excellent breeding but thinks nothing of calling him a 'dirty little boy' and a 'ragged little beggar', and then to the Ladies' Aiders, where in an interesting take on the hypocrisy of Christian charitable work (developed further in *Pollyanna Grows Up*), they decide that no one has any space for him in their homes. These good Christian ladies seem to care more about heading the list in a report than they do about homeless children on their own doorstep. Jimmy Bean is disappointed but unsurprised at their decision. He is a tough kid who insists that he wants no charity and is prepared to work hard for his keep. Mr Pendleton, realising that Pollyanna is not going to be his adopted child, is now asked by her to consider Jimmy instead. Although he is at first unwilling to exchange a sweet cheerful girl of good background for a dirty little boy whose beginnings are unknown, it is not too long until the crabby grown man has a 'child's presence' and the orphan boy has a 'real home'.

At this point in the story, when almost all the unhappy citizens of Beldingsville are now as glad as can be, Pollyanna falls in front of a car and loses the power of her legs. The reasons for this are not immediately clear. Pollyanna, who her creator clearly saw as loveable, charming, good and sweet in every way, did not need to be taught a lesson in unselfishness and humility, and in 1913 with *What Katy Did*, *Heidi*, *Jack and Jill* and *The Secret Garden* all published, paralysis followed by cure was not exactly an original plot device. It is true that there is still some unfinished business in the story which the accident helps to reconcile: Pollyanna still has to initiate her frosty aunt into the pleasures of the 'Glad Game' and finally turn her overdeveloped sense of Christian duty into real love, John Pendleton has not yet made the final decision to give a home to orphaned Jimmy Bean, and romance must be rekindled between Aunt Polly and Dr Chiltern. But it hardly seemed necessary to put poor Pollyanna flat on her back to do this. Surely Aunt Polly would learn to love her niece – how could she not when Pollyanna was so affectionate and so hungry for love? Mr Pendleton was about to give Jimmy a home anyway, and the coy Polly Harrington had already been seen blushing when Dr Chiltern spotted her wearing a rose in her newly curled hair.

Perhaps Porter understood that all this 'gladness' was not really enough to move the story along and something more dramatic was needed in order to add a little darkness to this otherwise very light tale. When Porter throws into the sentimental stew the possibility that her endlessly cheerful heroine might never walk again she is, in a rather heavy-handed way, showing that she understands that before readers can get the happy ending they desire and expect, the heroine must enter some dark place. A paralysed Pollyanna was by this stage a fairly conventional way of giving the reader a little of what Northrop Frye has called 'a movement of descent into a night world.'[6] Just as in a fairytale, in which the innocent maiden must meet dragons, witches and beasts and struggle free from their clutches, so Pollyanna has to meet her own demons.[7]

When Pollyanna is run over (and her misjudgement of the speed of a car coming towards her may well have been intended as an early road safety message to young readers), her *gladness* is put to the ultimate test. At first everyone fears she is dead, she is so white and still, but there appear to be no broken bones and the cut on her head is very slight. Her legs, however don't *feel* at all, and any reader of *The Daisy Chain* or *What Katy Did* will suspect the worst.

No one can bear to tell Pollyanna that her paralysis has been caused by damage to her spine. She believes that she has broken her legs and can be *glad* that, like Mr Pendleton's legs, they will get better again. A long waiting period follows and, like Katy Carr, Pollyanna grows pale and thin: 'The nervous activity of the poor little hands and arms only emphasized the pitiful motionlessness of the once active little feet and legs now lying so woefully quiet under the blankets.' When a specialist is called from New York, he confirms the prognosis that Pollyanna will never walk again – medically accurate both then and now. However, drama rather than medical plausibility is the business of the sentimental novelist, and a cat's insistent paw and nose edging the door open means that Pollyanna overhears what was never intended for her ears. With Aunt Polly in a dead faint, she cries to her nurse, 'Miss Hunt,

6. Northrop Frye, *The Secular Scripture – A Study of the Structure of Romance*, Harvard University Press, Cambridge, MA, 1976, p29.
7. A conversation between A.S. Byatt and Ignes Sodre, *Imagining Characters: Six Conversations About Women Writers*, Chatto and Windus, London, 1995, p247.

you *did* hear her! It *is* true! Oh, it *isn't* true! You don't mean I can't ever walk again?' And a few minutes later: '"How am I going to school, or to see Mr Pendleton or Mrs Snow, or – or anybody?" She caught her breath and sobbed wildly for a moment. Suddenly she stopped and looked up, a new terror in her eyes. "Why Miss Hunt, if I can't walk, how am I ever going to be glad for – *anything*?"'

The whole of Beldingsville is affected by this news. To think that they will never see that little smiling face again seems 'unbelievable, impossible, cruel'. When Mr Pendleton hears the news he cries, 'never to dance in the sunshine again! My little prism girl!' For the first time Pollyanna loses her ability to be cheerful. She is humbled in her 'bed of suffering' and realises that it isn't quite as easy as she once thought to tell life-long invalids that they ought to be glad that other folks aren't like them. She does, of course – as Eleanor Porter herself advocates – try to 'greet the unknown with cheer'.[8] Like her own convert to cheerfulness Mrs Snow, she sits up in bed knitting wonderful things out of bright coloured worsteds, glad that at least she has the use of her arms and hands.

But it is, of course, inconceivable that the novel could end here. The sentimental novelist is hypocritical and will do whatever is needed to give the reader a 'happy ending'.

The true artistic impulse is largely cruel – or at least relentless. To bring a novel to a climax, the artist must drive the situation, and probably the characters to extremes... The sentimentalist, on the other hand, is a non-artist who won't take responsibility for being ruthless. He won't drive his situations to the point of

---

8. Eleanor Porter, quoted in the introduction to the 1994 Puffin edition of *Pollyanna*.

artistic inevitability. Instead he appears to hold his hand in compunction. He resigns himself much too soon to the will of God; but covertly he is manipulating the will of God to suit what he is too hypocritical to admit is really his own taste.[9]

The reader waits for Pollyanna to walk again, and the method of her recovery is not really important. It happens when Jimmy Bean, now happily settled in his new home, overhears Dr Chiltern tell an astonished John Pendleton that is is a matter of life and death that he sees Pollyanna because he believes that there is a very good chance of her walking again. When asked how this can be, he explains with suitable vagueness:

I mean that from what I can hear and learn – a mile from her bedside – that her case is very much like one that a college friend of mine has just helped. For years he's been making a special study. I've kept in touch with him, and studied too, in a way. And from what I hear – but I want to *see* the girl!

Jimmy rushes off and tells Aunt Polly, who swallows her pride and asks Dr Warren to bring in Dr Chiltern for a consultation. Within two shakes, a 'wonderfully tremulous, wonderfully different' Aunt Polly tells Pollyanna that a) Dr Chiltern is soon to become her uncle and b) that she is going to be carried in cars and carriages to a great doctor far away.

Eleanor Porter, having done her job at bringing the novel to a suitable closure with everything tied together in a literary pink satin bow, perfumed with rosy petals and sweetened

9. Brigid Brophy, 'A Masterpiece and Dreadful', 1965, in Virginia Haviland, ed., *Children and Literature – Views and Reviews*, The Bodley Head, London, 1973, p66.

with cachous, then seems to lose the courage of her own convictions, and Pollyanna is not even granted a 'miracle cure' scene. All we have is her letter to 'Aunt Polly and Uncle Tom', written from a hospital, in a town, with a doctor, all nameless: a place where one patient 'walked last week' and another 'hopes to walk next month'. Perhaps Porter realised that the less said about this anonymous doctor, whose medical skill seemed to be confined to smiling a lot, the more likely the reader would be to swallow it. Pollyanna's letter and the book end with this unsurprising thought.

> Oh I'm so glad! I'm glad for everything. Why, I'm glad now I lost my legs for a while, for you never, never know how perfectly lovely legs are till you haven't got them – legs that go, I mean. I'm going to walk eight steps tomorrow.

The Hollywood film version deals with Pollyanna's temporary fall in a more literal way. Forbidden by Aunt Polly to go to the town carnival, Pollyanna climbs down the tree outside her room. Climbing back into the top floor of the house, she reaches out to rescue the doll she has just won (the doll she never had in the charity barrel) and falls to the ground. In the days that follow her accident, Pollyanna is depressed and will not be roused. Aunt Polly blames herself for not giving her enough love. The issue of whether Pollyanna will or will not walk again is kept deliberately hazy and Dr Chiltern tells Aunt Polly, 'We can only do so much for her with surgery. A great deal depends on her... What that child needs now is a shot in the arm of hope.' The whole of Beldingsville, including a miraculously walking Mrs Snow now descend on Harrington house, bringing presents and memories of how Pollyanna has spread cheer. The film ends with Pollyanna going off on the train. The audience does not need to see her 'cured'. With all that love, what other ending could there possibly be?

Pollyanna Grows Up: A Sequel with a Difference

Pollyanna Grows Up, written on demand from enthusiastic readers two years after the publication of the first novel, contains many of the elements common to the sequels of the classic family story or domestic drama – the end of the time of freedom, the sobering of the energetic young girl as she enters womanhood, the obsession with birth and 'good breeding', a certain amount of genteel poverty and, in the final pages, the marriage proposal. Conventionally enough in a sequel, Pollyanna is required to travel, first to Boston for a brief period to stay with a 'thoroughbred gentle-woman' and then, when she is 14, to Germany for six years to live with her uncle and aunt. These new places help to calm her exuberance a little and, although the book ends with her being 'glad, *glad*, GLAD for everything, now!', she is exposed to some sobering experiences which make it hard for even Pollyanna to be cheerful all the time.

Her six-year trip to Germany, explained away in a line or two, means that Pollyanna goes away as a girl and returns a young woman of 20 although she is still described by the men in the story as their 'little girl'. When Pollyanna returns to Beldingsville with her newly widowed and impoverished Aunt Polly, (Dr Chiltern has died unexpectedly and Aunt Polly has lost all the Harrington money invested in the railways), she tries hard to learn the skills of housekeeping essential to even a woman of 'good background'. She develops a passion for cooking and 'keeping house' and tries, not very successfully, to turn Harrington House into a boarding house for paying guests of a certain class. In her efforts to earn her own keep, Pollyanna also tries her hand at writing but, unlike Jo March in *Little Women*, her stories are rejected by the publishers.

The novel ends conventionally with Pollyanna's impending marriage (and two more besides), Aunt Polly financially more secure, and everything in its place. But along the way, *Pollyanna Grows Up* grapples with two issues which are most unusual in a child's novel of the period: the real life of a person disabled by poverty and the stark social inequality in a developing America.

Having given us a heavy dose of disease cured by love in the first volume, Porter takes a most unusual step in the second. In the character of Jamie we meet a child who cannot walk and who grows into adulthood without any hope of cure. There is nothing metaphorical about Jamie's impairment, unless we are willing to include the freedom of his spirit which can, of course, soar wherever he tells it to go. Porter may well have been influenced by writers and social reformers such as Douglas C. McMurtie. Published in New York, Boston and London at the beginning of the twentieth century, McMurtie was prolific in his writing and efforts on behalf of disabled children. In 1912, he told the story of 'a crippled boy raised from absolute dependence and given an education'. Unusually for the day, he advocated the non-residential system and laid out both the ethical and the practical principles involved in the 'restoration of crippled children to places as useful members of the community'.[10] Jamie is a character who doesn't follow any of the patterns of disability in children's literature of the time. Instead, we have an evocative portrait of the tragedy model of disability: a child and then a young man who we are told constantly 'will always be a

10. Douglas C. McMurtie, *Bibliography of the Education and Care of Crippled Children*, Douglas McMurtie, New York, 1913.

cripple', is forever 'tied helpless to a pair of sticks' and who
arouses pity and distress when anyone looks at him.

We first meet Jamie early on in the book when Pollyanna,
having been cured of her own inability to walk, still
sometimes remembers what it felt like to have 'legs which
didn't go'. She is living in the lonely, miserable house of Mrs
Ruth Carew, a wealthy but depressed widow. Pollyanna's job
is once more to bring light where hitherto there has been
darkness. (Literally, too: Mrs Carew has been in the habit of
keeping all the blinds down.) One of the sources of Delia
Carew's misery is her long-lost nephew Jamie, who was taken
off by his father several years ago after her sister Doris died.
A great deal of money has been spent in the effort to trace
him, but all attempts to find him have failed. In a plot which
is almost too difficult for the author to handle, this search for
the *real* Jamie and the final discovery that it is not 'crippled'
Jamie who is the rightful heir to a family fortune and noble
heritage but the tall, manly, physically perfect Jimmy Bean,
is all part of the portrayal of the non-walking Jamie as tragic
and emasculated.

Pollyanna discovers Jamie on one of her walks to the
Boston Public Garden. He is described first as a 'white-
faced boy in a wheelchair' and later as a 'lame boy', who is
wheeled into the park each day by his 'adopted' brother
Jerry and then is left all day to read from his books and
feed the squirrels with what little food he has. He is a
lonely child, orphaned some years ago, and is often hungry
and in pain. He lives with Jerry, who sells newspapers, and
a woman he calls 'mumsey', who took him in after his
father died. Mumsey makes some sort of living washing
and cleaning but she is not well herself and they are 'very
poor'. Jamie and Pollyanna are both lonely children and
although their lives could hardly be more different, there is

an immediate bond between them. He can talk even faster and longer than Pollyanna and can weave marvellous stories. She plays the 'Glad Game'; he has a 'Jolly Book'.

The presentation of Jamie's impairment is unusually realistic. Whereas today the majority of disabled people in the 'developed world' are older, in the first half of the twentieth century most disabled people were children. Poverty, poor diet, insanitary conditions and lack of appropriate medical treatment resulted then in disabling conditions, much as they do now in the poorer countries of the world. Conditions caused by malnutrition such as rickets and untreated accidents often caused permanent impairment in young limbs, and such children often did not survive into adulthood. Wheelchairs were only available if you could afford them, and so poor disabled children were often confined to their homes, unable to go to school or play with friends, living in poor-quality housing where their health was very unlikely to improve.

In *Pollyanna Grows Up*, Jamie has been poor as long as he can remember. He could walk a little when he was younger but his legs 'wasn't right'. Then he had a fall and his condition worsened so that he cannot walk at all. When Pollyanna tells him that there had been a time when she was in much the same situation and is sure that the doctor who cured her would be able to do the same for Jamie, he reminds her: 'He couldn't – you see; I couldn't go to him anyway. T'would cost too much. We'll just have to call it that I can't ever walk again.' Jamie has obtained his wheelchair in the only way possible for a boy in his situation – through charity. Jerry told someone who wrote about it in the newspaper and 'a whole lot of men and women came one day toting this chair and said 'twas for me.' Jamie was so grateful that it took 'a whole page of my Jolly Book to tell about that chair.'

We are constantly reminded that life for Jamie can be nothing but terrible and that the only thing which saves him is his imagination. In spirit and ambition he is the centre of brave deeds and wonderful inventions but in reality he is 'only a crippled boy in a wheelchair'. With Pollyanna's eyes full of tears as she listens, he tells her:

> You can't do nothing... You just have to sit and think; and times like that your think gets to be something awful. Mine did anyhow. I wanted to go to school and learn things – more than just Mumsey can teach me; and I thought of that. I wanted to run and play ball with the other boys; and I thought of that. I wanted to go out and sell papers with Jerry; and I thought of that. I didn't want to be taken care of all my life; and I thought of that.

From the first, Pollyanna is sure that Jamie is the long lost nephew of Mrs Carew, and there are lots of heavy hints to suggest that this might be true. But when Mrs Carew first meets him she is deeply shocked and cannot believe that this 'ignorant, sickly, crippled boy' is her dead sister's son. Out of duty, she eventually offers him a home, making no secret of her doubts about whether he is really her nephew, but Jamie refuses because he can see that she does not really care about him. Porter does not allow us to forget Jamie's impairment in her description of his refusal:

> 'And it isn't as if – as if I was like other boys, and could walk, either,' interrupted the cripple feverishly. 'You'd get tired of me in no time. And I'd see it comin'. I couldn't stand it – to be a burden like that. Of course, – if you cared – like Mumsey here –.' He threw out his hand, choked back a sob, then turned his head away again.

Weaved through the story of Jamie and his eventual adoption by Mrs Carew is an interesting look at charity doled out by wealthy Americans in the early twentieth century and Porter's own version of a certain kind of philanthropic socialism. *Pollyanna* also dealt with charity and the hypocrisy of those who cared more about the reputation of their organisation than they did about the needs of children nearer to home. In Boston, through her friendships with Jamie and Sadie, a shop assistant she also meets in the park, Pollyanna meets real hardship and oppression and learns about the loneliness and vulnerability of young women in a big city. The poor are described in stark, cruel terms. When Pollyanna goes with Mrs Carew to Jamie's tiny room, which is 'scrupulously neat' even though it is 'pitifully bare', the children in the broken-down tenements are described as 'filthy', 'sordid', 'ragged' and 'shrieking'. As they walk up the broken stairs she hears babies wailing piteously, men cursing and 'everywhere was the smell of bad whisky, stale cabbage, and unwashed humanity'.

For the first time, Pollyanna comes face to face with real poverty: people who live in terrible conditions in tiny, cold rooms and who do not have enough to eat. She is aware of the contrast between her own life in the grand house on Commonwealth Avenue and the lives of all the 'sick looking men, unhappy looking women and ragged children out there on the street'. She loses her faith in the powers of the 'Glad Game' to make things better since the only glad thing she can think of is to be happy that she has what they don't. She does not know, as the reader does, that the owner of this tenement building is her guardian Mrs Carew, and Mrs Carew is herself unaware that she is the landlord until she hears the name of her agent. Chastened, she instructs him to make the necessary improvements although the difference this will make to the lives of her tenants could only be very small.

Eleanor Porter's portrayal of the inequalities in society is a long way from what one of her characters, John Pendleton, laughingly calls Pollyanna's 'rabid socialism', and there are certainly no references to any radical social changes. Porter's interest, and the interests of her class, only touched at the edges of the problem of social inequality. The poor in this book remain poor, unless they have the helping hand of charity. Her concern was with the problems of philanthropy – how the wealthy of America dispensed charity to those who were seen to be worthy, what George Bernard Shaw described ironically as the 'deserving poor'. She saw inequality and poverty as a social ill which could be alleviated by wealthy people becoming more involved in how their money was spent, and whilst she was critical of the poor who wouldn't help themselves, she was also highly critical of the wealthy who gave money indiscriminately to charitable institutions without taking time to listen to the people who might be the recipients of this giving. When Mrs Carew listens to Mrs Murphy ('Mumsey') she learns that poor people would rather accept help from a friend who cares and whom they can in time repay, than from a rich woman who patronises them without understanding their lives. And from young Sadie Dean, the poor shop assistant, she learns that what young, lonely women who are trying to earn their living really need is a bright and comfortable place to live, with people who have the 'heart' and 'interest' to listen to their problems and who care about how their money is spent.

Pollyanna Grows Up is essentially a book in two halves. The first half deals with Pollyanna's time in Boston and the second, six years later, is concerned with her return to Beldingsville as a young woman of 20. Mrs Carew is now taking an active role in charity work. Instead of just donating her money to anonymous institutions, she runs a home for respectable working women like Sadie who have not yet fallen into disgrace. She is constantly on hand, giving advice and hearing their problems. Sadie is now her full-time assistant, much changed in appearance and manner. But the biggest change is in Jamie. By this stage living with Mrs Carew, he is properly fed and looked after. With the best medical treatment, he is no longer using a wheelchair but is able to walk with the help of crutches. But it is also clear that we are not supposed to view this ability to get around on his legs as a cure, or even to think of it as walking. As Mrs Carew's sister says in a letter to Pollyanna:

– poor Jamie. The greatest sorrow of his life is that he knows now he can never walk. He was here at the Sanitorium under Dr Ames for a year, and he improved to such an extent that he can go now with crutches. But the poor boy will always be a cripple.

Jamie's disability – not that this word is ever used – is his personal tragedy. Both financially and emotionally he is the recipient of other people's charity. The other characters might care about him and even love him but their strongest emotion when they look at him is an overwhelming feeling of pity. Jamie does not ask for this; he wants to be considered on the same terms as others and to earn his own living. But the constant pity he sees in other people's eyes means that he learns to define himself in their terms. In safer hands, Jamie could stand as a metaphor for the romantic idea of the artist as a perennial stranger, but in this story, he is denied his own voice.[11] He is always the outsider and is only able to describe himself as others see him. Physically imperfect and essentially lonely, he shares their view that the only way to look at him is through his crippled body and the only way to escape this view is to consider the freedom of his imagination and his *soul*. However clever and 'naturally refined' Jamie is, he can never be a proper man.

Set up against Jamie in order to constantly remind us of this point, we have the image of the truly *manly* young Jimmy, the adopted son of John Pendleton. This is the Jimmy Bean who first appeared as the neglected orphan in *Pollyanna*. In the second half of *Pollyanna Grows Up*, these two young men are constantly set against each other for our comparison, and the differences between the two James' can be seen as a study of both disability and masculinity and their interaction.

Firstly, there are the names: Jamie is the feminised adaptation of James whilst Jim or Jimmy is more plain speaking and boyish. Recounting a conversation with his real father, long since dead, Jimmy Pendleton tells Pollyanna, 'He said Jamie wasn't no sort of name for a boy, and that no son of his should ever be called it. He said 'twas a sissy name, and he hated it'. Jamie Carew, we understand, could never be a Jim.

Their appearance also reflects the masculine–feminine divide. After the gap of six years between *Pollyanna* and *Pollyanna Grows Up*, Jimmy is a 'tall, good-looking young fellow with peculiarly frank eyes and a particularly winning smile' and is a skilful rider of a 'mettlesome thoroughbred'. Jamie is also handsome and 'distinguished

---

11. Angela Carter, 'Walter de la Mare: Memoirs of a Midget', 1982, in *Expletives Deleted*, Chatto and Windus, London, 1992, p52.

looking' but in a more romantic, Byronesque sort of way. When Pollyanna goes to meet him at the station she sees 'his dark eyes, rather pale face, and dark, waving hair', which she finds most attractive. But unlike Jimmy, who makes a 'handsome pair' with his horse, Jamie can never be seen without a 'glimpse of the crutches at his side' at which Pollyanna always feels a 'spasm of aching sympathy contract in her throat'. Despite this, Porter asks us to believe that both young men are suitors to Pollyanna.

Jimmy's ambition is to be an architect, the kind of architect who builds bridges and dams. This is seen not as a desk job, but somehow physical – a job which involves spanning rivers and crossing chasms. We imagine him, like Colossus, standing astride the world. When Jamie first hears Jimmy's ambition he 'closed his eyes as if at the sight of something that hurt'. Jamie eventually achieves considerable success but in the more feminine and romantic pursuit of writing. Along with Pollyanna, he enters a story-writing competition but whereas she fails, he wins the first prize of $3,000 and at the same time learns that his manuscript has been accepted by a big publishing house. Yet he is never allowed to forget that it is not really a man's job; dams and bridges are part of the physical world but poetry exists only in the imagination. Describing his achievements at the very moment of his success he cannot help but remind us that all his life he 'has been in a prison', that Mrs Carew took in a 'lame boy', that he is a 'crippled lad', still 'tied to his crutches' and 'tied to two sticks'. Describing his success to Jimmy he says:

It's not much to you of course. You have two feet and your freedom. You have your ambitions and your bridges. But I – to me it's everything. It's a chance to live a man's life and do a man's work, perhaps – even if it

isn't dams and bridges. It's something I've proved now I
can do!

As a kind of set piece to illustrate the tragedy of Jamie's
existence and the impossibility of him ever being a real man,
Eleanor Porter takes all her characters on a two-week
camping trip in the mountains. In this scene we have the
typical 'paradise' of the open air signifying freedom and
renewal, but this is not to be the setting for miracle healing
and closure. Instead it is used to reinforce Jamie's inadequacy.
John Pendleton, who is falling in love with Mrs Carew,
Jimmy, Jamie, and solicitous, thoughtful Sadie Dean all
make a trip 40 miles from Beldingsville. With painful
accuracy, Pollyanna observes what no one seems to have
thought of: that the rough and uneven landscape where they
are setting up camp is a difficult place for Jamie to be:

> It was then that Pollyanna began especially to notice
> Jamie and to fear for him. She realised suddenly that the
> hummocks and hollows and pine-littered knolls were
> not like a carpeted floor for a pair of crutches, and she
> saw that Jamie was realising it too. She saw also that he
> was trying to take his share in the work; and the sight
> troubled her.

Sadie is the only one who does not seem to burden
Jamie with pity and, instead of taking things from him,
gives him things that he can carry. But we are constantly
reminded of his inadequacy, and towards the end of their
unpacking Pollyanna is distraught that no one thought of
how hard it might be for him and notices again, 'that
unmistakably he was getting very tired, and that his face,
in spite of its gay smile, was looking white and drawn, as
if he were in pain'. Only when they are sitting round the

camp fire and Jamie is telling stories can Pollyanna 'once more forget – Jamie's crutches'.

The camp is generally enjoyable and fun. Everyone confides in Pollyanna but the time she spends with the two Jameses is quite different. Jamie talks to her about how he is now sure that he is the real Jamie Kent, Mrs Carew's nephew, and how hard it would be to bear if he were not. She is shocked to hear for the first time about the bitterness he has felt since boyhood about the crutches, even though 'they're a whole lot nicer than the wheelchair'. But to Jimmy Pendleton she need not *talk* to be happy; he was always so comfortable and comforting – just like a real man: 'Jimmy was delightfully big, and strong, and happy... Jimmy did not have to swing himself painfully about on a pair of crutches – all of which was so hard to see, and know and think of.'

Everything comes to a head in a hero-proves-manliness-by-rescuing-damsel-in-distress scene. It is the last day of the trip. The whole party is on a two-mile tramp to catch and fry some fish and Pollyanna, detecting on Jamie's face the expression that is only seen when he is attempting something which taxes his skill to breaking point, stays at the back of the party with him, offering the occasional steadying hand. But then Pollyanna, 'looking particularly attractive in her scarlet sweater', decides to scramble over the stone wall to pick some flowers. She has both her hands full when she hears the hideous bellow of an angry bull. With the hoofbeats gaining on her she 'dimly, hopelessly' sees Jamie's agonised face and hears his hoarse cries which are trying to alert her to the danger. She runs as never before and when the hot breath of the maddened animal is almost upon her, she feels herself 'held close to a great sobbing something that she realised was Jimmy's heart'. Pollyanna is rejoicing in the splendour of Jimmy's strength and bravery, when she becomes aware of Jamie's inarticulate, choking cry. When the pair ask whether he is hurt, he cries:

> Hurt? Am I hurt?...Do you suppose it hurts to see a thing like that and not do anything? To be tied helpless, to a pair of sticks? I tell you there is no hurt in all the world to equal it.

Later she notices that his hands are bleeding when, in frustration at his inability to save her, his nails had cut right into his flesh.

After this it is clear that Pollyanna could not possibly marry Jamie. Our heroine needs a hero and it is clear that Porter has in mind someone who can stand and protect, not someone who must wait and watch. After some tortuous chapters where Pollyanna seeks Jamie out because she feels so sorry for him and Jimmy becomes an 'anxious-eyed young man whose visions were of a feared rival bearing away the girl he loved', we learn that Jamie is really in love with Sadie Dean. This is a relief to everyone since Jimmy has been torturing himself with the thought that as a man 'he is honour bound to step to one side and give the handicapped Jamie full right of way'. Actually Sadie, who we knew all along loved and admired Jamie, is quite a catch. Throughout the story she is about the only character in the book who does not view Jamie's life as a tragedy and who does not seem transfixed by his inability to run and jump about.

In a story obsessed with pedigree and birth, our masculine hero marries his social equal, but Jamie, whose heritage is unclear, marries someone of lowlier birth. Throughout the story, there is the puzzle of who is the genuine nephew of Mrs Carew. It would have to be a pretty obtuse reader who hasn't guessed it by this stage, but we finally get the proof that Jimmy, not Jamie, is the real James Kent after he proposes to Pollyanna. She accepts with delight but Aunt Polly, snobbish to the end, strongly objects on the grounds that as far as she knows he might be nothing but 'a rough little runaway urchin from an Orphan's Home'. Jimmy feels he has no alternative but to open the package from his father which has been locked in the Pendleton safe until he is 30, and there finds certain proof that he is the real nephew. His pedigree could hardly be sounder, with a father who comes from 'good stock' and a mother who is a member of the Boston Weatherby's, a family which can be traced 'back to the Crusades'. Jamie, despite the fact that Mrs Carew and her sister believe he must have good blood in him somewhere because he seems to have natural refinement and 'everything that is best in music, art and literature seems to appeal to him', is once more made the outsider, never to know his real family. He is displaced in Mrs Carew's heart and family by the true hero, Jimmy. In a final act of patronage, proving that he is a real man and not a boy, Jimmy himself decides that it is best to keep this a secret from Jamie and, just in case we've forgotten, he reminds us why:

> It's the fact that he isn't the real Jamie himself – and he with his poor useless legs! Why Uncle John, it'll just about kill him. I've heard him talk. I know… Great Scott! I can't take away from him this.

Mrs Carew thinks this is very fine of him. It is to be kept a complete secret from everyone – except Mrs Carew herself, her sister Delia Weatherby, John Pendleton, Pollyanna and Aunt Polly.

The novel ends with Jimmy and Pollyanna in the foreground and Jamie once more relegated to the background. Eleanor Porter tried her best to give her readers a disabled character who had a difficult life but who made it on his own talents, but it seems impossible for her to overcome her obsession with crutches and the state of non-walking. Even when she has Jamie happily in love, winner of a big literary prize and capable of earning his own living, she can only describe him in terms of his 'useless legs', the fact that he was a 'poor crippled boy' or that he is always 'tied to his crutches'.[12]

Jamie is unusual in a children's novel of the period in that he neither dies nor is cured. There are no miracles for him even at Dr Ames' amazing New York clinic where everyone seems to be the subject of some wonderful and instantaneous cure which enables them to get up and walk. But Jamie's problem is essentially different to Pollyanna's in the earlier novel. Whereas Pollyanna was completely whole and walking one minute but in an instant became dramatically, mysteriously paralysed, Jamie's impairment is founded in poverty, appalling housing conditions, ill health and an untreated accident. Such a mundane and unromantic condition (possibly spinal tuberculosis or the very common 'hip disease') does not easily lend itself to metaphors of instant transformation and renewal in the same way as an unknown, almost magical condition like a damaged nervous system or a broken spine.

The portrayal of Jamie is also unusual in that his impairment is not located in his mind like Colin Craven's in *The Secret Garden* but in his real, physical body. This means that he cannot be cured by a change of heart or an act of will. Instead of a miracle cure we have the other

---

12. As stated at the beginning of the book, 'cripple' is seen as a pejorative word and rarely used by modern writers. It is curious then that the back cover blurb of the 1994 reissue of *Pollyanna Grows Up* begins with the words, 'Her crippled legs cured, Pollyanna takes her glad heart...'.

popular stereotype of the disabled person, of a person 'confined' within a physically damaged body whose only possibility of freedom is spiritual. Porter is not alone in finding it impossible to look beyond physical impairment or to see that there might be more obvious good things about a disabled person than his other-worldliness. Things aren't easy for a chap who can't walk (unless like Douglas Bader, a British hero of the Second World War, he can do it on two false legs), and it is reassuring to those discomforted by the sight of a 'broken' body like Jamie's to think that in another, more spiritual dimension, 'his soul is so free'.

Porter does not cure Jamie, partly so that we can see that a real heroine like Pollyanna needs a real hero like Jimmy Pendleton but also because she wanted to describe some of the results of poverty in early twentieth-century America. These two halves of the book – the conventional, romantic, snobbish sequel to a successful children's domestic drama of the period, and the chapters which deal with social injustice and what she sees as the appropriate role of charity – do not sit easily together.

In the end, we are left with the conclusion that to be a whole man in Pollyanna-land, you have to be able to save the girl you love from a raging bull. Serious, thoughtful Jamie is not interesting enough for Pollyanna, or perhaps he is too interesting. A girl, we are shown, needs a man like Jim – a horse-riding bridge-builder. A romantic hero with handsome dark eyes, wavy hair and a whacking great publishing contract is no good to a girl at all.

Chapter 6

Misrule, Rebellion and Death:
Seven Little Australians by Ethel Turner

Children, you are very little
And your bones are very brittle;
If you would grow great and stately,
You must try to walk sedately.

You must still be bright and quiet,
And content with simple diet;
And remain, through all bewild'ring
Innocent and honest children.

From 'Good and Bad Children', in Robert Louis Stevenson, *The Child's Garden of Verses*, 1885

The family in *Seven Little Australians* lives in a house called Misrule. It has a different name over the door but no one uses it. Misrule and unorthodoxy are the order of the day, and author Ethel Turner is determined that the seven Woolcot children are seen as quite different from their counterparts in English family stories. First published in 1894 when Turner was only 22 years old, the book was an instant hit in Australia. This was closely followed by successful publication in England and America, and the book has since been translated into countless languages. It was dramatised for the stage a year after publication, made into several television productions, and more recently a musical. Continually in print in Australia, but not always in favour in England, it has recently been published by British Penguin as part of the Puffin Classics list.

It is interesting to speculate why *Seven Little Australians* did not achieve the same recognition in Great Britain as the novels described in earlier chapters. Perhaps it has something to do with the marginalisation of the Australian experience or Turner's own desire to distance herself from similar English stories (she does not mention American ones). She suggests that, unlike their English counterparts, Australian children are not 'darkened' by history or dull weather. Instead they sparkle in the brilliant sunshine. They alone will 'advance Australia'.

However different Turner wanted this story to be, it is still set within the conventional framework of the family story. Turner has created a character much like the lively Katy in Susan Coolidge's *What Katy Did*, although Judy Woolcot is even naughtier, more energetic and messy. Turner's story uses a number of traditional devices: the motherless family, a large brood of children who have plenty of time to get up to mischief and, at the centre of it all, the engaging heroine – spirited, clever, with a wild streak – who never really means to get into scrapes. But the ending is quite different. Turner brings the story to its first climax when Judy develops tuberculosis as the result of an unusually cruel father who has punished her misdeeds by sending her away. This serves to bring Judy back to the heart of the family where she longs to be, but unusually, it does not tame her. The second crisis occurs in a truly dramatic accident in which Judy breaks her spine saving her baby brother and then dies. Unlike other novels of the period, Judy does not have a time of enforced passivity in order for her to rise again as a cured and tamed young woman. Turner intended high drama, but we can also see Judy's death as a failure of the writer's courage. Unable or unwilling to allow Judy to become as spirited a woman as she was a child, Turner denies Judy her adulthood.

Feminist writer Dale Spender describes the effect that reading *Seven Little Australians* had on her as a child growing up in Australia and how it affected her experience as a reader. Until then she had had no experience of death, did not know that ordinary, strong girls whom you loved and admired could die so suddenly without any reason.[1] Turner creates characters whose worries and hopes seem as real as those of any writer informed by a more modern psychological understanding of children's behaviour. Like most of the writers of her day, her writing is not free from the didactic morality and middle-class snobbery of her age and, like Frances Hodgson Burnett's comments on the population of India in *The Secret Garden*, Turner's portrayal of the one aboriginal character in the story is essentially patronising and colonial. But the relationship she draws between the members of this idiosyncratic family, especially the relationship between the 'particular and rather irritable' father and his independent, free-spirited daughter, is something that any writer would be proud of. Despite Turner's obvious desire to take the framework of the English and American family story and give it a good shake, the balance between the conventional and the unusual is fairly evenly weighted. Like other domestic dramas, the plot is not concerned with sensational actions and adventures but with the inner conflict of characters, their own idiosyncrasies and the pleasures and trials of family relationships.[2]

In the first chapter, Turner takes the role of the kindly narrator observing a 'real' family, similar to Susan

1. Dale Spender in interview, Sixth International Feminist Book Fair, Melbourne, Australia, July 1994.
2. Walter McVitty, 'Ethel Turner', in D. L. Kirkpatrick, ed., *Twentieth Century Children's Writers*, Macmillan, London, 1978, p1266.

Coolidge's introduction to *What Katy Did* which no doubt followed the model set by Louisa May Alcott in *Little Women*. Turner self-consciously tells the reader that in Australia there is no such thing as a model child.

> It may be that the miasmas of naughtiness develop best in the sunny brilliancy of our atmosphere. It may be that the land and the people are young hearted together, and the children's spirits are not crushed and saddened by the shadow of long years' sorrowful history. There is a lurking sparkle of joyousness and rebellion and mischief in nature here, and therefore in children.

The children of Misrule are particularly uncrushable. They are as lively and individual as the children of any American or English family story and they rush around, not caring too much what they look like or that as a result of their 'very third-class daily governess who lived in mortal fear of her ignorance being found out by her pupils', they are only half-educated.

As in the best of such stories, each of the seven children has a distinct and different character and although there is a good deal of squabbling, they support and care about each other. Meg, the eldest, like her namesake in *Little Women*, is good-hearted but rather dreamy. The General is the youngest, a fat, smiley baby boy and half-brother to the other six children. There is a four year old, known confusingly as Baby. Bunty is next, the far from perfect six-year-old boy, with many of the characteristics of the overlooked middle child. He is the black sheep of the family and it is no surprise when he becomes the difficult and disturbed adolescent of the sequel, *The Family at Misrule*. Ten-year-old Nell is the pretty one 'with a face like a child-angel on a Christmas card'. Pip is serious, the sensible eldest son and the only one of the children who goes to school. He is very close to his sister, thirteen-year-old Judy. She is the central character in the story and by far the most interesting: the classic rebellious storybook heroine, granted her time of misrule and adventure.

Judy, at this crucial transitional age, is as wild, untidy, loving, generous, lively, clever and reckless as any heroine of the novels of the time. She is full of the 'rough, noisy and bouncing behaviour' which Charlotte Yonge believed girls over the age of 12 must overcome in favour of 'retenue and self control'.[3] Together with her brothers and sisters, she has a great deal of independence, time to play and time to get into trouble. Their rambling Sydney house is a paradise for children, and they enjoy all the fresh air and freedom to play which are a requisite in stories of the period. The house is surrounded by a huge wilderness of a garden, paddocks, numberless sheds for hide and seek and, best of all, the water of the Parramatta River. Like Katy and Jo, Judy runs rather than walks, and her appearance is interesting but unconventional:

> If she did not dash madly to the place she wished to get to, she would progress by a series of jumps, bounds and odd little skips. She was very thin as people generally are who have quicksilver instead of blood in their veins. She had a small, eager, freckled face, with very bright dark eyes, a small determined mouth and a mane of untidy, curly dark hair that was the trial of her life.

> Without doubt she was the worst of the seven, probably because she was the cleverest. Her brilliant inventive powers plunged them into ceaseless scrapes, and

---

3. Charlotte Yonge, 'The Monthly Packet', 1875, quoted in J. S. Bratton, *The Impact of Victorian Children's Fiction*, Croom Helm, London, 1981, p180.

although she often bore the brunt of the blame with equanimity, they used to turn round, not infrequently, and upbraid her for suggesting the mischief.

Like other heroines, Judy may be externally naughty and anarchic but she still has the internal values of tenderness, love, sympathy and intelligence required in middle-class girls.[4] She loves and quarrels with her siblings in equal measure and dotes on the baby, covering him in passionate kisses one minute, passing him on to someone else the next. What she does lack is the practical, loving guidance provided by a good parent. Her mother is dead and her 20-year-old step-mother, Esther, is just a 'lovely, laughing-faced girl, whom they all adored'. Esther's role in the story is romantic and decorative. She always looks beautiful, wears yellow silk dresses and wide-brimmed hats, but is incapable of offering them more than loving pats and her sweet smile. Like most fathers in stories of this time, the Woolcot's father is physically present but emotionally absent, except for shows of astonishing anger and ill-nature. The children have to look to each other for moral guidance and, unsurprisingly, this often leads them into trouble.

The family are of 'good stock' but live in genteel poverty. There is the normal amount of middle-class preoccupation with refinement and breeding in the book and even more in the sequel. Good taste and modesty are championed, the outward show of the vulgar rich being as reprehensible as the improprieties of the gutter.[5] Three

---

4. Kimberley Reynolds and Nicola Humble, *Victorian Heroines: Representations of Femininity in Mid-Nineteenth Century Literature and Art*, Harvester Wheatsheaf, London, 1993, p34; Sheila Egoff, *Only Connect – Readings in Children's Literature*, Oxford University Press, Oxford, 1996, p23.
5. Walter McVitty, 'Ethel Turner', p1266.

chapters in the middle of the book concentrate on Judy's
16-year-old sister Meg and explore some of the issues of
propriety so essential in the transition between girlhood
and womanhood. Meg's friendship with the forward and
flirtatious Aldith has a lot in common with Katy's
friendship with the unsuitable Imogen and *Little Women*'s
Meg's experiences with the wealthy but slightly vulgar
Moffatt family.

Where *Seven Little Australians* is different is in degrees.
Judy is like other naughty heroines but gets into even bigger
scrapes. All children in family stories have problems
looking as neat and tidy as was expected, but the Woolcot
boys are dirtier, and the Woolcot girls have more tears in
their dresses and more jam on their aprons than any other
storybook children. Judy is described as coming to
breakfast each morning 'looking as if her clothes had been
pitchforked upon her', and even the beautiful Esther is
spotted wearing pins instead of buttons.

Unusually, there is very little religion in this book. When
Pip, Judy or Bunty get into trouble their worry is not about
what God might think but whether their father will find
out and whip them! The Woolcot children are more
inclined to look to each other in times of trouble than to the
guiding hand of their Maker. In fact, the only reference to
Christianity in the book is during Judy's death scene when
the terrified children appeal to God to make her better and
Judy, struggling to find some comfort or explanation for
the terrible thing that has happened to her, wishes that she
'had gone to Sunday school and learnt things'.

One of the most striking differences in *Seven Little
Australians* is that the father, Captain Woolcot, is more
irascible and more unpleasant than any parent in a
supposedly happy family story. He is much more like a real
Victorian father would have been: patriarchal, tyrannical,

surrounded by children who never quite live up to his expectations. He has been forced to move his 'graceless' family away from the army barracks and suffers this removal with a 'bitterness of spirit'. He also seems to spend more time and money on his thoroughbred horses than he does on his children. Apart from the odd pat on the baby's head, he doesn't enjoy their company and has put thick felt on the nursery door so that he won't hear their noise. He never sits down to talk to them, like the fathers in *Little Women*, *Heidi* and *What Katy Did*, and his response to their naughtiness is to punish them. They are banned from the pantomime they are longing to go to, the boys are harshly beaten and, most cruel of all, Judy is sent to boarding school, away from the family she loves best. Why the 20-year-old, laughing-faced Esther married him is incomprehensible. (And the knowledge that Ethel Turner was only two years older than Esther when she wrote this book does not shed much light on this mystery.)

When Captain Woolcot thinks about his children, which is rare, he realises that he doesn't understand them and that Judy mystifies him most of all. Her mother's dying words were 'be careful of Judy', but he has no idea of how to do this. Watching her trying to be 'very good' one day as she expertly scythes the wilderness of a garden whilst unaccountably speaking in an Irish brogue, he remembers that his first wife had often trembled for Judy's future:

That restless fire of hers that shone out of her dancing eyes, and glowed scarlet on her cheeks in excitement, and lent amazing energy and activity to her lithe young body, would either make a noble, daring, brilliant woman of her, or else she would be shipwrecked on rocks the others would never come up to, and it would flame up higher and higher and consume her.

The reader might long for Judy to grow up and become the 'noble, daring, brilliant woman' her mother predicted, but we also know that she is 'cast in so different a mould from the others' that it is much more likely that some of this excess of spirit will be stamped out of her. We know that in order to avoid Judy being swallowed up by this mixed metaphor of water and fire, some change will have to take place.

In *Little Women,* Jo's biggest crime is to forbid Amy from joining Laurie and her on a skating trip. When Amy nearly drowns, she is immediately penitent at her selfishness and resolves to be better. In *What Katy Did,* Katy causes chaos one wet playtime at school and an imaginative game with classmates gets seriously out of hand. Katy too confesses and repents. With more serious consequences, she ignores her aunt's instructions not to play on the swing, but the reasons for this ban were never explained to her. Judy's misbehaviour, however, has a totally different quality to it and is often a result of self-absorption and wilfulness rather than naïve exuberance.

The mischief that really gets her into trouble involves Pip, the General and Captain Woolcot. It is the day after the children's attempts (and failure) to be very good and win back the pantomime tickets. Judy remains wrathful:

'It's a shame,' she said, 'it's a burning, wicked shame! What's the use of fathers in the world, I'd like to know!... Think of the times we could have if he didn't live with us.'

That afternoon, Pip has to take his father's full-dress uniform into Sydney for a dinner at the barracks. His younger brother Bunty nearly ruined it the day before by covering it in varnish. He is going in the dogcart which has to be left in town in order to have the back seat mended. Impetuously, he invites his favourite sister 'Fizz', his own nickname for Judy, and thrilled with the prospect of adventure, she jumps up and joins him. Judy has promised Esther that she won't let the General out of her sight, and although Pip grumbles about this for a minute or two, baby comes with them.

Along the way they meet a genial old Colonel, a friend of the family, who gives them half a crown each – a fortune. Judy has an inspired idea for a way to spend the money: 'Bondi Aquarium – skating, boats, merry-go-round, switchback threepence a go!' 'Good iron', Pip whistles softly, until they remember the problem of the baby. Pip is used to bold proposals from his sister, but what she comes up with is beyond everything:

'Who is the General's father? Tell me that,' she said, in a rapid, eager way. 'And isn't it right and proper fathers should look after their sons? And doesn't he deserve that we should get even with him for doing us out of the pantomime? And isn't the Aquarium too lovely to miss?'

Pip has serious misgivings. He knows that his father will have no idea what to do with a baby for two whole hours, but the temptation is too great. When they arrive at the barracks, Judy unseen, slips along the veranda and leaves the military coat and the General on her father's bed. She finds a soldier and tells him to go and tell the Captain that 'the parcels have come'. Her plan is to return two hours later and pick the baby up, explaining that they didn't take him with them as it was raining and they were worried he might get rheumatism. 'Fizz'll get us hanged yet', mutters Pip, but Judy is the stronger character.

Of course, when they return from their wild afternoon,

things have not gone to plan. Judy overhears the soldiers laughing at her father's reaction to the appearance of the cheerful but grubby baby and at 'old Woolly's' embarrassment as he tried to cope with the 'jolly little beggar'. The children know that trouble is in store. As Judy remarks, 'It's about the awfullest thing we've ever done in our lives', and they are genuinely terrified when they catch sight of their father on the ferry 'looking as glum as a boiled wallaby'. Back home there is a fearful row. Judy tries to take the blame but Pip receives a thrashing. Her own punishment is the most cruel thing her father could do – she is to be sent away to boarding school. The family are distraught and Esther's pleas to her husband go unheard. Judy cannot be allowed to get away with this, and when Captain Woolcot insists to his wife that 'Judy was being ruined for want of a firm hand', the author adds her opinion that this 'indeed, was in a measure true'.

No one really believes it will happen but on the day of her departure, with her bags packed and ready in the hall, Judy finally realises that this is not just a threat to make her see the error of her ways. Broken-hearted, she takes the General into bed with her and covers him in kisses until he manages to struggle free. 'White as death and utterly limp', she makes a final attempt to plead with her father: 'If you'll let me stay, Father, I'll never do another thing to vex you – and you can thrash me instead, ever so hard.' But even the strongest willed heroine cannot triumph in the face of patriarchal tyranny. Surrounded by the tears of all his children, her father has the final word:

'I think you're all demented!' he cried. 'She's going to a thoroughly good home. I've paid a quarter in advance already, and I can assure you good people I'm not going to waste it.'

For the next three chapters, the reader has to be content with dreamy Meg's unfortunate friendship with Aldith, her romantic encounters with unsuitable young men, the repression of the merest hint of sexuality and a near-death experience with over-tight corsets! When Judy does resurface it is in typically dramatic style. She has run away from school, back to the family who are the centre of her world. It has taken her a week to get home and she has walked most of the 77 miles, stopping at cottages to ask for food and sleeping rough when she had to. She is thin, hollow cheeked, exhausted and half-starved, with a terrible wracking cough. But she insists that they do not tell her father that she is there. She plans to live in the loft for a week and then return to school before her complicated plan is discovered.

The children all rise to the occasion, taking things from the house, bringing her food and making a little home from home in the loft. Even Bunty with his reputation as a sneak manages to keep it a secret. Judy is the centre of their world and all their confidence depends on the brothers and sisters being together.

If Judy seems tamed by this experience it is only temporary. Although she is still pale and tired with a nasty cough, her high spirits have returned and she is enjoying the adventure tremendously. Before too long, she is planning a little trip outside, not just a short run, but an afternoon picnic by the river. But her plans are foiled by poor old Bunty. He has received a savage beating from his father for not owning up to damaging one of his prize horses. In bitterness, he cries out 'Judy's home!... She lives in the old shed in the cow paddock... She's gone to the picnic and she's run away from school.' In her picture of this sad middle child, Turner draws an extraordinary portrait of a complicated and unhappy young person.

Bunty is lonely in the middle of a big family and feels with some justification that no one really listens to him and no one really loves him.

When Captain Woolcot hears that Judy is back home, he exploits the situation for all it is worth. He goes with his wife to the site of the picnic and when he sees Judy flee, torments the rest of the children first by talking to them for an hour as if nothing has happened, and then by locking them in his study so that he can go to the loft and find Judy before they have time to alert her. His response to the sight of his daughter, lying asleep in her loft bed, is typically selfish:

> There will be no end to my trouble with her as she grows older,' he said, half aloud, feeling extremely sorry for himself for being her father. Then a great anger and irritation rose within him as he watched her sleeping so quietly there. Was she always to be a disturber of his peace? Was she always to thwart him like this?

When she wakes, he is too angry to notice her strained face and her hollow cheeks and coldly informs her that she will be returning to school that afternoon. As further punishment, she is not to be allowed home for the Christmas holidays and probably not for those of the following June.

For Judy, this 'was as bad as a sentence of death', and her response to it is dramatic:

> Such terrible coughing, a paroxysm that shook her thin frame and made her gasp for breath. It lasted two or three minutes, though she put her handkerchief to her mouth to try and stop it.

The idea of death is now brought into the foreground. For what Captain Woolcot notices reminds him not only of the death of his wife but also the possibility of losing his wild, exuberant daughter: 'For the handkerchief that the child had taken from her lips had scarlet, horrible spots staining its whiteness.' The reader needs nothing more than those scarlet spots on a white handkerchief to know that this is tuberculosis. Those spots of blood mean that everything must change. There can be no dogcart for Judy, no train journey, no return to boarding school but instead she is fully restored to her rightful place at the centre of the family: 'a warm, soft bed, and delicate food, and loving voices and ceaseless attention'.

As we have seen in Chapter 2, a diagnosis of tuberculosis or 'consumption' in the 1890s was the equivalent of a death sentence. In literature, the young consumptive tended not to be like Judy, full of energy and vitality, but was usually a born victim, sensitive and passive, not quite life-loving enough to survive, a pale, sweet-faced child who had insufficient energy to survive the horrors of the vulgar world. However, it would have been hard for Turner to change Judy into the delicate image of the suffering child. Judy's problem was not the insufficient will to live but an excess of energy and emotion. Temporarily, she takes on the romantic appearance of the classic invalid, but it doesn't last for long. Although she has a badly inflamed lung and what the doctor describes as a nasty case of that 'vile disease', there is scarcely any time before she is her old self again, 'full of naughtiness and even mischief'. As the doctor says,

Little Miss Judy is such a wild, unquiet subject. She would seem to be always in a perfect fever of living, and to possess a capacity for joy and unhappiness quite unknown to slower natures.

Judy has made herself ill by an excess of passionate feelings, a capacity for deep unhappiness and an inability to accept the separation from her family, and has only saved herself from death by her 'indomitable spirit and pluck'. Her distress is both physical and psychological. Once she learns that her father does not intend to send her back to boarding school, she mends rapidly. Her illness serves the purposes of moving her back to the centre of the story and also comforting the young reader with the thought that cruel adults will repent their actions (even if that repentence is only temporary). Judy is in the unusual position of a literary invalid scarcely changed by her illness, and the reader is relieved when the Judy who emerges from her bed is much the same as the one they knew before.

If anyone is to change from this experience, it is the father who caused such deep unhappiness, and for a time he cannot forget the shock he received when he saw those red spots on the white handkerchief. The doctor has warned him that there is always some danger of a re-occurrence of tuberculosis and suggests a change of surroundings, a long way from the sea air. Right on the button, a letter arrives from Esther's parents inviting all the family to their home in Yarrahappini, a vast, sprawling place in the outback on the edge of 'Never-Never Land'. But any hope that Judy's illness might have transformed her father permanently vanishes when he waves them all good-bye at the station and walks down the platform with a jaunty air at the prospect of two months of bachelordom.

Illness in children's stories can offer the possibility of new places and new adventures. In Enid Blyton's adventure stories of the 1950s, children always seemed to be getting serious bouts of influenza which necessitated a long convalescence somewhere much more interesting than home. Judy's illness allows Turner to explore a quite different world. We leave Sydney, which has seemed to the reader to be much the same as the New England towns of Alcott and Coolidge, and enter a world which is genuinely Australian. In these chapters the enormous 'squatter's paradise' at the heart of Australia comes alive.

The 15-minute drive from the gate to the front door of the property, the huge house with a veranda as wide as a room, the dusty animals, the scorched earth, the brilliant light, the horses for each of the children who want to ride, the 'jolly little stunner of a gun' for Pip to shoot rabbits, the 40-pound jar of currants for Bunty, the dangers of cattle drafting and the vivid scarlet and blue of the wild birds are all part of the children's new world. So too are a vivid collection of characters, who were to become an essential part of the Australian children's novel.[6] In this novel we have an English baronet with a mysterious past and a drink problem, a rough stockman who lives miles from the homestead and rarely speaks to anyone, and an elderly aboriginal, Tettawonga, who had valiantly saved Esther's mother from some tomahawk-carrying bushrangers and so has earned his right to his cottage, daily rations and the pipe which never leaves his lips.

If Judy is a little quieter, a little more accepting of the fact that Pip gets to do exciting things that she cannot, we are not told so directly. She is still the jolly, teasing girl she always was. The book moves towards its ending and the only hint that this will not turn out happily is in a little touch of foreshadowing several chapters earlier. When Esther receives the invitation from her parents and Captain Woolcot suggests that they might live to regret it, the author tells us that 'he never dreamed how much sadder or how much wiser Yarrahappini would be'.

---

6. Humphrey Carpenter and Mari Pritchard, *The Oxford Companion to Children's Literature*, Oxford University Press, Oxford, 1984, p34.

One day Esther leaves Yarrahappini, with her beautiful gown of daffodil silk and chiffon packed in a box, to stay overnight at a party 55 miles away. As compensation for having no part in this pleasure, the children are off to picnic at a remote spot called Krangi-Bahtoo. They are to be taken there by a wagon drawn by 12 yoked bullocks and left to picnic while the men go to collect the trunk of a huge fallen gum tree 6 miles further on. Mr Gillet, the sad-eyed English aristocrat, is the only adult to stay behind with them.

Metaphorically and literally, it is the scene of Judy's sunset. The children have eaten lunch and are off playing nearby, and Meg is involved in a long conversation with Mr Gillet about all kinds of difficult things like the death of his sister and the healing powers of a forgiving woman. Judy is playing with the General, a wonderful mucky game which starts with squashed bananas and involves lots of chasing, hugging, falling down, and getting up again.

> He looked up at her with an adorable smile.
> '*Baby*!' she said, swooping down upon him with one of her wild rushes. '*Baby*!'
> She kissed him fifty times. It almost hurt her sometimes, the feeling of love for this little, fat, dirty boy.

She is distracted for a minute by a tick working its way into her skin and when she looks up she sees that the General has crawled some distance away, believing that he is being chased by Judy.

At this crucial point, the author's voice intervenes to warn us that something terrible is about to happen: 'And then – ah, God! It is so hard to write it. My pen has had only happy writing to do so far, and now!' (This is not entirely true. In her desire to bring on the melodrama, Turner seems to have forgotten that she sent a distraught Judy to boarding school some chapters earlier.) We move swiftly towards an ending which would leave only the hardest-hearted reader dry-eyed. Judy pretends to run quickly after him but the whole world seems to rise up before her:

> There was a tree falling, one of the great, gaunt, naked things that had been ringbarked long ago. All day it had swayed to and fro, rotten through and through; now there came up across the plain a puff of wind, and down it went before it. One wild ringing cry Judy gave, then she leaned across the ground, her arms outstretched to the little lad with the laughing eyes and lips, straight to death.

The others, who are quite far off, hear the terrible noise and the wild cry and rush to the spot. Judy is face down under the tree and the General, a little shaken but quite unhurt, lies underneath his sister, protected by her body.

The children stare in stunned silence; we hear their frightened breathing and Judy's agonised moans. Mr Gillet takes the door down from the stockman's hut and with the help of Pip they carefully place Judy on this stretcher and carry her up the hill. It is five o'clock in the evening and the bullock dray is still a long way off. Even when it returns it will be too slow and jolting to take Judy back to the homestead. Gillet instructs Pip to run 10 miles to the nearest doctor whilst he will run 14 miles to Yarrahappini to bring back a buggy. He tells Meg to watch Judy and give her water if she asks, because there is nothing else she can do. '"She is dying?" Meg said. "Dying?"' Mr Gillet thinks of all the things that might happen in the long time he is away and dares not leave her or Pip unprepared:

'I think her back is broken,' he said, very quietly.

And whereas in other novels we might expect the following line to be 'it will be some time before she can walk again' or even, 'the doctor says there is no cure,' here we have something far more dramatic and conclusive:

'If it is, it means death.'

The next chapter opens with the 'dying glory' of the sunset and the 'wild, mournful, unearthly' sound of the curlew. In the vast emptiness of the outback, Judy realises that she is dying and is terrified:

Oh, Meg, I want to be alive! How'd you like to die, Meg, when you're only thirteen? Think how lonely I'll be without you all.

Their appeal to religion to offer comfort to a dying child is almost comical:

Meg, I'm so frightened! I can't think of anything but 'For what we are about to receive' and that's grace, isn't it? And there's nothing in Our Father that would do either. Meg, I wish we'd gone to Sunday school and learnt things. Look at the dark, Meg! Oh, Meg, hold my hands!

Meg tries to find the right words, but her 'Heaven won't – be – dark' is derided by the author as 'only a halting, stereotyped phrase'. Poor Meg tries all the hymns she can think of, but they are dismissed by Judy as 'for old people'. Then Meg remembers the 'most beautiful hymn in the world' and without a break in her voice, sings the first and last verse of 'Abide With Me'. Finally she remembers that Judy won't be lonely because she will be going to join her mother, and she asks her sister to remember Mother's eyes.

So Judy grows quiet and quieter still and with Meg's cheek on her brow, Nell holding her hands and Baby her feet, Bunty's lips on her hair and finally, Pip rushing back and falling down beside her, Judy dies. In the euphemistic language of earlier Victorian deathbed scenes, but without any comforting bright light or the possibility of seeing angels, we are told that:

> Like that they went with her right to the Great Valley, where there are no lights even for stumbling, childish feet.
>
> The shadows were cold and smote upon their hearts; they could feel the wind from the strange waters on their brows; but only she who was about to cross heard the low lapping of the waves.
>
> The family return to Sydney, slightly wiser and much sadder. The 1994 Australian Puffin paperback ends with a drawing of Judy's grave from the 1894 edition. She is buried in a shady corner of Yarrahappini in 'a fair green field with one little garden bed'.

Margery Fisher in, *Who's Who in Children's Books* says:

> The unashamed sentiment in the description of Judy's death certainly belongs to its period but no writer of any period would need to be ashamed of having put into the frightened, courageous girls mouth words so sincere, poignant and universally true to life.[7]

Of course Turner plays on our emotions, and no child who has read *Seven Little Australians* could ever listen to the hymn 'Abide With Me' again without thinking of poor Judy lying frightened in an open field far from home, waiting for death to come. It is melodramatic and sentimental in the spirit of the times, but the ending is not entirely one of feeling over reason. If we accept Brigid Brophy's definition of sentimentality as the writer not having the courage of her own convictions, then the ending of *Seven Little Australians* cannot be accused of this crime.[8] Turner takes this frightening, unexpected death pretty far along the road to reality, and it is a long way from Beth's drawn-out wistful parting scenes in *Good Wives*. In real life, of course, Judy would have been most unlikely to die from her broken back within an hour or two. True, kidney failure or infection may have finished her off within a few years or months, or, even in the worst case, within a few weeks, but with a broken back rather than a broken neck, she is unlikely to have met her maker under the same sunset.

A more interesting question is not how Turner describes Judy's death but why she decided to let her die, especially as she clearly had the sequel in mind. Her final words to the reader are: 'Some day, if you would care to hear it, I should like to tell you of my young Australians again, slipping a space of a few years.' Given this, it seems extraordinary that she chose to kill off by far the most interesting and lively character in the book.

The reader is prepared for there to be some kind of transformation, because as Kimberley Reynolds reminds

7. Margery Fisher, *Who's Who in Children's Books: A Treasury of the Familiar Characters of Childhood*, Wiedenfeld and Nicholson, London, 1975 p164.
8. Brigid Brophy, 'A Masterpiece and Dreadful', 1965, in Virginia Haviland, ed., *Children and Literature – Views and Reviews*, The Bodley Head, London, 1973 pp66–9.

us, conformity for the heroine offers the only successful means of resolving crisis and permitting a happy ending.[9] We know that in 1894, Judy was unlikely to have been allowed to enter adult life in her state of non-conformity. So we might expect the life-threatening bout of tuberculosis to be seen as a punishment for wilfully inappropriate behaviour and to be the point of transition, as in *What Katy Did*, but at this point in the novel, Judy bounces back and seems as full of energy and self-will as ever.

Judy's dramatic accident is shocking – the broken spine, the pain, the legs that have no feeling and won't move – but it is scarcely original. The reader might anticipate that this sudden spinal injury would lead to a descent into the night world – a conflict within the self, a period of thoughtfulness which would in turn lead to a return to the light – cure, resolution of conflict and the embracing of refined woman-hood. Anything is possible in the wild landscape of the outback, and traditionally the open air is the site of healing, not punishment. But this is not to be. The 'idyllic' world to which Judy returns is heaven.

This is doubly shocking because Judy does not appear to be the sort of character who dies in novels. She is flawed and complex, but Turner does not seem to subscribe to the simplistic view that she is either 'too bad' and needs to be punished or 'too good' and destined to be one of God's children.

Turner may have killed Judy for no more complex a reason than because she wanted to do something quite different with the Australian family novel. She tells her readers at the beginning of the story that she is not going to give them Sandford and Merton (edifying moral tales of

9. Kimberley Reynolds, *Girls Only? Gender and Popular Children's Fiction in Britain 1880–1910*, Harvester Wheatsheaf, London, 1990, p129.

the late eighteenth century), and it is unlikely that she wanted the reader to see Judy's death as a punishment for her earlier 'naughty' behaviour.

One reading of the ending is to view Judy's death as a sacrifice. In the tradition of Christian teaching, Judy dies to save another when, without any thought for herself, she flings herself under the falling tree and rescues her beloved baby brother. But another reading is to view Judy's death as the failure of the author's courage. It would have been far more intriguing to watch Judy grow into the 'noble, daring, brilliant woman' her mother imagined she might be. With a sequel in mind, Turner set up the possibility of doing something quite different to the earlier novels she criticises, and in Judy she created a character with the potential to be a really interesting young woman.

Although the ending is a dramatic and striking conclusion to a nineteenth-century domestic drama, ultimately Turner has settled for convention. Judy's death occupies the same function in the novel as difficult, creative Jo March going off to Boston with her head full of stories but returning to the family home ready to take up Beth's dustpan and broom and marry middle-aged Professor Bhaer; or spirited, untidy Katy Carr lying paralysed for years in her bed upstairs and getting up only when she has learned not to put herself first and is ready and willing to take on the sainted task of being the 'Heart of the Home'.

The sequel *The Family at Misrule* bears out these misgivings. There are no brilliant, daring women here. The two boys, Bunty and Pip, are allowed to have adventures, though not always happy ones. Bunty gets into serious trouble and is shown as a complex and difficult character. Pip conventionally grows into a fine, strapping young man. The author is spared the problem of what kind of woman Judy of the wild hair and wild spirit would have grown into. Her nearest sisters, Meg and Nellie, become exactly what the Victorian reader might expect. Nellie will be 'that gladdening thing, an exceedingly beautiful woman, and she will be more, a good woman and a noble'. And Meg, just like the Meg in *Little Women*, loses her dreaminess and becomes 'sweet and good and true and unselfish'. Her only concern about marrying the sensible, grey-eyed Alan is the unconceited worry that Misrule will find it hard to manage without her. From time to time Judy is mentioned and missed, but she is never copied.

Chapter 7

What Writers Did Next:
Representations of Disability in the
Second Half of the Twentieth Century

Social perception of disability is ambiguous, motivated by compassion and hostile forces, understanding and misunderstanding, curiosity and aversion. That the representations of these perceptions in literature should be paradoxical is not surprising.

Baskin and Harris, 1977

For the writers whose novels are discussed in the earlier chapters of this book, there was no such category as 'books about disabled children'. There were, of course books which included children who were ill or blind or unable to walk, but in the mind of the writer, the purpose of the story was never to show the kind of life a disabled child might live. The idea that these writers might be perpetuating a view about people with a real-life impairment, suggesting that such a life was hardly worth living, would probably have astonished them. Their aim was largely didactic and, within the framework of warm and affectionate family stories, young readers were learning lessons on how to overcome selfishness or too strong a will and how to conform to traditional roles and gender expectations. In such a context, disability and illness were mostly used as metaphors, devices to bring the character through a period of trial or desolation into the bright light of resolution and a happy ending.

In the second half of the twentieth century, writers still

aimed to teach young readers important lessons, but what they wanted them to learn was different. Books became less religious, less sentimental, less about being 'good' in the sense of refined and unselfish and more about a social and psychological exploration of the situations young people might face. This chapter explores the ways in which such developments in literature for children have altered the portrayal of the lives of disabled children in more recent books, and asks questions about whether attitudes and representations have changed much, if at all. It takes a small selection of the many hundreds of novels written over the past 50 or so years which include a young disabled character. Although all the books chosen have some kind of domestic setting rather than the more exotic locations chosen by writers of fantasy, science fiction or adventure stories, and most deal with family relationships, they are not 'girls' books' in the way that *Little Women* or *What Katy Did* were.

Most also deal with children who in contemporary jargon have 'mobility impairments'. Modern children's writing includes many books that feature characters who are blind, deaf, have learning difficulties and so on, and although some of these are discussed in the sections which follow, most of the books chosen deal with children who cannot walk, and wheelchairs – accepted or discarded – are an important element in these stories. This is partly because walking and not walking has been a central theme in the previous chapters of this book, but also since the symbolism attached to walking is so powerful it remains a popular literary device.

Over the last few decades, there has been considerable progress in our perception and understanding of issues around disabled people. Significant advances in medical treatment have meant that people born with an impairment are less likely to die in childhood and can expect a full and rewarding life, and we are moving towards the inclusion of disabled children into mainstream schools rather than shunting them off into 'special schools'. The civil rights movement has taught us that defining disabled people in terms of their medical condition is constricting and limited and that we also need to consider the ways in which attitudes and prejudice serve to disable others.

One might expect to see these changes in society reflected in books for children, but unfortunately this is not always the case. Writers who attempt to portray disabled characters with conviction and make the reader aware of some of the 'problems' they might face have often been limited by their own narrow view and lack of any real understanding of what it is like to be disabled. Such writers have been unable to break out of their own perception of the lives of disabled children as constrained and dependent, and set themselves problems in their stories that they are unable to resolve in any positive way. This has resulted in some rather joyless books with confusing messages.[1]

Another problem is that although the writers who include young disabled people in their stories almost always want to go beyond the tragic or evil model,[2] there is often a

---

1. A recent Canadian film adaptation of *What Katy Did* (shown on British television in January 2000) is an example of this confusion. Katy is injured and then cured as in the book, but cousin Helen is strangely altered. Instead of being the pure angel of the original, Helen is a woman with a passionate past. Along the way she gives Katy an anachronistic lecture on the prejudice faced by people who use wheelchairs (they are refused entry to Burnett's coffee shop!), but she has a fatal illness and is going to die. By the end of the story there are no surviving disabled people. Kill or cure is the message in this twenty-first century version of the nineteenth century classic.

2. This positive portrayal does not apply to disabled adults in books. In Philip Pullman's *The Tiger in the Well* (Penguin Books, 1991), impairment and evil go hand in hand. The arch villain is paralysed: 'his arms and fingers were no more than inert lumps of fat...helpless fingers huge and dead in his lap'. He is 'utterly unable to make the slightest movement' even though the gunshot wound that caused his paralysis is below his breast, which would actually mean that he would have full use of his arms and hands.

surprising lack of research and attention to detail, which means that these stories can contain quite startling inaccuracies. Characters who lose a leg in an accident are somehow up and walking on their own within a week. Others, capable of racing their wheelchairs around the street with the power of their own arms, nevertheless have to rely on the school bully to push them to the nearest classroom. This adds to the confusion and lack of any satisfying resolution in the modern tale.

In this sense the books of the nineteenth century often had more integrity than some more recent titles. Susan Coolidge and her fellow writers were clear from the beginning that they wanted to show their female characters how they should behave, and when they had learned this lesson they could be cured. Modern writers aim for greater realism, but sometimes still find it hard to imagine what kind of life there can be for someone who is disabled.

1920–55

In the years immediately following the publication of *Pollyanna Grows Up*, there were few titles that entered the canon of 'classic' children's fiction in the way that *Heidi*, *What Katy Did*, *The Secret Garden* or *Pollyanna* did. The 1920s and 1930s did not generate much that was new or innovative. In general, children's fiction tended to look back to the 'Golden Age' of literature, and the books that have survived from that period (*The Story of Doctor Doolittle* by Hugh Lofting, 1920; *The House at Pooh Corner* by A.A. Milne,1928; and *Mary Poppins* by P.L. Travers, 1934, for example) created worlds of fantasy rather than reflections of reality.

Although stories of the 1940s and 1950s tended to

move back towards realism, even the outstanding books of that period (C.S. Lewis's *The Lion, the Witch and the Wardrobe*, 1950; J.R. Tolkein's *Lord of the Rings*, 1944–45; Mary Norton's *The Borrowers*, 1952–61; E.B. White's *Charlotte's Web*, 1952) were still located in fantastical worlds. Of stories that included a character who was disabled, it seems that only Laura Ingalls Wilder's autobiographical *Little House* books (1932–43), which feature Laura's blind sister Mary, are still in print in Great Britain today. Where a disabled character was featured, two physical conditions tended to outweigh all others – polio and blindness.

Considerable historic precedence exists for the use of both blind and lame characters in fiction: both are very visible and both draw upon presumed sympathetic perceptions.[3] Poliomyelitis, a disease that in the previous century had been known as infantile paralysis, was a potentially fatal viral infection which dramatically affected the lives of thousands of children and adults, until it was halted with the advent of vaccines in the late 1950s and early 1960s. It is estimated that 600,000 people contracted polio during the twentieth century. In some countries of the world, children still die and become disabled by polio.

As a fictional device, polio had great dramatic potential. It was often used to illustrate the brave 'overcoming' of apparently insuperable odds. In reiterating the classic business of rising from crutches, calipers or wheelchairs, writers continued to ignore medical accuracy in order to allow their characters to 'walk' again. As Baskin and Harris suggest in *Notes from a Different Drummer*, an annotated

---

3. Barbara H. Baskin and Karen H. Harris, *Notes From a Different Drummer: A Guide to Juvenile Fiction Portraying the Handicapped*, R.R. Bowker, Reed Publishing, New Jersey, 1977, p44. In the 43 books listed by Baskin and Harris, 13 titles deal with characters who had survived polio and 10 titles had characters who were blind.

list of children's books divided into impairment categories, the patience, forbearance and modesty of such characters can be traced back to nineteenth-century tales, the message being that goodness and effort inevitably ensure success.[4] In many of these stories, characters only begin to recover when their interests and energies are directed away from their limitations and become absorbed in some new project. In novels of the Victorian period, this would have been expressed as learning not to put yourself first or dedicating yourself to what Charlotte Yonge called 'joyous usefulness'.[5]

Blindness in stories was reflected in excess of its actual occurrence and it continued to offer the metaphorical possibilities that have interested writers since storytelling began – that by not seeing the superficial world, one is able to see the essence. In the introduction to their second compilation, *More Notes From a Different Drummer*, Baskin and Harris note that blindness is the most commonly occurring impairment in books containing black people, often used as a device allowing characters to 'forget' their own prejudices about race.[6]

Lists such as *Notes from a Different Drummer* provide an important role in making interested readers aware of books available, but their intention is often social rather than

---

4. See Baskin's and Harris' comments on Ruth Sawyer's 1946 novel, *Old Con and Patrick*, ibid.

5. Charlotte Yonge, *What Books to Lend and What Books to Give*, 1887, quoted in J.S. Bratton, op.cit. Stories about 'overcoming' polio in this period were often inspired by assumptions about American president Franklin Delano Roosevelt (FDR) and the Warm Springs Foundation he set up. Roosevelt contracted polio when he was a young man and although he was unable to move without the aid of either a wheelchair or leg braces and full crutches, there was an agreement that no photographs would be taken of him looking 'crippled'. This helped to perpetuate the myth that FDR had overcome terrible obstacles by the power of his will in order to stand again. Of the thousands of photographs of him taken during this period, only two show him in the wheelchair he frequently used to get around the White House.

literary. Other lists include those published by organisations such as the National Library of the Handicapped Child (NLHC) and booklets produced by librarians, for example the London Borough of Islington's *Kids Just the Same*. These publications are mostly aimed at adults who have contact with disabled children, although there is a growing awareness that it might be important for non-disabled children to read them too. Their intention is to 'encourage teachers, reading resource staff, special education professionals and librarians to take a closer look at juvenile fiction containing characters with physical, mental and emotional impairments'.[7] The booklet produced by Islington describes the books listed as useful for 'children with or without a disability' and suggests that it might be helpful for 'parents, carers and children'.

Although such lists are well intentioned, they encourage the tendency to see novels with disabled characters as 'problem' or 'issue' books, of interest only to other disabled children and adults who work with them.[8] Such an approach tends to see disability in children's fiction as an 'equal opportunities' issue rather than treating the books as serious fiction, subject to the same literary criteria and thoughtful reviewing as any other book for young people.[9]

If the fiction of the 1940s and 1950s provided little change in representations of disability, autobiographical stories of

6. Barbara H. Baskin and Karen H. Harris, *Notes From a Different Drummer*, R.R. Bowker, Reed Publishing, New Jersey, 1977, p24.
7. Debra Robertson, *Portraying Persons with Disabilities*, R.R. Bowker, Reed Publishing, New Jersey, 1992.
8. John Quicke's book, *Disability in Modern Children's Fiction*, is one of the very few serious studies in this area and also takes a social/psychological/integrationist perspective rather than a literary one. It is concerned with 'how disability is portrayed in modern children's fiction with a view to suggesting criteria that the reader might employ when selecting books on the topic'. John Quicke, *Disability in Modern Chidren's Fiction*, Croom Helm, London, 1985, p166.

this period offered 'inspiration' of a more realistic kind. In the retelling of personal history, the resolution is rarely in cure since in real life neither trauma, self-will, nor religious miracles will heal eyes made blind by meningitis or limbs affected by polio. Two important autobiographical stories from the middle of the twentieth century are Laura Ingalls Wilder's fictionalised novels of her pioneering childhood in America, *The Little House on the Prairie* books, published between 1932 and 1943 and Alan Marshall's *I Can Jump Puddles*, published in Australia in 1955.

Laura Ingalls Wilder was born in 1867 but did not start writing until she was well into her sixties, so that her stories are set in the same period as described in *Heidi* and *What Katy Did*. The *Little House* books are written in the third person with Laura appearing as a character in the stories of her family.[10] Her sister Mary, who becomes blind following an illness, is not *the* central character in the *Prairie* books, but she is portrayed as a vital member of the family. She is saintly, serene and supported by religious faith in the best tradition of the fictional invalid, but this is tempered by a realistic portrayal of her daily activities and her fierce desire to gain an education at a college for the blind in Iowa. When, after considerable struggle, the family eventually save enough money for her to go, they all feel a profound sense of loss which has nothing to do with her blindness. Laura 'misses her so much that it aches'. Impressively, Mary is off to study 'political economy and literature and higher mathematics and sewing, knitting, beadwork and music', but these lofty aims are weakened by the fact that we only ever learn about the letters she is now able to send home

9. See, for example, Pat Pinsent, *Children's Literature and the Politics of Equality*, David Fulton Publishers, London, 1997, chapters 3 and 8.
10. Laura Ingalls Wilder, *These Happy Golden Years*, Puffin Books, London, 1972 (First published 1943).

to her family and the fancy beadwork she gives them as presents.

Alan Marshall's *I Can Jump Puddles* is an account of his life after he contracted polio in the epidemic which swept through the Australian state of Victoria in the early 1900s.[11] The book was not specifically written with children in mind, but it was dramatised for television in the 1970s and published in Great Britain by Penguin Books as part of their Puffin Plus series for 'young adult' readers. Like *The Little House on the Prairie* books, it deals with a family struggling to survive in a difficult environment – in this case the Australian bush. It is a story of disability and masculinity at a time when young men proved their manhood by being physically tough and fearless:

> I respected men. I regarded them as capable of overcoming any difficulty, of possessing great courage. They could mend anything; they knew everything; they were strong and reliable. I looked forward to the time when I would grow up to be like them.

Alan's role model is his father, a beer-drinking, fighting man who can break in even the wildest horse and whom Alan sees as 'typical of all men'.

Alan's journey requires him to test himself continually against this physical model of manhood. In this sense it is an 'overcoming' story, but since it is true, the overcoming does not take place through a miraculous recovery, but in coming to a position where Alan can say about himself: 'I'm not going to waste any more time on cures ... It holds me back,' and begin to plan the next stage in his life.

---

11. Alan Marshall, *I Can Jump Puddles*, Penguin Books, London, 1974, (first published 1955).

He faces the usual responses from others who regard him as a tragic victim and who endlessly suggest 'treatments' which they have heard will cure him, but at the same time he is not isolated from life and is fully accepted by his family and his friends at school. Walking with crutches, he can make his own way through miles of bush, shooting hares or accompanying his friend Joe each day as he drives his mother's ducks to the pond and then back home again. He even takes part in a testing, week-long trip into the 'maiden bush', where he acts as a helper to the tough men who cut and split trees. Yet despite such masculine, physically difficult endeavours, like Jamie Kent in Eleanor Porter's *Pollyanna Grows Up*, he is often referred to as 'the kid who'll never walk again' (see Chapter 5). In this culture, walking with crutches, or walking slightly bent because of a curved spine, is described as 'not walking'.

Unlike Jamie Kent, however, Alan does not see himself as a tragic figure who can do nothing but despise himself whenever he looks at physically stronger men. He sometimes sets himself almost impossible challenges in order to be seen as a 'proper' man, but is capable of recognising and taking pride in his own achievements. Whereas Porter sees Jamie as 'someone tied helpless to a pair of sticks', Alan Marshall recognises the need for his crutches and is positively delighted when his family save enough money to buy him an 'invalid chair'. This response to a wheelchair is unusual even today – the heavy, initially unwieldy chair is not seen as an object of shame or constriction, but as exciting and liberating:

After a few days I could race it up the road, my arms working like pistons. I rode it to school and became the envy of my mates who climbed aboard with me, either sitting on my knee or facing one another sitting on the goose-neck. The one in front could grasp the handles lower down than my grip and help work them to and fro. We called it 'working your passage' and I would give anyone a lift who worked their passage.

At the end of the story, Alan wins a scholarship to business college in Melbourne to study accountancy, with dreams of becoming a writer (in this sense, like Jamie in *Pollyanna Grows Up*) and with his family, he leaves the bush to begin a new life.

This type of story which stresses overcoming physical limitations with vigorous and muscular endeavour has more or less faded from books about disabled children, except in the genre of historical fiction. Rosemary Sutcliffe, herself disabled, is one of the best-known writers of historical books for children, and many of her stories have characters with physical impairments who have to fight to regain their position in a society where only the fit will survive.[12] *Warrior Scarlet* is set in the Bronze Age and tells the story of Drem, a boy with a withered arm who will be relegated to 'weave with the women' unless he can learn to fight with the men. Through energy and effort, Drem becomes the finest spear man and a rider who can control his fiery horse with the grip of his knees alone. Like his brothers, he is accepted as a warrior and is allowed to cross to the 'Men's side' and wear the scarlet in his cloak.

Books from 1960 Onwards

Over the past 40 years, the serious academic study of children's literature has become a rapidly expanding field,

---

12. Rosemary Sutcliffe, *Warrior Scarlet*, Penguin Books, London, 1958. Other titles by Sutcliffe which deal with this issue are *The Witches' Brat* (1970) and *Blood Feud* (1976), both also published by Penguin Books.

with university courses, journals and books contributing to the discourse. But such work has rarely shown any interest in disability as a topic for critical study. Even important overviews such as John Rowe Townsend's classic study *Written For Children* and Peter Hunt's more recent *An Introduction to Children's Literature* fail to mention it.[13] Unlike issues of class, gender and race, it is rare to find any acknowledgement of the fact that disability and cure are recurring themes in books for children or any interesting, literary discussion of their treatment.

One reference can be found in Humphrey Carpenter and Mari Pritchard's *The Oxford Companion to Children's Literature*. Its entry for 'disability' includes the statement:

> The growing concern in Western society during the 1970s for the physically and mentally handicapped led to a spate of books for children in which the nature of such handicaps was explained, and those suffering from them were presented as cheerful, normal people.[14]

This comment, both patronising and inaccurate, implies that no children's book written before 1970 ever included a disabled child and ignores not only the fictional characters in the novels discussed in the earlier chapters of this book, but also the many disabled characters in other enduring texts.[15] Carpenter and Pritchard's comment also suggests

---

13. John Rowe Townsend, *Written for Children*, Penguin Books, London, 1974; Peter Hunt, *An Introduction to Children's Literature*, Oxford University Press, Oxford, 1994.
14. Humphrey Carpenter and Mari Pritchard, *The Oxford Companion to Children's Literature*, Oxford University Press, Oxford, 1984.
15. The novels of Charles Dickens, which for many years were read as much by children as by adults, contain many young disabled characters (even if by the end of the story, these 'poor invalids' were usually dead!): Tiny Tim in *A Christmas Carol*, Smike in *Nicholas Nickleby* and Paul Dombey in *Dombey and Son* are just a few.

that post-1970, these characters were always cheerful and content with their lot. Unfortunately this is far from the truth. Particularly in the weaker stories of this period, the 'handicapped children' in novels often suffered from internalised oppression, hating themselves, believing that the problems they faced were all their fault and dreaming of how happy they would be if only they could walk.

Alongside these developments in critical study and particularly since the 1960s, there has been an explosion in the publishing of books for young readers and the creation of a new category – fiction for teenagers or 'young adults'. This coincided with the concept of teenagers as a discrete social group with their own needs and aspirations. Most of these books have had a short publishing history, rarely surviving beyond the first or second printing.

As the twentieth century progressed, there was a new kind of realism in children's books. Topics once considered too sophisticated, emotionally upsetting or demanding were now deemed appropriate for young readers. Divorce, death (which had been an important part of Victorian fiction but was less frequent in the first half of the twentieth century), racism, sex, child abuse and disability were part of a new climate which made it possible for writers to explore more complicated subjects.

However, such subjects did not lend themselves to a simple, sentimental ending. This provided the author with a paradox – the happy, or if not happy, optimistic ending, is an important element of children's fiction, yet this can be at odds with the demand for a realistic treatment of complex psychological and social situations. Whereas in Victorian fiction, one could rely on religion or at least parental advice to provide the moral solution, in the second half of the twentieth century, young people are seen as less passive and more responsible for making their own decisions. Rather than seeking solace in God or accepting the advice of the wise adult, adolescents have had to come to terms with the problems they face and reach their own inner peace.

For the modern writer who deals with disabled characters, neither of the classic optimistic endings – miracle cure or 'overcoming' by coping cheerfully with life's vicissitudes – will do. The weak writer will probably be happy with any ending, but good writers have tended to resist the romanticisation of their disabled characters and present something more angry and real. Post-1950, with the exception of some curiously old-fashioned books like Louise Cooper's *Heart of Glass*[16] – which exploits the cliched ending of the wheelchair user who is miraculously cured by a traumatic event – disabled characters in children's books are more likely to be shown battling with social injustice and their own physical conditions. Yet surprisingly, death still remains a popular option. *Sweet Frannie* and *No Time At All*, both by Susan Sallis, and *See Ya Simon* by David Hill are all examples of stories where a character who uses a wheelchair is dead by the end of the book.[17] All of these titles use the technique of either the whole or part of the story being 'dictated' by a friend of the disabled character, reflecting on their life and the good times they had together. It is interesting to think about whether these stories reflect reality – some disabled children do, of course, have life-threatening conditions – or are a result of the writer's inability to imagine a happy, full life as a grown-up disabled person.

---

16. Louise Cooper, *Heart of Glass*, Puffin, London 1996. Described in the Puffin Catalogue as a 'fantasy, romantic thriller with a supernatural edge', *Heart of Glass* is part of a series more concerned with atmosphere than medical accuracy.
17. Susan Sallis, *Sweet Frannie*, Puffin Books, London, 1981; *No Time At All*, Corgi, London, 1994; David Hill, *See Ya Simon*, Viking, London, 1993.

Second-Fiddle Stories

Writers have always used the concept of the 'outsider', presenting a character who for one reason or another is on the edge of society. Earlier chapters considered the ways in which Jane Eyre, Jo March in *Little Women*, Katy in *What Katy Did* and Judy in *Seven Little Australians* failed to fit in with the model of refinement and self-sacrifice expected of women and how writers resolved this 'problem'. Post-1970, the outsider became a very popular literary device, particularly in novels aimed at adolescent readers. The teenager with divorcing parents, the one who has been ill-treated by adults, the black teenager (for some writers being black was in itself a 'problem' category), the one painfully exploring their sexuality, all offered the possibility of a complex exploration of the journey a troubled character had to make in order to achieve some kind of resolution.

A disabled character would appear to satisfy the classical requirements of the 'outsider' and, theoretically at least, this offers many possibilities to the writer. A disabled teenager might well have reasons for feeling lonely, not part of the crowd, subject to other people's judgements and prejudices. But the role of 'outsider' *within* the novel relies on the character being at the centre of the story with their views seen as valid. Too often in fiction, the disabled character is the 'outsider', not only in terms of characterisation, but also in terms of their marginalisation in the story itself. The disabled character is not the one with whom the reader is asked to identify; it is not their psychological journey which drives the narrative. Like Beth in *Little Women* and Helen in *Jane Eyre*, their role is purely to service the emotional growth of the non-disabled protagonist as he or she become happier and better adjusted.

This trend has given rise to a phenomenon which Pat

Thomson has dubbed 'second-fiddle books'. Such books do not usually concern themselves with cure or resolution for the disabled child:

> There is still a tendency for a book with a disabled character in it to be a 'problem' book, and there is an infuriating genre which might be deemed a 'second fiddle' book. In these, there is indeed a disabled character but they exist only to promote the personal development of the main, able-bodied character. Thus Samantha becomes a better person through having known someone in a wheelchair. Bully for Samantha but what about the person in the wheelchair?[18]

Susan Sallis' *An Open Mind* is a good example of a 'second-fiddle' book.[19] The story is told through David, who is disturbed by the thought of his father's impending marriage and is unhappy with life in general. Although Sallis' intention is also to open the reader's mind to the hopes and fears of Bruce, a boy with cerebral palsy, (referred to throughout the novel as 'spastic'), it is David's voice and David's views which are central.

In this story, Sallis employs a popular plot device in the 'second-fiddle' novel – the school project. The school project, usually social studies or citizenship, is a device by which the central character, sometimes troubled and difficult (male), sometimes worthy and charitable (female), goes off to a 'special school' or day centre, meets a disabled person, learns to be a bit more humble and goes back to school a better, wiser person. In *An Open Mind*, David's project takes him to the special school where he

18. Pat Thomson, 'Disability in Modern Children's Fiction', *Books For Keeps*, no.75, July 1992, p24.
19. Susan Sallis, *An Open Mind*, Penguin Books, London, 1978.

meets Bruce, the son of his father's new girlfriend. The story has many engaging moments and Bruce is realistically portrayed but the lessons we learn about him are designed to make the reader feel, as David's teacher puts it, how lucky we are, and wonder 'whether we owe them anything'.

Bruce is the brave, long-suffering type, patient and cheerful, never complaining. When Dave tells him about his proposed trip to the country, he observes that Bruce 'never hinted at feeling – well, deprived, before, and he didn't really this time. It was just so obvious he couldn't rough it in some cottage like we were going to do.' But in the name of realism, Bruce is not allowed merely to be cheerful and long-suffering in the mould of Tiny Tim. In the second half of the story, he feels guilty and wretched at the thought that his mother will not marry the man she loves because she doesn't want Dave's dad to be 'Lumbered with – with – with a – with a!' He cannot bear to name himself, he only has the language used by other people. He asks Dave whether he thinks people ought to be kept alive when they're no use to anyone, and decides that it would be best if he stopped taking his medication and let himself die in order to 'give his mum a clear field'.

In the end, we are told that everyone who knows Bruce really does care for him and loves him as he is, but Bruce himself fades out of the picture. Under the pretence of a 'modern' treatment of this subject, Sallis follows the traditional plot device of using the ill or disabled character as a catalyst for change in the protagonist. Bruce is still the 'other', self-hating, seeing himself only as a burden. The last words we have from him are when he tells Dave that he is 'no *good*' and Dave insists that this is nonsense because he 'makes people better than they were before'. At the end of the book, it is Dave's, not Bruce's sense of himself which is the issue. It is Dave who has developed into a more feeling kind of person, one who realises that people are the most important thing in his life.

Bring in the Spring by Hannah Cole is another story about a 'one-afternoon-a-week school project'.[20] Bel, a teenager who is not particularly happy with her home life, goes along to the 'special school' with her friend Clare in order to discover 'what that sort of school is like'. At first Bel is unenthusiastic, repulsed by the idea of 'children dribbling', but as the story develops she becomes more and more involved with Sarah, one of the pupils. The story, told in the third person, opens with two women from the residential home where Sarah lives, speaking about her as if she can neither understand nor hear them. They see her as a burden and avoid her when they can. Seeing her for the first time, Bel thinks, 'There was a handicapped child, coming towards them, in a wheelchair. She looked weird, poor little thing. Such thin legs in tight red trousers, and her head all sideways'.

But as Bel gets to know Sarah, she begins to recognise what none of Sarah's teachers, helpers or psychologists have been able to see: that she is intelligent and, alert, and, with help, can communicate with others. Hannah Cole works hard to make the thoughts and feelings of Sarah, a child without speech because of cerebral palsy, come alive to the reader. When Sarah sees a worker stealing the children's pocket money from the residential home where she lives, the reader is with her in her frustration at not being able to make herself heard. Sarah is not a stereotypically sweet and cheerful 'invalid'. She is angry when she feels let down and Bel has to learn to live without the gratitude she expected.

---

20. Hannah Cole, *Bring in the Spring*, Julia McRae Books, London, 1993.

The story ends with Sarah reunited with her mother and the school project coming to an end. Bel's journey has been about finding the confidence to pursue what she believes is right even when it makes her unpopular, and overcoming her abhorrence of people who are different. Sarah's is in finding a psychotherapist who can see that she is intelligent and will help her communicate, and in being accepted by her mother and taken home.

The reader of *Bring in the Spring* will have learned much about recognising the talents and intelligence of someone who looks different and cannot communicate in the ordinary way. But, despite such good intentions, Sarah's role in the novel is a passive one. We sympathise with her and long for people to see what she is capable of, but it is Bel who moves the story along, and however much the reader learns about children with communication difficulties and the prejudices they face, it is unlikely that Sarah the character, rather than the issues her presence raises, will exist long in the reader's mind.

Integrity or Misrepresentation

One of the strong points of Hannah Cole's novel is that she is clear that Sarah has a life worth living and her problems are mostly created by others who are too impatient and unwilling to listen. Many writers of the new wave of books in the 1960s, 1970s and beyond have been unable to create a disabled character who is not weighed down with feelings of inadequacy and self-hatred. Although they seek to portray a strong, independent disabled person, they have not been able to break out of their perception of the wheelchair as the symbol of dependency and restriction and of the life of such a person as essentially tragic. This has given rise to books with confusing mixed messages.

Some of these books have had short publishing histories for good reasons. Both Myra Schneider's bluntly titled *If Only I Could Walk* and Cordelia Jones' *The View from the Window*, published in 1978, are attempts at a realistic approach to people who use wheelchairs, showing how much they want to be treated just the same as everyone else.[21] Both, however, are caught in a depressing, dreary perception of the awfulness of life for a disabled person. In each of these books, the central character sees herself as a young woman who can never hope for a normal, loving, sexual relationship. Schneider's character proclaims, 'Why don't you speak the truth, I'm too handicapped to have a boyfriend', whilst in *The View from the Window* we are given the view that:

> Someone who marries a cripple must have something wrong with them. He must need to be indispensable to someone ... there's something morbid, unhealthy about wanting to devote the whole of your life to a woman who's crippled. It's not a natural form of love.

The 'happy ending' to *If Only I Could Walk* involves the central character realising that she shouldn't reject the advances of the boy with a stutter just because he too is an outsider (this theme is developed in later books such as Judy Blume's *Deenie* and Cynthia Voight's *Izzy Willy Nilly*), and concludes with the self-denigrating comment that 'She might not be able to stand or walk or dance but she was no longer just a spectator at the edge of the ring.'

Jay Ashton's *Killing the Demons* appears on many 'recommended' lists.[22] Ashton seeks to establish Sam, the protagonist, as a troubled but strong, independently

---

21. Myra Schneider, *If Only I Could Walk*, William Heinemann Ltd, London, 1978; Cordelia Jones, *The View from the Window*, André Deutsch, London, 1978.
22. Jay Ashton, *Killing the Demons*, Oxford University Press, Oxford, 1994.

minded character who becomes reconciled to her new life, but the messages in this book are muddled.

Sam is a troubled teenager who has become disabled after the car accident which killed her baby brother. She feels responsible for his death and is full of self-hatred, longing to escape from her 'useless legs'. The book's intention is to show the process by which Sam comes to accept that her brother's death is not her fault, and by the end of the story she is reconciled to a more fatalistic 'things happen' approach to this issue. She is, however, never really reconciled to her own situation as a disabled person.

Sam's freedom from the restrictions of the world she finds so unpleasant is through the make-believe world made possible by her computer; this 'escape' from life through technology is becoming a popular device in books about disabled children. *Killing the Demons* interweaves the fantasy world of medieval computer games and the difficult self-hating one of a teenager who in her own words is 'stuck in a wheelchair'. Through the computer, Sam can 'walk again'. She can also run through forests, ride horses, climb ladders into beautiful bedrooms and slay the demons of the title, one of whom is inevitably a 'hunchbacked dwarf'.[23]

One of the confusing messages in this story is how the writer wishes us to see Sam. Sometimes we are asked to see her as physically strong and capable of getting herself wherever she wants, whilst at other times, she seems totally dependent on others and is by implication, defenceless against their bullying and abuse. On the one hand, we learn that her arms are strong enough to wrestle her father and she can push herself for miles along the pavement, up and down kerbs, in order to prevent her friend's brother

---

23. See for a discussion of the hunchback in literature, pp129-33.

joining in a car theft. But when she is at school, she somehow becomes incapable of wheeling herself along the flat school corridor and into the lift. Sam can 'whip the wheels of her chair round and shoot up a ramp' but after every lesson she must wait for a volunteer to push her to the next lesson.

Presumably in order to explore the kind of bullying to which children who are different are subjected, Ashton has Cherill, a particularly unpleasant girl, seize her wheelchair from behind and

> with an alacrity that should have been a warning. She marched to the end of the corridor then, instead of taking the lift, pushed the chair until its front wheels hung over the top step of the concrete staircase.

It is hard to imagine why physically strong Sam not only fails to tell her to get lost, but also continues to let Cherill push her around, physically and emotionally. The writer seems to be struggling with the idea that a disabled person with strong arms and an active brain may well be able to do things on her own without the assistance of a 'carer', and this ill-researched picture serves to persuade the reader that life for a wheelchair user is essentially unhappy and dependent.

Sweet Frannie by Susan Sallis is another book which received widespread recognition and has been praised for its 'lack of sentimentality and use of the contemporary idiom'[24] and for the characterisation of a paraplegic 16-year-old girl who is assertive, rebellious and 'bubbling over

---

24. Pat Pinsent, *Children's Literature and the Politics of Equality*, p127.

with life'.[25] Interestingly, although it has been nominated for awards and has found its way onto many recommended lists, Baskin and Harris are vitriolic in their review of the book.[26]

Sallis uses a number of conventional devices from an earlier era of children's fiction. Frannie is an orphan, abandoned by her mother on the steps of the Social Security Office 'without a name or pedigree or legs that worked'. The book starts with Fran's 'coming home' but, unlike Pollyanna or Rebecca of Sunnybrook Farm, Fran is not seeking the love and acceptance of a frosty maiden aunt. Instead, she is starting a new life at Thornton Hall, a residential home for disabled people – the not-so-modern equivalent of the Victorian orphanage.

The book has a sharp-edged, first-person narrative. Fran does not like being patronised or pushed around. Sallis wants to give us an attractive and lively character who is proud of her independence and her beautiful hands and arms. Yet she constantly contradicts herself by insisting on Frannie's hatred of her 'heavy and useless legs'. At one point, she bizarrely suggests that these might have been replaced with 'tin ones' if it hadn't been for Frannie's weak heart, as if artificial legs could walk on their own without the need of nerves, muscles and messages from spinal cord to brain.

Part of Frannie's self-hatred for her body is her disgust at her incontinence, about which Sallis seems positively obsessed. We first meet this on page 10, when Frannie describes herself as coarse because she is always wetting her knickers, and then again on pages 16, 23, 42, 44, 57, 68, 111, 118, 123 and 138! Despite interpretations of the

---

25. John Quicke, *Disability in Modern Children's Ficiton*, p108.
26. Barbara H. Baskin and Karen H. Harris, *More Notes from a Different Drummer*.

book which have seen the portrayal of Frannie's sexuality as positive and unusual, Sallis constantly contradicts this view. Frannie loves being kissed by another resident of Thornton Hall, the handsome Luke Hawkins, but when her doctor suggests Luke is not as committed to her as she is to him, indeed would never have fallen for her if 'his legs were still there', she retorts, 'Maybe I should just let him touch me up a bit? After all I couldn't feel a thing and if he could get his hand through my plastic pants and the sani pads it might just give him a bit of a thrill!' She has a 'pulsating, beating, body' but, inexplicably, she says that 'love play' and 'the French kiss' can never be for her because she has 'no feeling below hip level'.

The whole story is coloured by the knowledge that Fran is going to die. Since we know from the beginning that 'her days are numbered' because of a heart complaint which seems to have no connection with her paraplegia (as in Victorian novels, no medical condition is specified), the reader is not asked to think about what kind of life this feisty, attractive, young disabled woman might have ahead of her.

Fran's spirited nature is complicated by the disgust or pity she feels when she looks at the other disabled people who live there: 'I knew these were attractive girls but my mind wouldn't get past those frightful hands fastened almost straight onto their shoulders'. She seems to love Luke because he is not really 'one of them'. True, he has had both his legs amputated following a car crash, but with Fran's help, he is soon going to be out of that wheel-chair and up walking on two legs, albeit artificial ones. About this Fran is insistent: 'You've got to Hawkins! You must walk again! How the hell can you carry me over the threshold if you can't walk!' The story ends with a warped 1980s version of the 'miracle cure'. Luke, still in his wheelchair, returns from his parents' home to Thornton Hall in order to comfort Frannie after the death of a foster aunt. Outside her room he turns to face her.

'Watch this Fanny.'
I watched.
He took the rug from his waist. He wore jeans and at the end of the jeans were black shoes. Slowly, smiling at me, he leaned down and pushed his left shoe over to his right and tucked the step of his chair out of the way. Then he knocked his left leg to the ground and followed it with his right. He sat up and placed his hands on the arms of his chair. Then he shoved. A grunt came from him and he stopped smiling, but he was up. He was standing free of the chair. He had no sticks, no crutches. He was free. Hawkins was free.

Miraculously, he lifts Frannie and carries her over the threshold.

The final section is in Luke's voice telling us that Frannie has died. Although Sallis clearly wanted the reader to see her as a strong, spirited, independent girl, it is impossible not to see her death as the price to be paid for the redemption of another. Her death has allowed handsome, sensitive Luke to become free of the burden of a life with her. Presumably he will continue to love and miss her, but we assume he will soon be walking his way into a new relationship with a girl who can walk on two legs and does not wet her pants.

Like many other books dealing with impairment, Sallis suggests that an enlightened way to look at disabled people is to see the person not the disability or, as she says in the novel 'see Frances Adamson not a paraplegic'. Acceptance in these terms means accepting the person despite their impairment. The real self, the one that matters, can never incorporate the braces, crutches or wheelchair. The real 'you' is the one within; the spirit rather than the corporal body. There is no perception of physical difference as an integral part of the whole person, not something which must be hidden away and ignored.

See Ya Simon by David Hill is set in Australia and is another book where the disabled character is dead by the end of the story, but at least the Simon of the title is not tortured by self-loathing. He is funny, sharp and alarming, although our response to him is tempered by the knowledge that he is not going to live to be an adult. Hill uses the technique of narrating the story of Simon through the voice of someone close to him, but this is not a 'second-fiddle' book. Near the beginning of the story his friend Nathan tells us, 'Simon's my best friend and sometime in the next year or two years, he's going to die.' The book is dedicated to someone who died aged 15, so Hill's intention may well be to re-create the 'real life' of a boy with muscular dystrophy. Although Simon dreams of walking or running in slow motion (the most popular cliché attached to the non-walker, closely followed by dreams of flying), he faces his waking world with brutal and sometimes very funny honesty and refuses to be patronised. In one of the few clearly political points in the book he says, 'What does the Telethon do. It treats us like outsiders. Makes you feel that as long as you go aaww and feel sorry for us, we'll be okay. We don't want your bloody self pity...we want your world!' The book starts with a description of him 'cheating' to score a goal, making everyone laugh. Unusually, his wheelchair is seen as something which gets him around, not something to be ashamed of. When talking of the girls they fancy, Simon jokes, 'A girl is naturally going to be impressed by a guy who's got his own set of wheels.'

The ending is sharp and sad and somehow manages to avoid the sentimental: 'He was bad tempered and funny. He was fierce and tough and brave. He was my friend. I'm proud I knew him, and I'll never forget him. See ya Simon.' Although the story is narrated by another, Simon is a real, memorable character who stays in the mind long after the reading is finished.

Another book with considerable integrity is *Flawed Glass* by Ian Strachan.[27] This adventure story is set on a Scottish island, and Strachan's central character, Shona, has serious problems of physical co-ordination and communication. But what Shona wants most is to be accepted and understood. Strachan's description of her is mostly sensitive and engaging, and the language he uses to describe her speech is startling and evocative:

> Only Shona knew that the words lay stored away in her head, neat and tidy as the clothes in her bedroom chest of drawers. It was just that when she opened her mouth to use them they flew out like clothes from the washing machine the day the door burst open in mid-spin.

As with Sarah in *Bring in the Spring*, people are unaware of Shona's abilities or how to help her. Nevertheless she is learning all the time and storing up things in her head. The story ends, like most adventures, with things neatly tied together. Despite many physical difficulties, Shona types a readable message into a computer which saves her father from ruin after he is wrongly accused of theft. She isn't cured at the end, she doesn't die, but she does find a good friend.

---

27. Ian Strachan, *Flawed Glass*, Methuen, London, 1989.

Accident and Illness

Most of the books discussed so far have dealt with characters who are disabled from the beginning of the story. However, a number of writers have taken a different line, choosing to investigate the emotions and psychological journey of a character who becomes disabled during the story. In these 'right of passage' novels, the protagonist has a disabling accident or illness, often a paralysing illness, and has to embark on a painful process until they reach some kind of accommodation to their new situation. These books, usually aimed at female 'young adult' readers, explore changed self-image, loss of self-esteem, relationships with family and friends, sex and romance and the adjustment to the physical loss of mobility. Sometimes they also look at the political and social aspects of becoming disabled – the barriers, prejudices and exclusion that a disabled person faces – but this is rare. The theme of walking and not-walking can be part of these stories along with the use of crutches, walking stick or wheelchair but, although these modern stories avoid miraculous healing or easy resolution, there is almost always some kind of physical cure. *Deenie* by Judy Blume and *Izzy Willy Nilly* by Cynthia Voight, both by leading American writers for teenagers, are two important books which deal with this subject.[28] *Calling Tracy* by Clare Cherrington is a simpler story aimed at younger readers, and among the more recent titles for the young adult market is *Fighting Back* by Wendy Orr.[29]

28. Judy Blume, *Deenie*, Piper Books, Heinemann Ltd, London, 1988 (first published 1973); Cynthia Voigt, *Izzy Willy Nilly*, Lion Tracks, London, 1989 (First published 1986). Peter Hunt in *Introduction to Children's Literature* makes the interesting observation that the same age group which was reading *Little Women* in the 1880s was reading Judy Blume in the 1980s.
29. Clare Cherrington, *Calling Tracy*, Hamish Hamilton, London, 1993; Wendy Orr, *Fighting Back*, Orchard Books, London, 1998.

These stories are about a fall from grace and, in order to emphasise the perceived tragedy of such a fall, the central character is often a more-than-average girl. She is either a champion of some kind, physically active and terrifically successful, or she is especially beautiful. Deenie is gorgeous, and her mother has plans for her to become a model before she is diagnosed with adolescent idiopathic scoliosis. Izzy is very pretty, very popular and a cheerleader when she is injured in a car crash with her date, who has had too much to drink. Tracy is a star skater before a fall from a tree, and Anna in *Fighting Back* is a karate champion until she is badly injured in a car crash. All of these stories contain a lot of information about visits to doctors and time spent in hospital, and much greater care is taken with medical accuracy than was the case in some earlier books. There is the odd inconsistency or lack of accuracy, but it is rarely significant to the development of the story.[30] All are direct, first-person accounts with the voice of the newly disabled girl absolutely central to the story.

The accident or illness in these books is almost always portrayed as a tragedy which must be overcome. The supposition is that the character has become a member of a club that no one wants to join, and the corollary is that they start to feel ugly and useless, full of self-loathing. When Deenie slashes at her hair after learning that she has to wear her brace for the next four years, she says, 'If I was going to be ugly I was going to be ugly all the way...as ugly as anybody'd ever been before... maybe even uglier.' The writers engage in a creative struggle with the world they imagine a newly disabled person has to face, and this struggle is more about individual issues such as self-esteem

---

30. In *Izzy Willy Nilly*, for example, Izzy manages to get out of bed and go to the bathroom without any help only a week after her leg is amputated – a most unlikely event.

and individual prejudice than the wider social issues of discrimination and exclusion. There are few attempts to look at the social pressures faced by disabled people or the ways in which prejudice limits possibilities.

In these books, characters take into themselves the words they have heard to describe disabled people. Throughout *Izzy Willy Nilly*, Izzy constantly refers to herself as a 'cripple'. Shortly after her accident she thinks,

> I couldn't think what to do with my life, what to want to do because all the things I wanted to do required normal people and I wasn't normal any more. I was abnormal – who would want to ask me to dance with him now? Who would want to go out with a cripple?

When her friends abandon her, Izzy thinks, 'I could understand it. I mean I wouldn't have wanted to be friends with a cripple either.' She sees it as impossible that she could be both 'crippled' and a 'real person'. Anna in *Fighting Back* is also unable to see how she can be both 'normal' and 'permanently impaired':

> Which word is worse, permanent or impaired?
> Impaired's an ugly word. Worse than handicapped.
> Disabled. Invalid.
> Am I disabled? How could I be?
> I'm still the same person – just can't do a few things...
> When do you stop being normal and turn into a handicapped person?

These books are not religious in the way of the Victorian novel, but they have their own morality. Part of the lesson the characters are expected to learn is to remember how unkind they have been to disabled people in the past. Izzy remembers how awful she was to a girl whose face has been burned and how her eyes were drawn to stare at her. 'I had never spoken a word to her. Because she was so horrible to look at.' Judy Blume foreshadows Deenie's diagnosis by having her observe at the beginning of the book: 'I try not to look at Old Lady Murray because she's so ugly she makes me want to vomit. She has a big bump on her back and can't stand up straight.' And a few pages later: 'Our town doesn't have school buses, except for the one that picks up the handicapped kids. They come to our school from all over.' She avoids Gina, a girl on her street who was knocked over by a truck and is in the 'special class' at her school because she 'wouldn't know how to act or anything'. At the end of the book, she looks into the classroom and sees Gina working on the blackboard and thinks, 'I wonder if she sees herself as a handicapped person or just a regular girl, like me.'

These books are the nearest equivalent to the domestic dramas of the nineteenth century. Although time is spent in hospital and in the doctor's waiting room, the main setting is the family home and the most important relationships are with the protagonist's parents, siblings and friends. Mothers and fathers in these stories usually manage to hide their feelings and support their child in the face of 'tragedy', but friendship is more complicated. Just as Katy in *What Katy Did* and Meg in *Little Women* have to learn that the best friendship is not with the showiest, most flamboyantly dressed girls, so Izzy and Deenie discover that the prettiest, most popular girls can sometimes let you down, and that real friendship can be found with girls you previously rejected. So, Izzy becomes friends with awkward, clumsy but intelligent Rosamunde, a girl from a much poorer background (as her mother continually reminds her), one who Izzy herself describes as 'not good looking' with 'fuzzy hair, a big nose and a bad figure'. And Deenie pals up with Barbara, a girl with eczema. At the start of the book Deenie is repulsed by this girl:

> I named her the Creeping Crud because she's got this disgusting rash all over her. It's supposed to be some kind of allergy but who wants to take the chance of finding out by touching her? It could be leprosy or something like that!

But after she has the brace fitted and Deenie too becomes 'untouchable', she begins to see that Barbara is 'a really nice person'.

In all these books returning to school is an important part of the journey, and the 'first day back' provides an opportunity for the writer to explore the character's emotions when confronted by the reactions of others. In *Izzy Willy Nilly*, 'the worst thing was the sudden brittle silence that froze the air whenever I made an entrance'. Readers are asked to imagine how they might respond to a girl who previously had everything: pretty, nice, good figure, popular with boys and girls, who now has 'half of one leg just hanging down inside her blue jeans'. The assumption is we could never like this person. Deenie has to face endless questions from the other students, and when the principal offers her a free place on the bus for 'handicapped children', she realises with some horror that she has now joined the group she previously despised. Yet the first day back at school is usually the beginning of the character's growth towards greater self-confidence and, of course, it is friendship which provides the key to the next stage in their journey.

The ending of such stories can present problems for the modern writer since, unlike their Victorian or Edwardian equivalents, good writers today must base their endings on some kind of realism. However, most writers are reluctant to end the story without at least a partial cure, and this is most often brought about by medical science, with a positive attitude to healing and 'inner strength' taking an important second place. Although none are the same as they were when the story began, all the characters in these stories make some kind of recovery. Deenie is going to go through a difficult four years with her 'Milwaukee Brace', but at some time in the future her spine will be straight; Izzy will always be an 'amputee' and will never make cheerleader again, but she will get an artificial leg. Annie has, as her insurance form states, a 'permanent impairment' and lives with some pain, but at the end of the story she is walking again without any assistance.

Wheelchairs appear in most of these stories, although there is often some kind of symbolic rejection, not significantly different to what happens to the wheelchairs used by Clara in *Heidi* or Colin in *The Secret Garden*. Even in late twentieth-century novels where the writer consciously sets out to make the reader more aware of the issues disabled people face, the wheelchair is still viewed as a symbol of dependency and restriction. When Izzy's mother sends her wheelchair back to the hospital, she remarks,

> I was glad, even thankful to be on crutches. First thing Monday, my mother returned both the walker and the wheelchair so I knew she was as happy as I was to get rid of them. On crutches I could move from room to room without feeling too much of a cripple.

Her new-found friend Rosamunde admires the way she now sits 'on a real chair, just like a real person', as if the person in the wheelchair was not Izzy at all.

This is gentle compared to Anna's feelings of triumph when her wheelchair is sent back to the hospital. She seems to invest in the wheelchair some malevolent power to constrain her. 'The wheelchair's leaving. Cleaned, folded, packed into the boot of dad's car like a guilty secret. Tough luck chair. I win, you lose – I'm not a cripple after all.' Walking makes her 'normal', and her contempt (and by implication contempt for all people who use wheelchairs or crutches or sticks) extends to all the equipment she has used in the story. Of her walking stick she says, 'But that's temporary; I'll be getting rid of it soon. A stick makes me look disabled – spastic.'

In these novels, all of the central characters have a future ahead of them, and there is a tempered optimism in all the endings, often helped along by the prospect of a desirable new boyfriend. What is unusual in these books is the absence of role models to show what life could be like for a disabled person. Too often the young characters are left to struggle on alone. There are few 'enlightened adults' whose role is to provide the experience and guidance needed to show young people what might be possible for them as they grow up, in the way that Miss Temple does for Jane Eyre and Marmee does for Jo. Of course, one of the difficulties for the writer here is the idea that an adult disabled person might have the qualities that allow her or him to act as teacher and guide, so the character has to learn to do these new things without assistance and with only negative ideas about the lives of disabled people.

Different Lives

It may seem a strange decision to include my own work in this chapter, but *A Different Life* has many similarities to the books discussed in the last section, so to leave it out altogether seemed odder than including it.[31] In this book, fifteen-year-old Libby is not especially pretty or popular and not at all sporty. She becomes paralysed after a mysterious illness which is hard for the doctors to diagnose. The issues for her are the same as any of the characters in the other stories – friendship, boyfriends or the lack of them, parents, self-image, school and exams – but it is also an attempt to explore some of the issues of exclusion and prejudice faced by disabled people.

In this story, Libby does have someone who can act as her guide through the most difficult parts of her journey. Barbara is intended as a kind of modern version of *What Katy Did*'s cousin Helen. Disabled herself, she is certainly not saintly or angelic, but occupies a similar role in acting as an example of what life can be like. Her role in the book is not just to help Libby adjust to her new body, but also to talk to her about the ways she might deal with the injustices she is likely to face, such as being excluded from school because she uses a wheelchair. Just as cousin Helen explains to Katy that she will cope much better with life if she accepts that God has taken her to his 'School of Pain', so a century later, Barbara explains to Libby that what the doctors, nurses and physiotherapists are saying to her might not be the most helpful way to deal with her new world:

> People around you do what they think's best for you – it's just that their training, their goal in life is to restore you to a state that's as near to normal as possible, and for them 'normal' means walking. That's not their fault. It's the way society looks at the world. They want everyone to be 'normal'. Normally average. They think a wheelchair – using a wheelchair – must be the end of

---

31. Lois Keith, *A Different Life*, The Women's Press, Livewire Books, London, 1997.

the world. I didn't have any choice in looking at things in a different way.

Libby's wheelchair occupies a role more like that of Alan Marshall's wheelchair in *I Can Jump Puddles*. At the end of the story it is clear that this is not something to be sent back to the hospital or thrown away; it is something functional and practical which gets her around and will help her along the road to independence. There is certainly no cure at the ending of this story, and I have tried to leave it for the reader to decide how happy Libby will be with her different life.

Survival and Strength

Two books remarkable for their portrayal of a strong, engaging and memorable character with a future are by Australian writer, Morris Gleitzman. *Blabbermouth* and its sequel *Sticky Beak* are written in the first person with Rowena (Ro) at the centre of the story, and the reader is no doubt that she will survive, no matter what obstacles are thrown at her.[32]

Rowena's impairment has nothing to do with wheelchairs or walking – she was born without the ability to speak. She can hear and she can communicate but her vocal cords do not work. Although such a condition is rare (presumably it does exist, but it is certainly not common), it has the advantage of being full of metaphorical possibilities. She has a big personality and a lot to say – hence the ironic title *Blabbermouth*. Gleitzman's novels are not 'problem' or 'issue' books in the way of many which cover the same sort of subject. They take a distinctly

---

32. Morris Gleitzman, *Blabbermouth* (1995; first published in 1992) and *Sticky Beak* (1995; first published in 1993), both Macmillan Children's Books, London.

different approach since they are both serious and funny, personal and political. There is absolutely no question of whether Rowena has a voice in these stories. Her 'problem' is not her inability to speak, although this can present enormous inconveniences for her, and she doesn't hate herself for it. She is a whole person, not one struggling to have the 'self within' shrine through in order to overcome the deficits of the body without. She wants metaphorically and literally to be heard, she wants her dad to be less embarrassing, and most of all, she wants a real, true friend.

The book opens with Rowena's first day in her new school. When the class bully calls her horrible names, she stuffs a frog in his mouth and binds it with tape – her way of rendering *him* silent. She had previously attended a 'special' school which the government closed down and where her best friend Erin died a year earlier, a sadness which re-visits her when she is feeling lonely or insecure. Although she has some good memories of these times, being 'sent back to special school' is an anxiety which runs through both stories.

Like many an earlier character in children's fiction (Katy in *What Katy Did*, Clara in *Heidi*, Colin in *The Secret Garden*, Judy in *Seven Little Australians*), Rowena is a half-orphan. She has a father but her mother died when she was very young. However, unlike his Victorian equivalents, Rowena's father is far from absent. He is a loving, devoted and sometimes excruciatingly embarrassing parent. She communicates with her lurid, satin shirt-wearing, country-and-western singing, loud-mouthed father by sign language and with most other people by writing. Using sign language has a number of advantages. It means, for example, that Rowena and her dad can speak over the noise of the tractor on his newly acquired, weevil-infested apple farm.

Gleitzman takes one or two conventions from novels about disabled children and turns them inside out. The 'project' is an example of this. In her first week in school, Rowena is delighted to find a great friend in Amanda Cosgrove and is thrilled when Amanda invites her home to tea. That is, until she hears the dreaded words, 'Community Service Project':

My guts turned to ice.
Amanda must have seen the expression on my face because her voice went quiet.
'I thought you could be my project,' she said.
I stared at her while my guts turned to liquid nitrogen and all the heat in my body rushed to my eyelids.
Words writhed around inside my head, stuff about how if I wanted to be a project I'd pin myself to the notice board in the classroom, and if I wanted to be a tragic case I'd go on '60 Minutes', and if I wanted everyone to point at me and snigger I'd cover myself with Vegemite and chook feathers, but I knew she wouldn't understand all these signs, and my handwriting goes to pieces when I'm angry and disappointed and upset.'
'No thanks,' I said, and turned and ran.

Rowena has to make the difficult decision between friendship and pride and, like many children, perhaps girls in particular, she chooses friendship. In a wonderful parody of the benefits of charity work, Amanda's nauseating father introduces Rowena with the words, 'I'm going to ask each of our Helping Hands to bring their Community Service Projectee up onto the stage, and tell us a little about them, so that we, as a community as a whole can help them to live fuller and more rewarding lives.' But Rowena can never be a silent victim and with

Amanda translating for her, she explains to an astonished audience, 'I've got problems making word sounds... Perhaps you've got problems making a living, or a sponge cake, or number twos.' And then, 'You can feel sympathy for me if you want, and I can feel sympathy for you if I want. And I do feel sympathy for any of you who haven't got a true friend.'

Blabbermouth and the sequel *Sticky Beak* are essentially about communication, talking and learning to listen to other people. Rowena survives her own quite public mistakes, her father's continued wearing of loud shirts and singing off-key in public, his marriage to her primary school teacher and her complicated feelings about the prospect of their new baby. With its arrival only weeks away, she confesses to her father her concern that when they have 'a kid who can speak with its mouth, you won't want to spend heaps of time flapping your hands about with me' and later, her worry that the baby will be born, like her, with a hereditary 'speech problem'. She feels that she could help a baby who could not speak, 'Teach it sign language. Show it how to write really fast so it can get its order into the school tuck shop before all the devon and chutney sandwiches are gone. Demonstrate what you have to do with your nose when you're cheering your best friend up with a look'. But equally she worries, 'if that baby talks, what chance have I got?'

The ending satisfyingly combines sentimentality and pride. When the newborn baby, a much longed-for sibling (named Erin after her friend who died), lets out a howl that rattles the windows, Rowena – confident in the love of her dad and her new mum – holds the baby proudly and announces: 'This is my baby sister, and there's nothing wrong with either of us.'

What Happens Next?

A recent trend, particularly in books for younger readers, has been to include a disabled child in a secondary role, not merely as a catalyst for change or 'second fiddle' to the real protagonist, but as a real independent character in the story. There are several picture books for younger readers which have a character in a wheelchair and where the aim is to naturally incorporate them into the telling of the story, rather than making their presence some kind of issue or device. Jean Adamson has added a title to the famous *Topsy and Tim* series in which the children meet a new friend who uses a wheelchair, and *Boots for a Bridesmaid* by Verna Wilkins is a story where the fact that the mother of the bridesmaid uses a wheelchair is revealed only through the illustrations.[33]

In books for a slightly older age group, Philip Ridley's *Scribbleboy* is a good example of a story that includes a disabled child who is not a 'problem' and, although his wheelchair is more than incidental, the difficulties he sometimes faces are certainly not the main issue.[34]

Scribbleboy is a slightly surreal adventure about the wonderful graffiti which appears to brighten up a dull, concrete estate, and the characters are larger than life. The central character is Bailey, a new kid on the block, who feels sad and lonely after his mother leaves home and his eccentric father starts to act as if he is a character from the film *Top Gun*. His first friend is Ziggy, who is a mixture of confidence and sadness and also badly needs a new friend. Ziggy is introduced to the story like this:

A boy about 11 years old, thin, pale, with large brown eyes. He was wearing a green anorak, a white button up

---

33. Verna Wilkins, *Boots for a Bridesmaid*, Tamarind Press, London, 1995.
34. Philip Ridley, *Scribbleboy*, Puffin Books, London, 1997.

shirt, open at the collar, corduroy trousers and slippers.
His hair was jet black and very curly.
Bailey's first thought was: he's very short.
His second thought was: negative, not short. He's sitting down.
The third: why's the chair on wheels?
Then he realised: the boy was in a wheelchair.
'Welcome, welcome, welcome, New Kid!' cried the boy, approaching Bailey... 'My name is Ziggy Fuzz and, as the President of the Scribbleboy Fan Club, may I welcome you to... well, the fan club.'

There are discussions about how it feels to be Ziggy, but the development of the plot is about keeping the legend of the Scribbleboy alive and re-uniting families. Ziggy remains in the story right up to the end, not as the main character, but with an important role and issues of cure, doctors or walking again are never mentioned.

In a recent interview, Philip Ridley talked about his reasons for including disabled children in his books, one being that although he was a voracious reader, he has no memory of any disabled characters in the stories he read as a child. (Another was that two of his best friends used wheelchairs and this was a natural part of his world as a child.)

There has been, if not a conscious, then a kind of subconscious desire not to have disabled characters in books. Why are they not as frequent in books as they are in society? That's a question you have to ask. I think that we've still got a huge distance to travel. I think we're at the beginning of the beginning of this beginning to change.[35]

---

35. Philip Ridley on *You and Yours*, BBC Radio 4, 1st February 2000.

It seems likely that writers who are themselves disabled will make the most valuable contribution to this development in children's literature. Pat Thomson argues that we are unlikely to be fully satisfied with books about disability in modern children's fiction until disabled writers start to come through in greater numbers,[36] and it is true that when confident writers like Joyce Dunbar (*Mundo and the Weatherchild*) and Jane Stemp (*Waterbound*) use their own experience of disability to write stories for children, the result is perceptive and real even when, as in these titles, their medium is fantasy or futurism rather than contemporary realism.[37]

Comparisons are often made between disabled writers' contribution to literature and that made by black writers over the last few decades. Writers such as Joseph Lester (*Long Journey Home* and *Basketball Game*, Puffin Plus 1977), and Rosa Guy (*The Friends*, *Ruby*, *The Disappearance*, Puffin 1977), and Mildred Taylor's series of books starting with *Roll of Thunder Hear My Cry*, Gollanz 1977), began a development which brought not only a new subject matter to children's fiction but also a completely new way of writing about black people's experiences.[38] Their work dramatically transformed the face of books for children, and whether they were writing about black people's history and the experience of racism, or family life and the individual trials and tribulations of growing up, it was clear that these authors and their works provided a knowledge and insight as well as a literary experience which was quite different to that of previous books.

---

36. Pat Thomson, *Disability in Modern Children's Fiction*.
37. Joyce Dunbar, *Mundo and the Weatherchild*, Heinemann, London, 1985; Jane Stemp, *Waterbound*, Hodder Children's Books, London, 1995.
38. Joseph Lester, *Long Journey Home* and *Basket Ball Games*, Puffin Plus, London, 1977; Rosa Guy, *The Friends*, *Ruby*, *The Disappeared*, Puffin, London, 1977; Mildred Taylor, *Roll of Thunder Hear My Cry*, Gollanz, London 1977.

In a similar vein, disabled writers have argued that the disability movement, like any other movement struggling to get its voice heard, needs its own literature and that writers need to be able to 'name' their experience in order to understand it.[39] But just as black writers are not writing solely for the edification of black children, so the growing body of writers who are themselves disabled will want their books to be read and understood by all kinds of readers. It is to be hoped that like the best of black writers, disabled writers will write from a different perspective, less prone to stereotypes of tragedy and despair; less full of 'problems' and 'issues' for which there is no solution; with less 'blaming' of the disabled person as if there were no social factors involved. There is a wealth of experience and history to be written about; and disabled writers will certainly do this differently to other writers.

On the other hand, we do not want a situation, which some commentators suggest exists today, in which white writers do not feel that they can include black people in their stories, where men do not feel they can write about women and where almost nobody feels they can write about disabled people. The experience and the history of being disabled by attitude and prejudice, as well as the often tricky business of living with an impairment, are enormously varied, and this variety has huge potential in books for children. Young readers today need what they have always needed: good books that let the imagination do its own work and provide them with a valuable literary experience; books that teach them things they don't know about and help them to understand things they do; books that make them laugh or cry. They need books with lively,

---

39. Lois Keith, *Mustn't Grumble: Writing by Disabled Women*, The Women's Press, London, 1994, p3.

well-rounded, memorable characters. Some of these characters need to be disabled, and some of the books will be written by people who know about this from their own lives and experiences.

Conclusion

In the realm of metaphor, disease does not have to be cured by microscope or operation. It can be cured by forgiveness or love.

Journalist Linda Grant on the death of writer Kathy Acker, who believed that she could cure herself of cancer; *Guardian*, 2 December 1997

The Victorian novelist had no problem with the idea that literature for young people was first and foremost a tool to shape the young to the needs of that society. Moral messages were based on the principles of Christian teaching and religious ideas about responsibility and blame, innocence and evil. The novels of the day reinforced the belief that boys should be active and strong, girls must be tamed in order to render them fit for marriage, disability could be a punishment for inappropriate behaviour, and illness could be overcome with sufficient will or good thoughts. However, attitudes are often very slow to change, and what is extraordinary in these largely irreligious times is the resilience of the image of the person who miraculously walks again or that of the blind person who sees. There is still an enormous need to prove that there is some force beyond ourselves, some spiritual power we can tap into when all else lets us down.

In the Victorian novel, these images were useful symbols for proving the power of religious faith. Today, with the exception of evangelical Christians like Morris Cerullo who still claim that through a public display of faith, impairments can be miraculously cured, people in Western societies are less likely to put their faith in 'God's will' and are more likely to turn to medical science.[1] We rely on surgery and the chemical remedies prescribed by the doctor to cure our physical ills and are surprised and disappointed when their treatments let us down. We rely also on the psychotherapist or the counsellor to help with our emotional ills, believing that an understanding of the inner workings of our minds will help us to be happier and more fulfilled. But even medical science and the talent of the most skilled therapist have not been able to provide solutions to all the difficulties we face. At the beginning of a new century, when God and science both seem to fail in providing answers to all of our ills, people invoke a whole variety of 'forces', spiritual and personal, to cure and to heal.

'Miracle cure stories' remain as popular as ever. Newspapers and magazines, particularly those aimed at women, are still full of them. People are invited to talk about how they 'threw away that wheelchair' and walked again by the power of their own will, or 'proved the doctors wrong' when they were told that they would 'be confined to a wheelchair' for the rest of their lives. In these stories it is as if the wheelchair itself possesses some bad spirit which must be exorcised. Perhaps the collective psyche is so attracted to stories of 'mind over matter' and the 'power of positive thinking' because to the average person, the life of someone who cannot walk (whether real or fictional), seems un-liveable. We do not want to contemplate the idea that things people would never have wished for do happen and that there are some conditions doctors cannot cure.

---

1. Christian evangelist Morris Cerullo's publicity campaigns for his worldwide 'healing' tours in the 1990s featured advertisements showing wheelchairs upside down and thrown away and white sticks broken. The captions suggested that people would be 'walking away' following their receipt of the healing messages Cerullo had to offer.

It is not uncommon for people to suggest that being disabled, especially having to use a wheelchair, must be a fate worse than death. In a single day I heard three versions of this story. The first was a woman who suffered serious illness after silicone breast implants. In a newspaper article she stated, 'I stagger around on crutches now because I'm damned if I'm going to submit to a wheelchair at my age'. The second was a radio play about a father who relentlessly trained his disabled son to run a mile. The play ended in his triumphant statement, 'I've sent it back to the hospital, we don't have to have that damned wheelchair in the house any more.' The third was a story a woman told me about her mother who remained housebound for the last two years of her life, refusing to go out because she could not bear to see herself or be seen in a wheelchair.[2] 'Overcoming' or cure was what these people were hoping for; acceptance did not come into it. It seems that the public appetite for such stories is insatiable, with campaigns around rights and better access for disabled people being a lot less attractive to the press.

A recent 'cure' story which continues to receive enormous publicity and is in fact not a cure story at all is that of the actor Christopher Reeve. Reeve is always referred to in media coverage as Superman, one of his former acting roles, presumably to distinguish between his previous existence as an active, physically strong actor and his present life as a wheelchair user who has very little movement in his body. Ever since his accident in 1995, Reeve has received enormous publicity for his public statements that he is certain that he will walk again. Medical correspondents who usually report on these developments become over-excited by any kind of research that suggests cure, and headlines such as 'Cells from

---

2. Lois Keith, 'Encounters with Strangers', in Jenny Morris, ed., *Encounters with Strangers*, The Women's Press, London, 1996.

pigs could help Superman walk'[3] have continued to feed the public's expectations of a miracle.

When Reeve claimed that he would concentrate on raising money for research to find a cure for spinal cord injury and would be keeping his body exercised so that he is ready for surgery, people believed that this showed an enormously positive attitude to what seemed, to non-disabled people at least, a life hardly worth living. The language used by the media to describe his certainty that he would walk before his fiftieth birthday suggests that accommodating to a life as a disabled person and finding a new way to live is a sign of moral weakness. Reeve is seen to be giving the public 'a dramatic display of determination and optimism', his demeanor is described as 'remarkably animated' and he is reported as seeing himself as a role model for other disabled people because of his 'willpower' and 'discipline'.[4]

Disabled campaigners have, of course, viewed these events rather differently. In February 2000 Reeve appeared in an American advertisement on the day of the Superbowl, an occasion well known for its enormous viewing figures. The advertisement for an investment company showed a computer-generated image of Reeve 'walking' again to the applause of a crowd of glamorous onlookers. Disabled people have called this 'disgracefully misleading'. Writer Charles Krauthammer argues that in his Superbowl ad, Reeve is evangelising his imminent redemption:

---

3. *Mail on Sunday*, 15 November 1998. The report is usually much more cautious than the sensational headline in these articles.

4. *Observer*, 23 January 2000. Reeve himself seems to have taken on the view that acceptance is 'giving up'. In February 2000 he announced to viewers of the USA *Good Morning America* show, 'The biggest problem actually is people who have been in a chair for a long time, because in order to survive psychologically they've had to accept "ok, I'm going to spend my life in a chair".'

The false optimism Reeve is peddling is not just psychologically harmful, cruelly raising hopes. The harm is practical too. The newly paralysed young might end up emulating Reeve, spending hours on end preparing their bodies to be ready to walk the day the miracle cure comes, much like the millenarians who abandon their homes and sell their wordly goods to await Rapture on a mountaintop. These kids should instead be spending those hours reading, studying and preparing themselves for the opportunities in the new world that high technology has for the first time in history made possible for the disabled.[5]

Another aspect of the Reeve case is the emphasis on his 'willpower'. With little if any evidence to back up their claims, newspapers and magazine articles have been delighted to proclaim that Reeve has 'confounded doctors' and 'astounded the medical world', and that his 'incredible inner strength and personal drive' mean that a miracle must be imminent. A newspaper headline, 'A Will Not To Be Ill', led with an article which claimed that through his intense desire to hold his young son, Reeve had regained sensation in his arm.[6] It seems at best unlikely that someone with a complete spinal cord injury can regain feeling by an act of will, however much they long to hug their child, but the story received wide coverage. A *Guardian* journalist wrote:

This concept of mind over matter, that positive thinking not only helps maintain a healthy body but can also contain or even drive away disease and repair

---

5. Charles Krauthammer, 'Restoration, Reality and Christopher Reeve', *Time* magazine, January 2000, Associated Press, © Time Inc.
6. *Guardian*, 20 May 1997. In his autobiography, *Still Me* (1998), Reeve discusses his continuing hope for a cure but does not mention any increased sensation in his arms.

damaged tissue, has been gaining popularity, particularly over the last twenty years.

Of course it is not true to think that the idea of disease being 'driven out' by an attitude of will is a modern one. The belief in 'mind over matter' can be traced back to the Romans, but in these days of advanced scientific medicine it has taken on a new dimension. People who have seemingly incurable conditions are not seen just as being able to cure themselves through positive thinking but are also asked to take responsibility for becoming ill in the first place. This view is particularly applied to people who have cancer, a disease which has developed a metaphorical language of its own.[7] People who have cancer are deemed to be 'victims' who have somehow contracted this disease because of a problem in their inner self – too stressed, too tense, too weak, too emotional. 'Cancer victims' are seen as having somehow betrayed themselves and must be accountable for both the condition and its treatment. In the battling language which is often used in this field, the suggestion is that the cure has a moral basis – that brave and good people 'defeat' cancer; they 'beat' it; they do not let it 'conquer' them; whereas cowardly, undeserving people allow it to kill them. Through a variety of tactics people are encouraged to believe that they can, indeed should, take responsibility for their own state of health. They must, as Schopenhauer proclaimed, assume dictatorial power of the will, in order to subsume the rebellious forces of the body.

That there are connections between *some* diseases and *some* states of mind is widely accepted. Most people, scientists as well as 'the woman in the street', do believe that there is a link between negative emotional states such

---

7. See Susan Sontag, *Illness as Metaphor*, Penguin Books, London, 1983.

as worry, unhappiness or grief and physical conditions such as ulcers. But the rhetoric surrounding life-threatening illnesses, especially cancer, positions those who become ill as both worthy of blame for their condition and responsible for its treatment and cure. This would seem to contradict another commonly held view that cancer is caused by factors clearly outside of the individual's control, such as pollution and other environmental factors.

Within the 'mind over matter' approach to curing cancer, the self-help cancer movement has, over the last 20 years, recommended a variety of tactics, some sensible, others bordering on the bizarre. Meditation, acupuncture, vegan diets, carrot juice, coffee enemas, thinking of the body as a temple, visualising the illness and imagining healthy cells gobbling the diseased ones are just a few of the approaches advised. Patients are asked to believe that through positive thinking and belief in 'the self', they can regain control over their own body. In situations where the cancer continues to kill, it is not just medical science which is seen to fail, but also their own will to live. As John Diamond says, writing about his own experience of the disease, 'It leads to the idea of the survivor as personal hero – that only those who want to survive enough get through to the end, and the implied corollary that those who die are somehow lacking in moral fibre and the will to live.'[8]

It is interesting to observe that the less that is known about a disease and the more resistant it is to cure, the more people are likely to resort to non-scientific, superstitious or spiritual solutions. Few would try to cure chicken pox with willpower, yet for mysterious diseases like cancer, and even for incurable conditions like spinal cord injury, such interpretations thrive.

---

8. John Diamond, *Because Cowards Get Cancer Too*, Vermilion, London, 1999, p72.

In their need to seek alternative solutions, many have sought a non-scientific, more spiritual approach which goes beyond the more ordinary belief in will-power or 'mind over matter'. The broad title of 'New Age philosophy' might be used to describe this movement. New Ageism uses the teaching of a number of different religions and philosophies, ancient and modern, to promote the idea that the power to heal is within us all. Its vocabulary of 'unlocking our inner potential', 'spiritual growth and freedom', 'psychic healing' and 'enlightenment' encourages the idea that there are forces both within and outside ourselves which can be harnessed to promote healing, cure and happiness. Such a view of the world replaces traditional religion in providing formulas for dealing with the difficulties of modern life and promotes the idea that with the right approach and sufficient determination, health and happiness (and possibly wealth too) are within the grasp of the individual.

Such an approach to life is undoubtedly helpful and comforting to many, even if the language of the movement ('liberate your spirit', 'enrich your life', 'explore the mysteries of the soul', 'tap your inner resources', 'revitalise your body' and 'achieve good health') might feel a little too mystical for some cynics.[9] The view that individuals may well have better knowledge about themselves than professionals is empowering. People no longer feel that scientific medicine has all the answers, and many refuse to be at the mercy of 'experts' who have their own prejudices.

The trouble with a view of the world which continually tells us that the responsibility for healing can be found within ourselves, is that those of us who either cannot or do not want to be 'absolved' of our conditions are seen as

---

9. From a 1999 advertisement for the Mind, Body and Spirit Book Club.

failures. Placing all the responsibility on the individual is most likely to result as it has always resulted, in at best pitying and at worst blaming and excluding those who cannot or will not be 'cured'. As I write this, the newspapers are full of yet another story of another 'miraculous treatment' for spinal cord injury, a treatment which has, in fact, been around for years. The accompanying pictures show a French man who has had electrodes implanted in his leg, not yet walking. No story there, but still hailed as an important advance. This is unhelpful to disabled people who would much rather have *less* emphasis on medical cure for the impairments which remain resistant to such an outcome (and there are many of these) and much *more* on the social and political restrictions on their lives imposed by prejudice and access.

Nevertheless, healing – physical, spiritual and psychological – is likely to remain at the centre of human imagination and desire. There is no end to the sources in which people are willing to place their trust and perhaps that is why it is not so surprising that more than a century after the Victorian novels discussed in the first six chapters of this book, the healing parables have remained part of both our ordinary, and our literary and visual, vocabulary. As the last chapter showed, modern literature for children tends to avoid this device as a resolution to problems but in adult writing, particularly that which aims at 'universal themes', it has remained popular.

Two recent examples of this are Arthur Miller's play *Broken Glass*, first performed in England in 1994, and Lars Von Trier's 1996 film *Breaking the Waves*.

Arthur Miller's play, set in the 1930s, is about Sylvia Gellburg, an American Jewish woman living through Kristallnacht and literally paralysed by her inability to do anything to help the Jews in Germany. She is unable to move her legs and spends the entire play in bed or in a wheelchair. With the help of her doctor, she begins to understand that her paralysis is caused not only by her anxiety and fury at America's refusal to face up to what was happening in Germany, but also by other compromises in her life: her husband Phillip's self-loathing at being Jewish in an anti-Semitic world and his impotence at work and in bed. In the final scene, trying to reach her husband as he lies dying from a heart attack, she discards her wheelchair to walk again. As Paul Darke observed in his review of the play, 'one must never underestimate the power of a cliché.[10]

In *Breaking the Waves*, Von Trier gives us Bess, a young Scottish woman innocent to the point of simplicity and her new husband Jan, an oil rig worker. When Jan is paralysed by a drilling accident, we see him lying in a grim hospital bed, no wheelchair or rehabilitation in sight. With the unspoken assumption that their sexual life is over, he asks his wife to fulfil his erotic fantasies by having sex with other men. Believing that God has punished her for loving him too passionately and for praying too hard for him to be returned to her, she sacrifices her virtue and ultimately, her life. At first she tries to placate him by pretending that she has had sex with other men but when Jan's condition deteriorates, she begins to transform herself into a prostitute in stiletto heels and hotpants. As she describes her exploits to her husband, he begins to improve. Bess now puts herself in real danger, visiting sailors who she knows are sadistic and violent. Beaten almost senseless, she is taken to hospital where she asks to see Jan. She is distraught when she finds that he is still paralysed and, in the tradition of all tragic heroines, she dies.

---

10. Paul Darke, *Disability Arts Magazine*, Autumn 1994.

Jan's broken neck does not have to await medical research for that long-awaited cure. Miraculously, her death 'saves' him, and in the final scene of the film he walks to her funeral, completely redeemed by her sacrifice. (Although, it must be admitted, he does seem to be wearing a foam brace round his neck.)

Both play and film opened to considerable acclaim. Derek Malcolm, writing in the *Guardian*, began his review of *Breaking the Waves,* 'No film this year has held me in its grip quite so hard. If you haven't seen it, you'll miss one of the great cinematic events of the year.'[11] Arthur Miller's play was described as a fine, period play with resonance for the contemporary audience. Neither the unlikely and stereotypical theme of healing through love or through death of another, nor the religious and literary precedents for the character who miraculously walks again, was mentioned in any of these reviews.

Perhaps paralysis and disability were not a feature in the critical, intelligent reviews because they were not considered as part of the central theme of the works. Just as the reader is more likely to remember Heidi's pleasure and freedom in her Alpine loft than they are Clara's walking again, or the growth and beauty of *The Secret Garden* in Hodgson Burnett's novel rather than Colin discarding his wheelchair, so it is possible to view Sylvia's and Jan's rising to walk again as almost incidental. The issues in these works are intended to be the lofty ones of freedom and oppression, sexual repression, blame and responsibility rather than 'merely' physical cure. The writers are not really asking us to believe in 'miracle cure', and the sophisticated audience for which these works are intended understand that this device is used as a powerful

---

11. Derek Malcolm, *Guardian*, 18 October 1996.

metaphor. But for such a metaphor to work, it must be based on widely accepted images and beliefs: that to be made lame or crippled is some kind of punishment and to walk again is good and right. Such use of metaphor calls on the widely held belief that 'not walking' is a passive and unhappy state which renders the victim powerless, and that a release from this state is desirable above all else.

In our modern society, after many years of social progress about disabled people's right to be accepted and valued for who and what they are, one might expect a more enlightened approach to the treatment of disability in cultural works, a more complex exploration of this well-worn metaphor. However, it would appear that the 'Take Up Thy Bed and Walk' approach to story-telling has life in it yet.

Select Bibliography

Aiken, Joan, 'Purely for Love', in Virginia Haviland, ed., *Children and Literature, Views and Reviews*, The Bodley Head, London, 1973

Alcott, Louisa May, *Good Wives*, Simon and Schuster Pocket Books, London, 1995 (first published 1869)

Alcott, Louisa May, *Jack and Jill*, Little, Brown, Boston, 1928 (first published 1880)

Alcott, Louisa May, *Jo's Boys*, Puffin Books, London, 1983 (first published 1886)

Alcott, Louisa May, *Little Men*, Puffin Books, London, 1983 (first published 1871)

Alcott, Louisa May, *Little Women*, Puffin Books, London, 1958 (first published 1868)

Avery, Gillian, *Behold the Child – American Children and Their Books 1621–1922*, The Bodley Head, London, 1994

Bailen, Miriam, *The Sickroom in Victorian Fiction – The Art of Being Ill*, Cambridge University Press, Cambridge, 1994

Baskin, Barbara H., and Karen H. Harris, *Notes from a Different Drummer: A Guide to Juvenile Fiction Portraying the Handicapped*, R.R. Bowker, Reed Publishing Inc., New Jersey, 1977

Baskin, Barbara H., and Karen H. Harris, *More Notes From a Different Drummer*, R.R. Bowker, Reed Publishing Inc., New Jersey, 1984

Blume, Judy, *Deenie*, Piper Books, Heinemann Ltd, London, 1988 (first published in 1973)

Bratton, J.S., *The Impact of Victorian Children's Fiction*, Croom Helm, London, 1981

Briggs, Julia, 'Reading Children's Books', in, Sheila Egoff, ed., *Only Connect – Readings on Children's Literature*, Oxford University Press, Oxford, third edition, 1996

Brontë, Charlotte, *Jane Eyre*, Puffin Books, London, 1991 (first published 1847)

Brophy, Brigid, 'A Masterpiece and Dreadful', 1965, in, Virginia Haviland, *Children and Literature, Views and Reviews*, The Bodley Head, London, 1973

Burnett, Frances Hodgson, *The Little Hunchback Zia*, St Hugh's Press Ltd, London, 1946, (first published 1916)

Burnett, Frances Hodgson, *The Lost Prince*, Puffin Books, London, 1971 (first published 1915)

Burnett, Frances Hodgson, *The Secret Garden*, Puffin Books, London, 1988 (first published 1911)

Byatt, A.S. and Ignes Sodre, *Imagining Characters: Six Conversations About Women Writers*, Chatto and Windus, London, 1995

Campbell, Susie, *Jane Eyre*, Penguin Critical Studies, Penguin Books, London, 1988

Carpenter, Humphrey, *Secret Gardens: A Study of the Golden Age of Children's Literature*, George Allen and Unwin, London, 1985

Carpenter, Humphrey and Mari Pritchard, *The Oxford Companion to Children's Literature*, Oxford University Press, Oxford, 1984

Carter, Angela, 'Walter de la Mare: Memoirs of a Midget', 1982, in *Expletives Deleted*, Chatto and Windus, London, 1992

Coolidge, Susan, *What Katy Did*, Puffin Books, London, 1994 (first published 1872)

Coolidge, Susan, *What Katy Did Next*, Puffin Books, London, 1994 (first published 1886)

Coolidge, Susan, *What Katy Did at School*, Puffin Books, London, 1994 (first published 1886)

Diamond, John, *Because Cowards Get Cancer Too*, Vermilion, London, 1999

Dusinberre, Juliet, *Alice to the Lighthouse: Children's Books and Radical Experiments in Art*, Macmillan Press, London, 1987

Eagleton, Terry, *Myths of Power: A Marxist Study of the Brontës*, Macmillan, London, 1988

Egoff, Sheila, ed., *Only Connect – Readings in Children's Literature*, Oxford University Press, Oxford, third edition, 1996

Enright, D.J., ed., *The Faber Book of Frets and Fevers*, Faber and Faber, London, 1989

Enright, Elizabeth, 'At 75, Heidi Still Skips Along', 1955, in Virginia Haviland, ed., *Children and Literature – Views and Reviews*, The Bodley Head, London, 1973

Fisher, Margery, *Who's Who in Children's Books: A Treasury of the Familiar Characters of Childhood*, Wiedenfeld and Nicholson, London, 1975

Frye, Northrop, *The Secular Scripture – A Study of the Structure of Romance*, Harvard University Press, Cambridge, MA, 1976

Gilligan, Carol, *In a Different Voice: Psychological Theory and Women's Development*, Harvard University Press, Cambridge, MA, 1982

Gleitzman, Morris, *Blabbermouth*, Macmillan Children's Books, London, 1995

Gleitzman, Morris, *Sticky Beak*, Macmillan Children's Books, London, 1995

Gordon, Lyndall, *Charlotte Brontë, A Passionate Life*, Vintage, London, 1995

Gordon, R.G. and M. Forrester Brown, *Paralysis in Children*, Oxford Medical Publications, Oxford, University Press, Oxford, 1933

Gorham, Deborah, *The Victorian Girl and the Feminine Ideal*, Croom Helm, London, 1982

Gubar, Susan and Sandra Gilbert, *The Madwoman in the Attic: The Woman Writer and the Nineteenth Century Literary Imagination*, Yale University Press, New Haven, CT, 1979

Haviland, Virginia, ed., *Children and Literature – Views and Reviews*, The Bodley Head, London, 1973

Hill, David, *See Ya Simon*, Viking, London, 1993

Hippocrates, *Aphorisms*, ?460–?377, quoted in D.J. Enright, ed., *The Faber Books of Frets and Fevers*, Faber and Faber, London, 1989

Hunt, Peter, *An Introduction to Children's Literature*, Oxford University Press, Oxford, 1994

Jones, Helen L., 'The Part Played by Boston Publishers of 1860–1900, in the Field of Children's Books', *Horn Blood Magazine*, June 1969

Jordan, Alice M., 'Children's Classics', 1947, in Virginia Haviland, *Children's Literature – Views and Reviews*, The Bodley Head, London, 1973

Keith, Lois, 'Take Up Thy Bed and Walk (or How to be a Good Girl)', *Books For Keeps*, No. 75, July 1992

Keith, Lois, *A Different Life*, The Women's Press, Livewire Books, London, 1997

Keith, Lois, 'Encounters with Strangers', in Jenny Morris, ed., *Encounters with Strangers*, The Women's Press, London, 1996

Keith, Lois, ed., *Mustn't Grumble: Writing by Disabled Women*, The Women's Press, London, 1994

Kirkpatrick D.L., ed., *Twentieth Century Children's Writers*, Macmillan, London, 1978

Lamb, Charles, 'The Convalescent', 1833, in D.J. Enright, ed., *The Faber Book of Fevers and Frets*, Faber and Faber, London, 1989

Maddox, Sam, *Spinal Network*, P.O. Box 4162, Boulder, CO, 1993

Marenholtz Buelow, Bertha, Maria van, Baroness, *Child and Child Nature*, translated by Alice M. Christie, W. Swann Sonnenschein, London, 1879

Marshall, Alan, *I Can Jump Puddles*, Penguin Books, London, 1974 (first published 1955)

McMurtie, Douglas C., *Bibliography of the Education and Care of Crippled Children*, Douglas McMurtie, New York, 1913

McVitty, Walter, 'Ethel Turner', in D.L. Kirkpatrick, ed., *Twentieth Century Children's Writers*, Macmillan, London, 1978

Moers, Ellen, *Literary Women*, The Women's Press, London, 1976

Morris, Jenny, *Pride Against Prejudice: Transforming Attitudes to Disability*, The Women's Press, London, 1991

Nodelman, Perry, 'Utopia. Or How to Grow Up Without Growing Up', in Sheila Egoff, ed., *Only Connect – Readings in Children's Literature*, Oxford University Press, Oxford, third edition, 1996

Orr, Wendy, *Fighting Back*, Orchard Books, London, 1996

Picardie, Ruth, *Before I Say Goodbye*, Penguin Books, London, 1998

Pinsent, Pat, *Children's Literature and the Politics of Equality*, David Fulton Publishers, London, 1997

Porter, Eleanor, *Pollyanna*, Puffin Books, London, 1994 (first published 1913)

Porter, Eleanor, *Pollyanna Grows Up*, Puffin Books, London, 1994 (first published 1915)

Quain, Richard, ed., *A Dictionary of Medicine, Including General Pathology, General Therapeutics, Hygiene, and the Diseases Peculiar to Women and Children*, Longmans, Green and Co., London, 1800

Quicke, John, *Disability in Modern Children's Fiction*, Croom Helm, London, 1985

Reynolds, Kimberley, *Girls Only? Gender and Popular Children's Fiction in Britain, 1880–1910*, Harvester Wheatsheaf, London, 1990

Reynolds, Kimberley and Nicola Humble, *Victorian Heroines: Representations of Femininity in Mid-Nineteenth Century Literature and Art*, Harvester Wheatsheaf, London, 1993

Rich, Adrienne, 'The Temptations of a Motherless Woman, 1973', in *On Lies, Secrets, and Silence: Selected Prose 1966–1978*, W.W. Norton and Company Inc., New York, 1980

Ridley, Philip, *Scribbleboy*, Puffin Books, London, 1997

Rieser, Richard, ed., *Invisible Children Report on the Joint Conference on Children, Images and Disability*, Save the Children and The Integration Alliance, London, 1995

Robertson, Debra, *Portraying Persons with Disabilities*, R.R. Bowker, Reed Publishing, New Jersey, 1992

Sallis, Susan, *Sweet Frannie*, Puffin Books, London, 1985 (first published in 1981)

Saxton, Martha, *Louisa May Alcott, A Modern Biography*, The Noonday Press, Boston, 1995

Selway, Deborah and Adrian F. Ashman, 'Disability, Religion and Health: a literature review in search of the spiritual dimensions of disability', in *Disability and Society*, vol. 13, No. 3, June 1998

Showalter, Elaine, *A Literature of Their Own, British Women Novelists from Brontë to Lessing*, Virago, London, 1978

Sontag, Susan, *Illness as Metaphor*, Penguin Books, London, 1983

Spyri, Johanna, *Heidi*, Regent Classics, Thames Publishing Company, London, (translator and date not listed) (first published 1880)

Spyri, Johanna, *Heidi*, translated by Eileen Hall, Puffin Books, London, 1994 (first published in 1880)

Stemp, Jane, *Waterbound*, Hodder Children's Books, London, 1995

Stevenson, Robert Louis, 'Ordered South 1881', in J. D. Enright, ed., *The Faber Book of Frets and Fevers*, Faber and Faber, London, 1989

Stevenson, Robert Louis, *The Child's Garden of Verses*, Longman & Co, London, 1885

Sutherland John, *Can Jane Eyre be Happy? More Puzzles in Classic Fiction*, The World's Classics, Oxford University Press, Oxford, 1997

Thomson, Pat, 'Disability in Modern Children's Fiction', *Books For Keeps*, No. 75, July 1992

Thwaite, Anne, *Waiting for the Party: The Life of Frances Hodgson Burnett*, Virago, London, 1974

Townsend, John Rowe, *Written for Children*, Penguin Books, London, 1974

Tritten, Charles, *Heidi Grows Up*, W.M. Collins and Sons Co. Ltd., London and Glasgow, 1958

Turner, Ethel, *Seven Little Australians*, Penguin Books, Australia, 1994 (first published 1894)

Turner, Ethel, *The Family at Misrule*, Penguin Books, Australia, 1994 (first published 1895)

Wilder, Laura Ingalls, *The Little House on the Prairie*

Wilder, Laura Ingalls, *These Happy Golden Years*, Puffin Books, London, 1972 (first published 1943)

Wilkins, Verna, *Boots for a Bridesmaid*, Tamarind Press, London, 1995

Yonge, Charlotte, *The Daisy Chain or Aspirations. A Family Chronicle*, John W. Parker and Son, London, 1856

Zipes, Jack, 'Taking Political Stock: New Theoretical and Critical Approaches to Anglo-American Literature in the 1980s', in Sheila Egoff, ed., *Only Connect – Readings in Children's Literature*, Oxford University Press, Oxford, third edition, 1996

Index